The Global Crisis in Humanity

The Global Crisis in Humanity

IN OUR EVOLVING TRANS-CULTURAL WORLD

Vincent L. Lombardi

ISBN-13: 9781979231749
ISBN-10: 1979231745

Contents

Frontispiece

The revelation which belongs to the new aeon can be none other than a divine-human revelation. It cannot be thought of or expected without creative human activity. A process which makes ready for the era of the Spirit is taking place. . . . It is a revelation in Spirit and in Truth and in it the link between the human and the divine is realized; in other words, God-manhood will be made manifest.

– Nicolas Berdyaev, *Truth and Revelation*

To believe that the body must be resurrected is to say, therefore, that eternity is not a cancellation of time and history but that history is fulfilled in eternity. But to insist that the body must be resurrected is to understand that time and history have meaning only as they are borne by an eternity which transcends them. They could in fact not be at all without that eternity. For history would be meaningless succession without the eternal purpose which bears it.

– Reinhold Niebuhr, *Beyond Tragedy*

He who does not realize to what extent shifting fortune and necessity hold in subjection every human spirit cannot regard as fellow-creatures nor love as he loves himself those whom chance separated from him by an abyss. The variety of constraints pressing upon man give rise to illusion of several distinct species that cannot communicate. Only he who has measured the dominion of force, and knows how not to respect it, is capable of love and justice.

– Simone Weil, *Poem of Force*

Globalization, understood as the coming together of humankind entails many beneficial aspects and needs to be honed carefully, not rejected in a wholesale manner. It needs to be combined with *egalization* to *globegalization*, which means giving all citizens of the world equal chances for building dignified lives. The introduction of the terms *egalization* and *globegalization* is therefore crucial if we wish to forge more effective analysis and action.

– Evelin Lindner, *Beyond Humiliation*

Introduction: The Global Crisis in Humanity in Our Transcultural World

I

The twentieth century has become in retrospect a transitional interval bridging the end of the modern world with the onset of our transcultural world. The modern world has ended, and we recognize on the horizon the beginning of a world beckoning us to rise above the false presumption that we live in a meaningless and purposeless universe. As will be discussed in depth throughout this book, the remarkable discoveries of the twentieth and twenty-first centuries disclose that energy, spirit, and freedom comprise the foundation of the cosmos and universe. Human life possesses a cosmic, eternal character. When we observe human creations—a skyscraper, for example—its source, rooted in energy and the outpouring of human consciousness that brought it into being, is nowhere in evidence in the temporal-spatial reality. The principles of architecture, science, mathematics, and human energy embodied in it remain mute in the skyscraper we observe. Moreover, without continual injections of energy, human creations fall into an entropic state—decay and return to nature. Innovative conscious breakthroughs give rise to new discoveries and inventions. This is also true of existing cultures globally. History is a chronological record of significant events that do not in themselves disclose the human consciousness and spirit embodied therein.

Our plight is not primarily a crisis in humanism—the severing of reason and religious dogma—but a global crisis in humanity: a process of dehumanization in which the will-to-justice is overwhelmed by the will-to-power. The global crisis in humanity sheds light on history and demands an assessment of the source of endless wars and revolutions in an age of globalization in which the various world cultures and civilizations have become interconnected and interdependent. History is the record of human events issuing from human creativity: an underlying mystery that proceeds from the realm of human consciousness and stands in the temporal-spatial world as objective reality. We tend to take the empirical world, our own creations, as the fundamental reality, with a disregard for its cosmic and eternal foundation.

In his *Nature and Destiny of Man*, the eminent theologian Professor Reinhold Niebuhr declared before the end of World War II that modern technological civilization had brought all civilizations and cultures, all empires and nations into closer juxtaposition to each other, despite the fact that this expansive intimacy brought about tragic wars. "The spiritual hatred and the lethal effectiveness of 'civilized' conflicts, compared with tribal warfare or battles in the animal world," he maintained, "are one of many examples of the new evil which arises on a new level of maturity."[1]

Niebuhr presumed humanity was headed for a universal culture or a world government as the natural and ultimate end which would give meaning to the whole historical process. Humanity had sought redemption by regarding the process of history itself as securing the fulfillment of human life. He maintained that the "new and urgent task" confronting humanity with progressively difficult tasks makes our very survival dependent on creative solutions. He saw clearly that history "moves towards more inclusive ends, towards more complex human relations, towards the technical enhancement of human powers and the culmination of knowledge."[2] He also understood that humanity mistakenly regarded the process of history itself as the means to human fulfillment. Our human plight, he alleged, lies more deeply ingrained in us than a mere idolatry of and pride in culture. It was a fundamental mistake, he cautioned, to believe that humanity could solve its "problem either by an escape from history or by the historical process itself." This oversight goes beyond "the pride, not of particular men and cultures," but the pride "of man as man."[3]

As early as the 1940s, Niebuhr addressed the possibility of the development of a world community. "The convergence of two forces of universality, one moral and the other technical, creates such a powerful impetus toward the establishment of a world community that the children of light [those of a naïve optimism] regard it as a practically inevitable achievement. As always, they underestimate the power of particular forces in history."[4] Many among the children of light mistakenly assumed that the primary basis of unity and the source of cohesion resided in geographic boundaries, ethnic homogeneity, common experience, and tradition. But the task in building a world community, Niebuhr reasoned, is humankind's final necessity and possibility. "It is a necessity and possibility because history is a process which extends the freedom of man over the natural process to the point where universality is reached. It is an impossibility because man is, despite his increasing freedom, a finite creature, wedded to time and place and incapable of building any structure of culture or civilization which does not have its foundations in a particular and dated locus."[5] For Niebuhr, the perpetual problem of establishing a world community remains humanity's interminable hope.

It is to Niebuhr's paradoxical challenge of humanity's final necessity and possibility, though well-nigh thought improbable, that this book seeks to provide a hopeful yet cautious response: a revolution in which humanity awakens to its divine character and its human personality endowed with a creative vocation. As Martin Luther King Jr. acknowledged, our hope lies in our revolutionary spirit. He professed a ceaseless opposition to poverty, racism, and militarism and called our attention to the adage that the arc of the moral universe is long, but it bends toward justice. Humanity is confronting a judgment not only upon the end of the modern world, but upon the chronicle of history itself in which we embrace, hopefully, the possibility of the onset of a transcultural world.

<h1 style="text-align:center">II</h1>

During the eighteenth and nineteenth centuries, humanity became more and more conflicted about the rise of humanism: the belief in the self-sufficiency of human beings stripped of a higher nature—a spiritual grounding. By the end of the nineteenth century, a global crisis in humanity erupted among theologians, religious philosophers, secular philosophers, scientists, and social thinkers in the humanities and liberal arts. These intellectuals conceived a likely transfiguration of consciousness that questioned the modern materialist conceptions of the nature of the universe. Immanuel Kant's distinction between the realm of phenomena and the realm of noumena (things-in-themselves); Georg Hegel's assertion of the goal of history and the embodiment of the world spirit; Søren Kierkegaard's declaration that God participates in history incognito; Vladimir Solovyev asserting God seeks union with and seeks to be born in Man, and Man seeks union with and seeks to be born in God; Karl Marx's vision of brotherhood in a united world federation; Fyodor Dostoevsky's portrayal of suffering, salvation, and the return of the Grand Inquisitor; Friedrich Nietzsche's anticipation of the Übermensch (Superman) as the supreme manifestation of the evolutionary process; Leo Tolstoy's articulation of the resurrection; Sigmund Freud's discovery of the unconscious; Ralph Emerson's focus on contradictory and compensatory forces in life—all were charged with great expectations of a future that guides human action; all affirmed the possibility of the revelation of meaning as a path toward greater perfection; all provided a steppingstone to existential self-validation.

Let's not omit twentieth-century thinkers and their contributions. Among them Hermann Hesse's idea of destiny, Thomas Mann's magic mountain, Miguel de Unamuno's immortality, Ortega y Gasset's perspectivism of a non-relativistic human character in which absolute truth is derived, and the warning in the dystopias of George Orwell and Aldous Huxley regarding the loss of Western humanistic values—all affirmed the possibility of the revelation of meaning, not only of the past but of the future. Their prophetic visions sought to unite past and future as both unfold in the present. In so far as human life is essentially action and movement inspired by goals, they applauded great expectations that stimulate activity and suffuse life with meaning and purpose.

These nineteenth- and twentieth-century thinkers draw our attention to a vision of truth, meaning, and purpose underlying the historical process that lies fallow for many today. Their way of life guided by a purpose outside itself is alien to our present existence. It is not so much the transcendent end per se that gives meaning to life but the enthusiasm sparked and the communion enjoyed in life's journey.

III

Ample optimism had prevailed in the expansion of freedom stemming from the Renaissance of the fifteenth century and continuing up to World War I, despite the presumption that humanity was living in a purposeless and meaningless universe. With the onset of World War I, the ancient cardinal virtues—wisdom, temperance, courage, and justice—were gradually abandoned for intractable utilitarian values that fashioned and fostered a heightened sense of crude individualism and a prideful confidence in reason. The line between war and peace in democratic societies presumably facilitated greater awareness and an informed citizenry. During the first two decades of the twentieth century, humanity witnessed the end of the modern world, substantiated by the enormous violence and destruction suffered during World War I. The peace agreement signed was barely dry when the world relapsed into the more horrific World War II.

Globally, today, humanity continues to find itself caught up in wars, revolutions, and mounting chaos while simultaneously compelled to counteract threats both at home and abroad. The constant preparation to counter these unrelenting dangers has led to the production of ever more powerful technologies of death and destruction. The race to create more lethal means of destruction poses a threat to our biosphere, hydrosphere, atmosphere, and geosphere and thereby to the very survival of life on Earth. Nations continue to develop advanced armaments and destructive technologies devastating to resources of human and planetary life. The development of weaponry during World War II had advanced to a level whereby it was possible not only to slaughter human beings en masse, but to wreak massive destruction on the human habitat and its ecosystems. In a systematic extermination, millions of innocent people were forced into Nazi concentration camps set up in Germany, Poland, and across Europe during World War II. Massive groups of prisoners were incarcerated and slaughtered in the Holocaust without trial or judicial process. The wholesale destruction of two cities, Hiroshima and Nagasaki, justified the use of the newly invented atomic bomb by the United States, which brought World War II to a prompt ending.

These woeful horrors were unfortunately disregarded. Warfare in the latter half of the twentieth century endured the absolute evil of the sovereign power of the people. By the onset of World War II, society had shed any semblance of the practice of laissez-faire economics, despite the fact that citizens en masse sustained the belief that free-market economics comprised the mainstay of democracy. The American philosopher and political theorist James Burnham predicted that the democratic society, with its specious free-market economics, had already consolidated itself into a managerial society by the beginning of World War II. The economic order was restructured, creating state monopolies in its enterprises and in producing war goods with managers and bureaucrats fused into a single class with a united interest.[6]

The aftermath of World War II gave rise to the onset of the so-called Cold War between the United States and the Soviet Union, two superpowers armed with nuclear deterrents; their standoff resulted from mutually assured destruction. Competing ideologies that gave rise to the Korean War and the Vietnam War that followed which incurred an estimated 54,000 American soldiers killed in Korea and 58,000 in Vietnam over the course of ten years. Unfortunately, the United States at the onset of the twenty-first century recklessly declared a "war on terrorism" in response to the 9/11 destruction of the World Trade Center Towers and got itself mired in two unnecessary, protracted wars in the Middle East—in Afghanistan and Iraq. The path to large unwinnable wars could have been and should have been avoided, assuming the U.S. had sought, in partnership with the major world powers, an international intelligence network of Middle East nations seeking relief from the destruction of their homeland and the copious death of their citizens. Such an alliance held the prospect of furnishing a communitarian means of arresting the spread of terrorism in the Middle East, in a world engaged in horrifying and endless warfare, revolutions, unmanageable internal turmoil, and appalling terrorism in countries involved hopelessly in sectarian warfare in Sunni and Shiite Islamic rivalry.

IV

Despite the world's nations being mired in wars during the latter half of the twentieth century (in Korea and Vietnam), a reformist outlook gave rise to a professional and entrepreneurial spirit. Among intellectuals, political thinkers, philosophers, religious writers, and researchers in the natural and social sciences, a transcultural world was evolving, questioning the absolute sovereignty of the nation-state system that inflicted horrifying destruction globally. My endeavor in this book is to introduce and confirm what can best be categorized as a "transcultural evolution" and the possible establishment of a world community, inclining humanity to rise above its war-engineered and war-weary nation-state system that is ravaging planetary life and resources.

This coalescing of the major domains of knowledge, revolutionary in scope, will be referred to throughout this book as a transcultural evolution. The major domains of knowledge encompass and integrate the profound revelations of the cosmos and universe—energy, spirit, and freedom—brought to light during the early decades of the twentieth century. Resolute hope in transcending the nation-state system of the modern world requires, in addition to humanity expanding literacy to the children of every nation, embracing mandatory spiritual literacy—the establishment of a transcultural ethical necessity that respects the mores, customs, and traditions of people globally. Spiritual literacy rises above and beyond its embodiment in mystical revelations of religion alone, prone to sectarian divisions and political power. In spiritual literacy lies the key to knowledge of the human personality, our creative vocation rooted in the cardinal virtues (prudence, justice, fortitude, and temperance), buttressed by the moving power of the theological virtues (faith, hope, and love). Spiritual literacy is grounded in the discovery of the eternal character of the cosmos and the universe.

The global crisis in humanity in our transcultural world, our present plight, is the paramount challenge of our time. In the following chapters, the transcultural evolution, which differs fundamentally from the modern materialist interpretations of the cosmos and the universe, will be addressed in depth.

V

Chapter 1 focuses on two opposing global revolutions: a global crisis in humanity, which threatens our very survival, and a transcultural evolution, which illumines, enriches, and edifies our spiritual character and creative vocation in the stewardship of planetary life and the world's resources.

Chapters 2, 3, and 4 focus on the mystery of life's origin and the advancing knowledge in cosmology, astronomy, astrophysics, and anthropology. Our transcultural evolution elevates consciousness beyond the disclosure of Einstein's discoveries and quantum physics. Einstein's theory of relativity projects the physical sciences into the realm of the metaphysical.

Chapter 5 considers the global crisis in humanism of the nineteenth century. It examines the underlying dark night of the soul, disclosing the plight of despair of Leo Tolstoy—one of the Russian writers considered among the greatest authors of all time—and his awakening to the eternal.

Chapter 6 examines the contributions of the Russian essayist and philosopher Fyodor Dostoevsky, whose psychological penetration into the human soul has had a profound influence on comprehending the global crisis in humanity of the twentieth century. Chapter 6 also includes the contributions of the German philosopher and cultural critic Friedrich Nietzsche, who exercised a profound influence on Western philosophy and modern intellectual history. The ingenious and inspired views of these thinkers—Tolstoy, Dostoevsky, and Nietzsche—encouraged higher learning that expands impressively our vision of the future.

In contrast, many among the world's citizens tend to have a vacuous vision of a world community. Humanity has become more and more predisposed to utilitarian values as the highest achievement, devoid of an awareness of the transcendent mystery in life. The upshot, as American historian, moralist, and social critic Christopher Lasch declared, is the fostering of aspirations that promote self-condemnation and self-contempt. Modern advertising as a lure, Lasch warned, "compels not so much self-indulgence as self-doubt that creates needs and generates new anxieties."[7]

Chapter 7 critiques Adam Smith's moral philosophy underlying the nature of man, society, and laissez-faire capitalism.

Chapter 8 reviews the plight, transformation, and outcome of capitalism, dispossessed of its foundation in the cardinal virtues, and its embrace of utilitarianism. In his *Acquisitive Society*, British economic historian R. H. Tawney provided a profound judgment on both capitalism and socialism. The Great Depression inspired John Maynard Keynes to conceive a macroeconomic analysis based on utilitarianism, beyond the microanalysis of the business firm set forth by Adam Smith, as a means of finding a way out of the collapse of capitalism.

Chapter 9 sets forth Karl Marx's critique of the social, economic, and philosophical analysis of the unfolding of history which, he presumed, would give rise to a world federation of democratic states.

Chapter 10 reviews the plight of the democratic society.

Chapter 11 concerns the plight of our planet, the prospect of a New Renaissance, and the awakening to the Era of the Spirit.

VI

In the twenty-first century, humanism divorced from knowledge of the spiritual reality turned out to be a fear-provoking breeding ground for social and political revolutions within nations, and wars between and among nations. As spiritual beings, we cannot be reconciled with or subordinated to the power of social institutions which are, in reality, human creations. To do so would be to live in a state of idolatry, entranced by human creations. The spirit stands supreme beyond the willfulness of the political realm, as well as beyond economic institutions that belong to the means and not to the end of sustaining the fulfillment of life. Even in democratic societies, supreme authority continues to maintain itself by propaganda and political deception.

History teaches that all religions—including Christianity, one of the most universal messianic religions embodying spiritual knowledge of personal, social, and human evolution—have been, to a greater or lesser degree, afflicted with sectarianism. This does not deny the fact that religion has provided ample enrichment to human life by its mystical insights apropos the eternal. Yet the sacred and spiritual ground of religion taken literally becomes a virulent source of sectarian divisions, as well as a scourge on human freedom.

This book addresses the truth embodied in our evolving transcultural world that extends beyond religion while, at the same time, reaffirming the meaning of its mystical revelations. This provides an answer to the final question about reality: Is there a genuine reality? The answer is, unequivocally, yes. The genuine reality is the eternal reality grounded in energy, spirit, and freedom that cannot be discerned by our five senses, focused and fixed on the temporal-spatial reality. Nor can the eternal be ascertained from conclusions derived strictly from subjective or objective data. Truth and wisdom lie beyond data of factual and historical reality. They establish anthropological proof of the fact that humans belong to two worlds—time and eternity. This view rises above modern humanism, which embraces the belief that human beings are merely bound to the world of time and human needs. Our transcultural world affirms the mystical premise that human beings are a microcosm of the macrocosm, validating that wisdom and freedom—the most precious needs of the soul—do not derive from the temporal-spatial world but are inherent in the cosmos and universe. As the nineteenth-century philosopher Søren Kierkegaard claimed, human beings are a synthesis of the finite and the infinite.

Yet another profound mystery related to spirit and energy unravels two phenomena which in the world of appearances have little to do with one another. I'm referring to the discovery that the energy and spirit inherent in atoms, molecules, and cells have a common wellspring with the creative energy inherent in human beings. Scientific findings acknowledge that parallel phenomena—energy and spirit—result in a positive outcome for both the crisis in humanism (of lesser significance) and the global crisis in humanity (of world-shattering consequence). They establishes that atoms, molecules, and cells—components inherent in human life—contain within themselves energy and wisdom which are fundamental components of the universe. By splitting the atom, scientists discovered that energy contained within it is released. Spiritual energy within human beings also contain enormous hidden wisdom and creative power. The creative wonders of the atom and the human being—the foundation of the universe—are by their very nature both interrelated and interconnected.

VII

Reinhold Niebuhr called our attention to a caveat, namely that the "ultimate proof of freedom of the human spirit is its own recognition that its will is not free to choose between good and evil. For in the highest reaches of the freedom of the spirit, the self discovers in contemplation and retrospect that previous actions have invariably confused the ultimate reality and value, which the self as spirit senses, with the immediate necessities of the self."[8] Niebuhr acknowledged that we are caught in an ultimate paradox: in the final exercise of freedom, we cannot escape; the fact that "Man is most free in the discovery that he is not free."[9] But the self in contemplation and the self in action must not be taken as a distinction between the self as spirit and the self as natural vitality; that is to say, as Freud's superego—the self in bondage to the vicissitudes of time and history.

"There is only one self," Niebuhr emphasized. "Sometimes the self acts and sometimes it contemplates its actions. . . . When the self in contemplation becomes contritely aware of its guilt in action it may transmute this realization into a higher degree of honesty in subsequent action."[10] The human spirit aware of this propensity is able to reign over both external worldly and internal psychological influences. Our spiritual depth thereby provides us with the realization of knowledge of the meaning of the inward and outward dynamics in the living moment. Guilt is consciousness of a sense of wrongdoing. Conscience—knowledge with respect to Truth and the Good—activates the spirit with respect to the suffering of guilt and its expiation in repentance. Through guilt, the self's spiritual sensitivity illuminating reason is able to distinguish between genuine guilt—actual wrongdoing, violating truth and wisdom—and conformity of thought to various social forces.

In conscience, the spiritually literate person understands that the perpetrator of a crime (the criminal) and the victim (the person injured) must both be treated with love and compassion by virtue of their human dignity and their divine-human nature, even though one must be punished for the crime. Punishment meted out, however, cannot violate the law of love and empathy, even if the wrongdoer is unrepentant. Otherwise, those administering punishment fail in their responsibility, falling short of truth, justice, and goodness. Guilt is to the soul what pain is to the body. The former stirs the spirit rooted in conscience; the latter stirs consciousness arousing reason and the will. For the spiritually illiterate, conscience is informed not by the spirit but by belief and faith, whether grounded in religious dogmas, scientific discoveries, cultural values, or social mores.

VIII

My teaching experience belies the view that spiritual and ethical values cannot be taught in higher education or, indeed, to children from an early age. I have found that students at university respond enthusiastically and come alive when exposed to courses in existential and phenomenological psychology, which broach the profound relationship between the psyche and the spirit. An assessment of the spiritual reality and the need for spiritual literacy will hopefully disabuse the reader of the shortsighted view that the moral and spiritual reality should be excluded from public education.

Some forty years ago, my colleague Professor Emeritus Ronald Puhek established the Michigan Institute of Existential Metapsychology. His weekly seminars are to this day well attended. He has written numerous works advancing spiritual literacy. The Institute's goal is the search for truth, which can be incorporated into one's life. His books were first used as tools in ongoing weekly seminars for professional and nonprofessional people. He has been successful in helping to transfigure the consciousness of many of the Institute's participants. The impact on their lives has a radiating influence, initiating and broadening concentric circles relating to knowledge of the spiritual reality. Their personal lives stand as a witness to spiritual literacy for their children, members of the community they interact with, and those they serve in their professional work. Puhek's creative endeavors span the spectrum of spiritual literacy. From one of his earliest works, *The Metaphysical Imperative: A Critique of the Modern Approach to Science*, to one of his latest, *True Friendship*, one encounters the outpouring of a gifted mind. Puhek's creative efforts include the major domains of knowledge—religion, philosophy, the sciences, and the liberal arts.

Physician, psychologist, and social scientist Dr. Evelin Lindner and her cadre of physicians and associates conversant with the humiliation and ignominious treatment of human beings worldwide have a deep grasp of spiritual literacy's potential in coping with the global crisis in humanity. Lindner's 2012 book, *A Dignity Economy: Creating an Economy that Serves Human Dignity and Preserves Our Environment*, is a well-researched, serious, and sober response to the world crisis looming on the planetary horizon. It calls our attention to the possibility of extensive damage to or destruction of our ecosystems. Her work is not only a clearinghouse of knowledge of creative thinkers around the world. It is a thoughtful deliberation of their concrete contributions in establishing a collective stewardship of the global community. In association with other physicians, scholars, and colleagues, Dr. Lindner has helped establish the World Dignity University and an international "dignity and humiliation network." She and her associates understand thoughtfully and thoroughly the fact that the crisis facing humanity provides us with an unparalleled opportunity and responsibility to confront the challenges besetting the human family, the ecosystem, and planetary life. "We face a window of opportunity," Lindner counsels, "whether we use it or not. And we'd better use it."

The crux of the alienation of human beings from the product of their work, from their activity of production, from their intuitive intelligence, from one another, and from planetary resources, Lindner maintains, is the indignity and humiliation that saps and drains our creative participation in the destiny of the world. Her recent book, *Honor, Humiliation and Terror, An Explosive Mix and How We Can Defuse It with Dignity* is an incredible contribution to human welfare.

She transcends pessimism and optimism as well as realism and idealism and is not swept away by dreamers who either consider force a solution or are blinded by the fantasy of crude individualism and self-regulating markets. She clarifies the irresistible pull toward irrational behavior reinforced by the "legitimizing myths" that promote a herd mentality; human beings denuded of their dignity and their creative vocation in a world of potential abundance. These legitimizing myths burst and shatter the unity-in-diversity of human existence—human solidarity rooted in freedom—through credulous economic and political ideologies, literalistic and ritualistic religions, positivistic and fragmented fields of science, philosophies captivated by modern science, and various art forms whose effects serve to narcotize consciousness.

Nonetheless, Lindner and her colleagues are able to celebrate the creative contributions of universal world religions; further our understanding of the eternal, transcendent reality; ensure the enrichment of the lives of members of the human family; promote discoveries in the social, biological, and physical sciences that foster our quest for truth and goodness; heighten our intuitive intelligence; and uphold the revelations of beauty in the liberal and fine arts that nurture a loving heart. Working on the world stage, Lindner and her colleagues enliven our spirit, enhance our hope, and bolster our trust in humanity. They also warn us to be careful, cautious, and thoughtful in parsing much of the nonsense that passes for "mainstream" thought today. She and her associates have created an awakening of humanity to the truth, reality, and dignity of all human beings unparalleled in the annals of postmodern history of the twentieth and twenty-first centuries. Lindner and her colleagues ensure the kinship of human beings as part of the global human family.[11] Dr. Lindner, as we now know, was nominated for the Nobel Peace Prize in 2015 and has been re-nominated in 2016 and 2017.

IX

Children at an early age not yet socially conditioned, in contrast to their elders, are still open to the mystery of the universe. They respond enthusiastically to the wonder of life. You'll note that in the following example of teaching a child the underlying creative source of life and being there is no mention of the word spiritual literacy or spiritual reality, no more than there is mention of the word "literacy" in teaching children to read. In being taught spiritual literacy, the child is encouraged to consider the invisible nature and source of energy and spirit underlying life and being.

The following passage taken from the Upanishads illustrates how to teach children about the spiritual reality through analogies.

The father is teaching his son:

"Bring me a fig."
"Here it is, father."
"Break it open. What do you see inside?"
"Some rather tiny seeds, father."
"Break one of them open. What do you see inside?"
"Nothing at all, father."
"From the inside of this tiny seed, which seems to be nothing at all, the whole fig tree grows. This is the Real. That is atman. That art thou, my son."[12]

In Hinduism, Atman is a symbol of the immanent spirit in human beings whose spiritual energy has the capacity to come into communication and communion with Brahman, the ultimate reality.

CHAPTER 1

The Crisis Threatening Humanity

I

Humanity faces a global crisis which threatens our very survival. The number of natural and human crises are not only escalating but becoming ever more destructive. The twentieth century has given rise to increasing anarchy, chaos, and turmoil—crisis within crisis within crisis—overwhelming the governing center of nations and the international community. Among them are the crisis in religions susceptible to sectarian divisions, including the eruption of violence within various Islamic factions in the Middle East; the global crisis in the breakdown of nations beset with escalating internal turmoil; the crisis in world capitalism mired in economic injustice and the unequal distribution of wealth; the crisis of power in the military-industrial complex, garrisoning the planet with weapons of mass destruction; the crisis in climate change and its effects on the world's ecosystem and the human habitat; the crisis in the management of long-life radioactive waste; the crisis of refugees penetrating national borders; the crisis of criminality and crammed prisons; the crisis in the use of psychotropic illicit drugs; the crisis in cyber security potentially leading to cyber warfare; and so on. The results of these crises give rise to what is referred to in this book as the *global crisis in humanity*.

Throughout the twentieth century, the rise of superpowers armed with nuclear arsenals at the ready, their wars, and proxy wars persisted as they furtively evolved under the radar of the powerbrokers engaged in the expansion of corporate capitalism globally. The worldwide risk of anthropocide and an ecocatastrophe became discernible for the first time in the aftermath of the two world wars in the twentieth century. By the twenty-first century, the global crisis in humanity had escalated. No longer could the role of peacekeeping and the safeguarding of human rights be secured and sustained by any single superpower or regional alliance of nations. The response to the disastrous 9/11 terrorist attack on the World Trade Center Towers embroiled the United States in two unnecessary wars branded as a "war on terrorism." Unfortunately, the United States soon found itself deeply mired in the benighted sectarian divisions and internal struggles within Islamic cultures.

On September 16, 2001, the George W. Bush administration put forth a Manichean response to the tragic terrorist attack on the United States, ostensibly accepted by both political parties and the mass of American citizens: "My administration has a job to do and we're going to do it. We will rid the world of evildoers." This simple-minded clarion call altered the U. S. global status as it soon became enmeshed in two ill-fated, preventable wars—in Iraq and Afghanistan—followed by the world financial crisis of 2008. Captivated by its audacity of exceptionalism, the United States was gravely compromised.

These dubious actions in the Middle East took place despite the bitter memory of the horrific United States catastrophe and defeat in the drawn-out Vietnam War. Much now known, or should have been known then, still haunts the American psyche. American investigative journalist and historian Nick Turse has released a startling study of the Vietnam War and a history of Vietnamese suffering, *Kill Anything That Moves: The Real American War in Vietnam*. While researching the history of the treatment of U. S. veterans for post-traumatic stress disorders, Turse discovered the records of the Vietnam War Crimes Working Group, furnished by a cadre of U. S. military officers who convened after the My Lai massacre to evaluate allegations of war crimes committed. Turse cross-referenced the information in these files with interviews of Vietnamese survivors. The records disclosed the unconscionable death and destruction wrought upon the Vietnamese people—allies of the United States against Japan in World War II.

Nick Turse described fierce bombings combined with ground operations, Operation Speedy Express, that ran from December 1968 to May 1969. During these operations, the United States brought to bear every weapon in its arsenal, with helicopter gunships firing off hundreds of rounds a minute, B52s shaking the earth with massive bomb loads, F-4 Phantom jets dropping vast amounts of napalm, navy ships hurling "Volkswagen-sized shells at targets miles away." Operation Speedy Express rained down death and destruction for six months across thousands of square miles, densely crowded with civilians. Revealed was the fact that the My Lai massacre was one of many My Lai massacres.[13]

II

Well steeped in depth psychology, psychiatrist Viktor Frankl brought to our attention the fact that "every age has its own collective neurosis." He realized the postmodern era to be an "existential vacuum," a "mass neurosis" or cleavage in the human psyche that has given rise to "a private and personal form of nihilism." Many today hold a nihilistic belief that "being has no meaning." The danger inherent in teaching of man's nothingness, Frankl alleged, is the outcome of the theory that man is nothing but a product of "biological, psychological, and sociological conditions, or the product of heredity and environment. Such a view of man makes him into a robot, not a human being."[14]

Humanity can no longer turn from the mounting, menacing, and mutinous turmoil encompassing human life, coupled with uncontrollable technological advances and their unintended consequences for our planet's ecosystems and the continued survival of planetary life. Cultures are in crisis and civilizations are crumbling from within. Rising fear, hatred, suffering, and dehumanization demand a moral and spiritual response. A world crisis has come to the fore, and the human capacity to acknowledge and confront it is a worrisome trial humanity must endure and hopefully transcend. Despite economic interdependence, mutual need, and dependence on planetary resources, nations continue to arm themselves with weapons of mass destruction. They fail to acknowledge that regardless of social, cultural, and political differences, citizens are obliged to share essential virtues of human life, especially an understanding of the eternal reality.

Steeped in political philosophy, Robert Kaplan claimed with the keen eye of a journalist that unmanageable anarchy gives rise to tyranny. Having traveled far and wide, Kaplan developed an informed realism balanced by a tolerant measure of idealism. Rising anarchy, he understood, is the outcome of nations disintegrating before our eyes. Any facile dreams of peace have been shattered during the post-Cold War era. "World War I delegitimized war," and "the end of the Cold War has spawned an equally dangerous notion—the delegitimization of great power divisions."[15] Kaplan had little confidence in the capability of the United Nations as a world body to resolve the issue of war and peace: "Rather than a better version of humanity, a world body merely reflects the global elite, as it is." He presumed that morality is unachievable without a global moral force necessary to foster peace. "Though the U.N. is certainly not about to dominate the world it carries within it the seeds of a banal, bureaucratically distant organization, inflexible because of the vast territory it would have to manage, and lacking accountability because of its received claim to progressive rationality."[16]

Kaplan presumed that the role of the United States was "necessary not only for minimal global security but for the health" of its own society. Yet he painted a pessimistic picture of "narcissistic isolationism" in a postindustrial world of miniaturized, concealable, deadly tools in the hands of stateless terrorists. He saw "legions of techno-optimists celebrating the expansion of world trade and claiming that human ingenuity will solve our problems." These same people neglected the fact that "human ingenuity comes too late." He disregarded the conventional wisdom that "mounting interdependency of financial markets make large-scale conflagration impossible," and that "beneath the surface of comforting, globalizing truths, the world is awash in dangerous new alliances."[17]

The lure of war and humankind's capitulation to the vicious cycle of wars cannot be understood fully from historical facts alone. The history of civilizations reveals the self's submission to the idolatry of culture that secretes the toxic cult of crude force. History teaches us nothing more than the fact that war is the fated destiny of the nation-state system, its presumption of sovereignty, and its power severed from truth and wisdom. Historical facts are the tip of the iceberg of the spiritual meaning of war.

Kaplan's assessment of the rising anarchy that breeds tyrannies, terrorism, genocide, and stateless forms of warfare globally must be taken to heart. They are akin to a ticking clock in a world mired in an entertainment culture devoid of understanding. Knowledge of history is a necessary aide-mémoire of the prevalence and the horror of war. History teaches that a "just war" doctrine is no longer justifiable in a world in which planetary life is at risk. Historical knowledge devoid of wisdom and conscience rooted in the eternal puts human life and nations on a dangerous course in a world armed with weapons of mass destruction.

American investigative journalist and academic Christian Parenti also assessed the growing chaos wrought by political, economic, and environmental disasters that gave rise to "catastrophic convergence." He was not referring specifically to several disasters happening simultaneously. Rather, he foresaw tragic conditions in which "problems compound and amplify each other, one expressing itself through another." He regarded the Cold War era of militarism with its traumas of the past that left behind damaged societies which "often respond to new crises in ways that are irrational, shortsighted, and self-destructive." The "Cold War sowed instability throughout the Third World; its myriad proxy wars left a legacy of armed groups, cheap weapons, smuggling networks, and corrupted officialdoms in developing countries."[18] Catastrophic convergence incited by climate change and the climate crisis "will require a relegitimation of the state's role in the economy." Planning and "downward redistribution of wealth" will be needed.[19] Parenti made clear the awful fix the world is in, given the looming global crisis in humanity.

Despite their profound sense of history, Kaplan as well as Parenti evaded the life and world of the spirit that lies deeper than cause-and-effect analyses of the world of time and history. Consciousness becomes structured such that its direction and content become drenched in the prevailing theories, philosophies, ideologies, and interpretations based solely on historical facts. The enemy is denigrated, dehumanized, and disregarded as fellow human beings. They are characterized not as persons or human subjects, but as objects of hatred. How else is the universal proscription against murder in all societies—the killing of fellow human beings—able to be bypassed without compunction? Both sides convert their enemy into heartless objects—*the* enemy of humanity. Both sides justify themselves as representing the good. An inverted moral consciousness afflicts warring nations.

III

There is no shortage of books being written about the twenty-first century that give us reason to address and assess two contradictory planetary outcomes: the life-affirming end of modern history with humanity graced in an uplifting apocalyptic age of spiritual evolution, on the one hand; and the life-destructive threat to planetary life and mass extinction, on the other. By falling back on history alone for answers, as though knowledge of history itself can assure us of the path we must traverse and the suffering we must bear, we find ourselves instead at a frightful impasse. The human mind in the postmodern era, keen on history and historical facts, has tragically failed to grasp the metahistorical and metaphysical underpinnings of reality—the spiritual contributions that issue from the heights and depths of human consciousness. Our hope and trust in humanity reside in our spiritual nature advanced by the discoveries of our transcultural world, still evolving and to be discussed in depth in succeeding chapters.

Military historian and Professor Emeritus, Andrew J. Bacevich focused on international relations and presents us with three interlocking crises facing the United States—a catastrophe in the making: an economy in disarray (no longer easily resolvable), government transformed into an imperial presidency (a democracy in form only), and a society enmeshed in endless wars (driven by a deep infatuation with military power). Bacevich regarded the revival of a distinctly American approach, the neglected tradition of the realism of Reinhold Niebuhr and the Niebuhrean perspective. "As pastor, teacher, activist, theologian, and prolific author, Niebuhr was a towering presence in American intellectual life from the 1930s through to the 1960s. Even today, he deserves our recognition as the most clear-eyed of American prophets."[20]

"Niebuhr's realism," Bacevich understood, "entertained few illusions about the nature of man, the possibilities of politics, or the pliability of history." Bacevich acknowledged Niebuhr's prescient view of the future: "Global economic crisis, total war, genocide, totalitarianism, and nuclear arsenals capable of destroying civilization itself—he viewed all of these with an unblinking eye that allowed no room for hypocrisy, hokum, or self-deception. Realism and humility formed the core of his worldview, each infused with a deeply felt Christian sensibility."[21] Niebuhr's realism embodied respect for power and its limits, sensitivity to the unintended consequences, aversion to claims of American exceptionalism, and skepticism of easy solutions; for at the end of the day, U. S. values, beliefs, and responsibility would be on trial.

Bacevich alleged that a return to those principles only can put the United States once more on a common ground in dealing with its urgent problems: a grand project of economic and political convergence and integration befitting globalization. "Realism in this sense implies an obligation to see the world as it actually is, not as we might like it to be. The enemy of realism is hubris, which in Niebuhr's day, and in our own, finds expression in an outsized confidence in the efficacy of American power, as an instrument to reshape the global order."[22]

Bacevich evaluated the limits of power, quoting from Niebuhr's books, including *The Irony of American History, World Crisis and American Responsibility, Moral Man and Immoral Society,* and *Beyond Tragedy.* We get a glimpse into Bacevich's grounding in the spiritual reality and his capacity to rise above a simple historical analysis. In his *Limits of Power,* Bacevich upheld that "Americans are increasingly inclined to write off the future. So they carry on heedless of the consequences even for themselves, no less for their children or grandchildren." His analysis identified the tragedy of our age, moving inexorably "to the end of history." Bacevich quoted Niebuhr from *Beyond Tragedy*: "social orders will probably destroy themselves in the effort to prove that they are indestructible." In a nuclear age, Bacevich's final warning should be gravely pondered: "Clinging doggedly to the conviction that the rules to which other nations must submit don't apply, Americans appear determined to affirm Niebuhr's axiom of willful self-destruction."[23]

The frightful reality we face concerns the dual connotation of "the end of history." It presumes the end of the modern era giving rise to a positive and uplifting rebirth in the postmodern world, advancing knowledge of the synthesis of religion, philosophy, the sciences, the liberal arts, and the humanities. Failing to awaken to the eternal and to the deeper meaning underlying history, we confront the dark clouds of ecocide—the extensive damage and destruction to the world's ecosystems—that casts a menacing specter on planetary life.

In his *Irony of American History,* Niebuhr also claimed that the United States as a world power would be "an inexorable fact for decades to come, whether within or without a fuller world constitution than now prevails." Niebuhr warned that even healthier "modern nations must be content with only approximate equilibria of power lest they destroy the vitalities of various social forces by too rigorous effort to bring the whole communal life under an equalitarian discipline." If the power of the United States "does disappear it will be eliminated by the emergence of new forces or the new coalition of older forces, rather than by constitutional contrivance."[24] Niebuhr also warned that "the fragmentary wisdom of any nation should be prevented from achieving the bogus omniscience, which occurs when the weak are too weak to dare challenge the opinion of the powerful."[25]

In his follow-up book, *Washington Rules*, Bacevich assessed the goal of U. S. power, what he called caveats of "a new trinity." His *first caveat* is the warning to reverse the self-defeating goal of hegemony. "The purpose of the military is not to combat evil or remake the world, but to defend the United States and its most vital interests." Any nation "defining itself in terms of military might is well down the road to perdition, as earlier generations of Americans instinctively understood." His *second caveat* is his warning to heed the primary duty station of the military. "Just as the U.S. military should not be a global police force, so too it should not be a global occupation force." Bacevich recommends dismantling the Pentagon's sprawling network of existing bases and establishing a military presence abroad only in specific circumstances after necessary public debate and congressional authorization. He endorsed the policy of the withdrawal of U. S. troops forthwith from the Persian Gulf and Central Asia.[26]

Bacevich's *third caveat* is his warning concerning the *just war tradition*. The U. S. must employ military might "only as a last resort and only in self-defense." He denounced the doctrine of the pre-emptive war policy advanced by the George W. Bush administration, arrogating to itself the employment of force against "ostensible threats even before they material-ize." Bacevich cited this reversal of the just war tradition as "a moral and strategic abomination, the very inverse of prudent and enlightened state-craft" that gave rise to "the misguided 2003 invasion of Iraq."[27] "Promising prosperity and peace, the Washington rules are propelling the United States toward insolvency and perpetual war. Over the horizon a shipwreck of epic proportions awaits."[28]

Bacevich's third book, *Breach of Trust: How Americans Failed Their Soldiers and Their Country*, indicted the U. S. public for becoming mentally and emotionally released from the preoccupation with the nation entering wars, in view of having an all-volunteer military. In this scenario, citizens generally tend to be relieved of fear that members of their family will be conscripted for military duty. This shift to an all-volunteer military dates back to the early 1970s when President Richard Nixon "accurately interpreted the popular will" to "jettison the tradition of the citizen-soldier" by "creating an all-volunteer force."[29] Eliminating conscription has lessened the nation's communal commitments once inspired by moral and personal virtues; the nation turned its focus inward and became mired in a utilitarian mentality, seeking diverse forms of entertainment.

"Americans accepted fighting for freedom as their job; today with freedom still their birthright, they expect someone else to do the fighting."[30] Bacevich regarded the all-volunteer military as a bad bargain—fiscally, politically, and morally—and "the warrior has proven a costly disappointment." Who benefits from the existing arrangement? Bacevich included "the national security state, the military-industrial-congressional complex, and the mushrooming private security sector . . . the people who wield influence within these institutions have no incentive for seeing anything amiss."[31] Bacevich claimed that in so far as the past continues to be prologue, the U. S. can look forward to "more needless wars or shadow conflicts sold by a militarized and irresponsible political elite; more wars mismanaged by an intellectually sclerotic and unimaginative senior officer corps; more wars that exact huge penalties without yielding promised outcomes, with the consequences quickly swept under the rug." The truth Bacevich endeavored to get across about the all-volunteer military concerned the fact that it immensely reduced the public's informed moral preoccupation with armed intervention. A broader approach, more inclusive of the public, is a return to "conscription, with *all* able-bodied young men and women eligible for service but only *some* actually selected."[32]

IV

Nick Turse brought our attention to the plight of the U. S. in his *Complex: How the Military Invades Our Everyday Lives.* He disclosed the hidden system that penetrates the lives of citizens, referred to as the Military-Industrial-Technological-Scientific-Media-Intelligence-Corporate -Complex. This covert system taking hold ideologically is a marriage of corporate capitalism and the military-industrial complex, which invades and pervades all aspects of the lives of its citizens. This current way of life perpetuates an untoward and problematic mentality difficult to reverse—a tendency toward total influence, "economic, political, even spiritual," first recognized and acknowledged by President Eisenhower in his farewell address in 1961 and extended extensively since. Eisenhower was prescient: "This conjunction of an immense military establishment and a large arms industry is new in the American experience. . . . Yet we must not fail to comprehend its grave implications. . . . In the councils of government, we must guard against the acquisition of unwarranted influence, whether sought or unsought, by the military-industrial complex. The potential for the disastrous rise of misplaced power exists and will persist."[33]

Turse claimed that this vast system—the conjunction of the military establishment and the large arms industry—is felt in every state, city, and office of the federal government. It is a symbiotic relationship not limited to megacorporations; it includes "thousands and thousands of small-towns and their niche contractors" and "numerous government agencies connected to the U. S. Department of Defense and allied entities such as the Central Intelligence Agency and the Department of Homeland Security."[34]

Turse concluded that collectively these government agencies form "the essential core of the military-industrial complex." Military contractors may "still reign supreme as the primary weapons-producing 'merchants of death,' but huge arms deals including firms like Lockheed Martin and Boeing, are now only a mere portion of the story. While they may still rake in the largest single sums of any Pentagon contractors their total take . . . is dwarfed by the combined totals of the rest of the DOD's [Department of Defense] contractors. These include big-name companies, small firms, and organizations you might never suspect of being on the military dole." A partial list runs the gamut from "California TriStar Films and Twentieth Century Fox to Velda Farms . . . from the National Vitamin Company of Porterville, California, to the American Meat Institute . . . and the American Medical Association. . . . These entities now form the bulk of the Complex, turning the iron triangle into a collection of 'iron myriagons' (ten-thousand-sided polygons)."[35]

According to Turse, the military-education complex has the potential to alter the landscape of higher education by manipulating research agendas, changing the course of curricula, and forcing schools to play by its rules. This has dangerous implications for higher education, enabling and enhancing military adventures for decades to come. Turse alleged that this cozy arrangement among the various organized entities will lead to new lethal technologies wielded against people across the globe. The reality citizens find themselves accepting grudgingly involves the fact that, "None of this, however, ever enters the realm of debate in the United States—which gives the idea of the ivory tower."[36]

Turse discovered the great boon to the expansion of the military-industrial complex brought about by the formation of the Department of Homeland Security 1993-2003: "'national security' was once the concern mainly of three agencies—the Department of Defense, the Department of State, and the Intelligence Community." As far as what happened since and what is supported in homeland security, Turse found the following: "57 federal agencies, 50 states, 8 territories, and 3,066 counties involved . . . 87,000 different government jurisdictions that will play roles in homeland security . . . the private sector will play a major role . . . and this role will not be limited to logistical support. Corporate America will be required to play a major operational role in homeland security."[37]

V

The disturbing geopolitical quandary the world confronts was discussed in depth by Zbigniew Brzezinski, former national security advisor during President Jimmy Carter's administration. Brzezinski claimed that the "World is now interactive and interdependent. It is also, for the first time, a world in which the problems of human survival have begun to overshadow more traditional international conflicts. Unfortunately, the major powers have yet to undertake globally cooperative responses to the new and increasingly grave challenges to human well-being—environmental, climatic, socio-economic, nutritional, or demographic."[38]

For Brzezinski, the onset and outcome of the Arab Spring was a reminder of a potentially political awakening of the Middle East currently mired in growing turmoil and the prospect of virulent sectarianism in Islam. Of the many conflicts besetting the region, Syria is currently trapped in a civil war with no end in sight, and the U. S. is entangled in the Afghanistan War—the longest war in American history. Brzezinski claimed that the world of the twenty-first century presents far different challenges than those of the past. "The world is now almost everywhere politically awakened—with millions stirring restlessly in pursuit of a better future. . . . Consequently, today's world is much less susceptible to domination by a single power, even by one as militarily powerful and politically influential as the United States."[39]

Consequently, he foresaw that the West remained enmeshed in an unstable economic and political world confronting a world crisis. Nowhere in his disclosure of the U. S.'s vulnerabilities or of the timeworn nation-state system did Brzezinski fully grasp the significance of transcending geopolitics. He failed to comprehend the need for a world order that safeguards planetary life and binds the consciousness of human beings trans-culturally. Cultures and civilizations are the creations of human beings in a world moving toward interdependence economically, socially, politically, and morally. Lacking knowledge of the eternal reality of the cosmos and universe, Brzezinski became incapable of overcoming a mindset shackled to the pervasive idolatry of one's nation.

German Professor of Philosophy Jürgen Habermas recognized that the supra-national response to the crisis of global power demanded "a new mode of politics capable of transforming mentalities." In contrast to Brzezinski, Habermas understood the necessity of bringing about a change in the structure and direction of consciousness to assuage the enormity of destruction inflicted by two world wars and constant warfare among nations globally. A change in mentality is no simple matter. It presumes a mass education of citizens living in differing and antagonistic civilizations. It also presumes confronting and remedying what appears to be an intractable world problem—"the monstrous injustice of a highly stratified world society in which even elementary basic goods and life chances are today unevenly distributed in an intolerable way."[40]

In principle, humanity undergoing a change in the direction, structure, and content of consciousness must aim, according to Habermas, "at civilizing the exercise of political authority no matter how farsighted it may be."[41] Practically speaking, another problem confronts the citizens of the world's nations. The fact that injustices and disparities cannot be expunged overnight in a world whose citizens have become habituated more and more to utilitarian values, heedless and bereft of knowledge of the ancient cardinal virtues. Yet Habermas understood that the fundamental problem is, at its root, spiritual and deeper than Brzezinski's geopolitical solution that rests fundamentally on power politics.

Habermas foresaw the possibility of a supra-national body with adequate power that extended beyond the United Nations; an intergovernmental agency to promote international cooperation inclusive of all nations, as well as an international court of justice. On a global scale, humanity would thereby overcome many culturally embedded violations of human dignity and human rights that must be addressed: impoverished social classes, unequal treatment of women and men, discrimination against foreigners, and cultural, religious, and racial prejudice and bigotry, etc.[42] Yet Habermas, like Brzezinski, failed to awaken to our transcultural world that discloses the fundamental properties of the cosmos and universe, as well as properties of our divine character as human beings. The transcultural world, to be discussed in depth in following chapters, subordinates the particularity and idolatry of culture to the universality of human existence. It establishes the imperative of spiritual literacy transculturally. From where we stand today, Niebuhr's warning some seven decades ago regarding human destiny encapsulated the unflinching mission ahead: the task of building a world community as humanity's final possibility and necessity.

VI

Professor of philosophy J. Glenn Gray thought deeply about the spiritual component of warfare. He helped unravel the complex spiritual mystery underlying warfare few of us would have imagined. In his book, *The Warriors: Reflections on Men in Battle*, he recalled the brutality and hatred as well as the love and beauty he experienced in a war environment as an intelligence officer in Europe during World War II.

"I have come to the extremity of knowing beyond all doubt that there is no other way for me to survive this period except the hard Christian way of finding the finer points in my associates and loving them for those characteristics. The bare cold, prophetic words of Auden, "We must love one another or die" have rung in my mind on several of these frigid, sleepless nights of late . . . you would have to see many things . . . to know why I should come to realize such a primitive truth as that I have only one alternative to death and that is to love, to care for people whom I, as a natural man, want to strike down.[43]

Gray realized that our nature is not merely human but divine. In awakening to his creative vocation and power of freedom, much limited on the battlefield, he confirmed the wisdom stirred by conscience: to love to the extent possible as a means of validating the meaning and purpose of life. "I am driven to the Christian way out. It is hard, yet there is great comfort in finding it. I sleep better now, and because I give love I find it oftener."[44]

When conscripted into the military, Gray had just received his Ph. D. in Philosophy from Columbia University. His military experience awakened him to religious revelations, symbolic embodiments of the world of the spirit and spiritual life. He envisioned the fundamental character of human beings, whether enemy or compatriot: "The search for the most familiar and evident of all truths the belonging together of the human species, in religious terms, the brotherhood of man, is rarely attended with success."[45] From his military experiences in a war environment, he was able to establish as an intelligence officer his love and brotherhood for both the captured enemy and his colleagues in the military. He had awakened to the spiritual reality and had grasped its primal source that illumined his soul and invigorated his mind and body under the most harrowing conditions on the battlefield.

Gray discovered that a decisive transformation ruptures the barrier between the self's consciousness and conscience, beyond Freud's superego; that is, beyond the self's conscience caught strictly in the grips of the values of culture, civilization, and social upbringing. The self no longer remains deaf and blind to its communal responsibility; one's life is no longer yoked to necessity, fate, and chance imposed by the world. The self responds to the call of conscience beyond the limited range of conformity to the herd, what psychiatrist Viktor Frankl called our collective or mass neurosis and what Christianity calls our fallen state. Under such conditions, we return to ourselves, delivered from our submergence in the world of time and its conforming forces.

Our true inner history of freedom and individuality is disclosed to us only upon awakening to conscience liberated from thoughtless conformity to norms, rules, laws, and social institutions. Prior to our awakening, we are, as Frankl claimed, robotized rather than humanized. Only when we awaken to conscience—knowledge grounded in the spiritual reality—do we become aware of a higher freedom enabling us thereby to discern true wisdom underlying social institutions tethered to the moral reality. Only then does our genuine struggle of freedom begin, as we rise above intellectual, moral, and natural necessity. Conscience becomes transfigured spiritually. Only then do we escape our idolization of the created world as an ersatz god stifling our creative vocation.

Awakening to the spirit and to conscience becomes a defining moment in our lives. It's as though a membrane in consciousness held intact by conformity to the outer reality ruptures and the spirit bursts forth. Our creative freedom frees up our capacity to enter the realm beyond the law and redemption: the realm of eternal values and the spirit with its outpouring of grace and ecstasy. Consciousness has overcome its muffled and dampened conditioning and is no longer submerged in the world of time. It has awakened to its divine inheritance of pure conscience, what Nicholas Berdyaev called the "superconscious," in contrast to our conscious and unconscious minds.

Gray clarified this state of awakening. "To an awakened conscience everything about human actions becomes then strange and nearly inexplicable. Why men fight without anger and kill without compunction is understandable at all only to a certain point. A slight alteration in consciousness would be sufficient to put their deeds in a true light and turn them forever from destruction." The "true light" is the self's entry into the life and world of the spirit. Gray expressed a fundamental truth in breaking the bondage of conscience to necessity imposed by the temporal-spatial reality—that is, Freud's superego. "It would require only a coming to themselves to transform killers into friends and lovers, for, paradoxical as it may seem, the impulses that make killers are not so different in kind from those that make lovers. I know no other explanation for the notorious linkage in war between the noblest and the basest deeds, the most execrable vices and the sublimest virtues."[46]

Herein we confront a profound metaphysical paradox. What precisely in spiritual awakening could possibly clarify the similarities between the impulses that make killers and those that make lovers? To turn a person into a killer, to induce a person to kill another person, is contrary to the universal moral proscription against murder in all social groupings, including primitive societies. For a person to kill another, he or she must be convinced that the enemy is an enemy of more than just one's community. The self must be convinced that the human being killed is *the* enemy of humanity. In other words, the self must be convinced that *the* enemy is the embodiment of evil—out of the pale of human existence. The enemy is thereby stripped of its humanness. In killing *the* enemy and ridding the world of evil, the soldier experiences communal ecstasy, the psychological state of being taken out of oneself by presumably carrying out God's work. However, the fact is well-nigh established that communal ecstasy is not genuine community with our human species, and this is called into question by soldiers upon returning to civilian life. The more spiritually sensitive among them soon fall into a stricken state of remorse with regard to the moral inversion experienced in the war environment. Their consciences become traumatized by the violence they participated in.

Disheartening also is the fact that many soldiers, unconscious of the evil they participated in, are self-wounded psychologically; the evil remains underground and inaccessible to their conscious minds. After the war, soldiers soon learn that *the* enemy country has taken its place once again as a friend or an ally and, thereby, a member of the "human family." Their former illusion on the battlefield—*the* enemy as the embodiment of evil—can be likened to the crucial impulses underlying the horrific acts of terrorism carried out by suicide bombers who unwittingly or intentionally surrender their lives to God, destroying what they have come to believe (or were made to believe) is sheer evil in the world, in return for a presumed eternal life in paradise. Here we see the kinship of soldiers in communal ecstasy forfeiting their lives for their comrades and suicide bombers destroying what is believed to be the embodiment of evil.

But what is it that makes lovers? Spiritually speaking, love is the moving power of life that has mystical and cosmic significance. Love has a divine predestination, as Plato disclosed in the *Symposium*. Love, especially erotic love, is the attraction to the good the self recognizes in the other, the beloved; the good the soul of the lover yearns for and is separated from reveals itself in the life of the beloved. The socialized self is a truncated self, a soul partially mesmerized and captivated by prevailing social values. The spellbound self is divided and suffers in a state of alienation, severed from its eternal character. Union with the other in erotic love anticipates self-completion. The self in love foresees the reunion of its cleaved self—the restoration of its wholeness. Love, therefore, is the self's emotional thirst for reunion of its divided self from bondage to the socially defined nature of the good. Lovers thereby become bonded in mutual ecstasy through the mutual anticipation of their pure and whole humanity, each helping the other toward the reunion of the self in plenitude and in freedom.

The impulse to kill and the impulse to love are both rooted in the socially defined good and constitute an emotional response to sever and detach the self from the bad and reunite with the good. In killing enemies, soldiers experience communal ecstasy. They are taken out of their mundane lives embedded in the temporal-spatial reality and rise above egoism to experience the presumed good of their community. They are bonded with their fellows who represent the good and envision *the* enemy as the embodiment of evil. In communal ecstasy, soldiers are willing to sacrifice themselves to save their comrades from the evil assaulting their community, a community which, in their inverted moral state, represents the transcendent Good. Here we realize a virulent form of misplaced idolatry of one's society and community. Gray alleged that the ultimate secret of comradeship that gives rise to sacrificing one's life for his or her comrades is "nothing less than the assurance of immortality that makes self-sacrifice at these moments so relatively easy."[47]

For two lovers, the whole world is transfigured with a ray of light coming from the ecstasy that anticipates self-completion, experienced in mutual erotic entrancement. Neither the souls of human beings whose impulses turn them into killers, nor the souls of human beings whose impulses turn them into lovers, are necessarily awakened to the spiritual reality. Conscience is caught in the grips of the world and its social institutions, social and political forces, propaganda, and contemporary customs and mores. During battle, soldiers are reduced to the lowest moral common denominator. Indeed, soldiers of each warring faction mentally and emotionally strip enemy soldiers of their divine inheritance in order to kill them without compunction. Tragically, soldiers of high moral and spiritual achievement on either side of the battlefield sometimes kill or are killed by a crude, psychologically degenerate enemy from the other side. Similarly, in the case of lovers, the erotic bond of love lovers share may be based on crude mores, low self-esteem, or a lack of moral maturity. Erotic rapture cannot be the sole determinant for the marriage of two lovers; true marriage requires reason and the guidance of wisdom. Gray alleged that an awareness of what is happening to soldiers in time of war and people in love requires "a coming to themselves," a spiritual breakthrough awakening their conscience. Ultimately, for both soldiers and lovers, this can only be actualized through freedom and spiritual literacy.

Unlike the experience of philosopher Gray, the vast majority of soldiers do not awaken to conscience. Many are traumatized upon homecoming, having to cope with their experience of evil on the battlefield. Psychiatrist Jonathan Shay has studied the disastrous war experiences of soldiers in depth, their combat traumas and tribulations that incur psychiatric symptoms upon homecoming. Shay admonished his readers to learn about "the psychological damage that war does."[48] He discovered a formidable list of symptoms soldiers experience upon homecoming. They include, among others, loss of authority over mental functions; persistent mobilization of the body and the mind for anticipated lethal danger; persistent activation of combat survival skills in civilian life; chronic health problems stemming from mobilization of the body for anticipated danger; a sense of betrayal and exploitation that destroys the capacity for social trust; alcohol and drug abuse; and suicidality, despair, isolation, and meaninglessness.[49]

This range of key symptoms suffered by many with post-traumatic stress disorder (PTSD) reveals that the moral and spiritual reality is a furtive underpinning of the life of citizens. Soldiers on both sides of the battlefield experience, psychologically, communal ecstasy, as they regard their respective nations as an ersatz God. Upon homecoming, many battlefield solders feel betrayed. According to Shay, this paradox is clear and should be taken to heart: fighting for one's country can render one unfit to be its citizen.[50] The universality of the moral and spiritual reality trans-historically and transculturally resounds profoundly in the lives of veterans upon homecoming throughout the ages, many in need of empathy and compassion to bring about a possible recovery from their psychological traumas. In his study going back to the Homeric period in the *Iliad* and *Odyssey* and continuing up through the contemporary world, Shay raised the fundamental question concerning the root causes of the felt betrayal experienced by soldiers upon their return to civilian life. The problem lies primarily in the realm of society's betrayal of the cardinal virtues, the realm of ethics, and the recognition of our humanness that transcends our national or societal origin. War eviscerates for both warring parties the trans-moral and trans-spiritual underpinnings of their respective societies.

In his book *Killing from the Inside Out: Moral Inquiry and Just War,* Professor Robert Emmet Meagher claimed that there is a crisis of suicides among young veterans who have suffered the trauma of war. Many veterans feel betrayed by their country. Meagher alleged that the just war theory has become a self-deluding lie and called for a rethinking of the largest standing military establishment in the history of the world—the United States.[51]

The global crisis in humanity and the lethal severity of the destructive power of contemporary warfare, which put planetary life at risk, have brought about a reality that calls into question any possible justification for war today. Knowledge of our transcultural world and the urgent exposure of children globally to spiritual literacy from an early age have now become imperative for the survival of humanity and planetary life.

CHAPTER 2

Human and Biological Evolution

I

All life-forms live within four spheres of planetary life: the geosphere, atmosphere, hydrosphere, and biosphere. Any damage to or destruction of any of these planetary spheres could bring about the annihilation of humankind and the extinction of all planetary life-forms. The distinguished paleontologist and priest Teilhard de Chardin envisaged human evolution and biological evolution as two phases of a single process. In his *Phenomenon of Man*, he coined the term *noosphere* to denote the sphere of mind as opposed to the biosphere or sphere of life. Human beings and all life-forms are not only nourished by the resources of the earth. The sun, as Plato taught in antiquity, also provides two necessary attributes to sustain planetary life: energy to transform matter into life-forms and light by which the eye is able to see. He made an astute observation about the miraculous nature of the human eye and its relation to the sun: the eye, a biological organ, contains in itself both the energy of the sun necessary for its generation and light endowing the self with vision. The Earth retains its procreative power in its dependence on the energy and light of the Sun.

Science in the twentieth century has discovered that the atom can no longer be exemplified as a microscopic and infinitesimal center of its own domain. Einstein's theory of relativity, Planck's quantum theory, Bohr's atomic theory, Heisenberg's uncertainty principle, Rutherford's discovery of component parts of the atom, Fermi's discovery of slowing down the neutrons penetrating the nucleus of the atom, Meitner's discovery of the process of unleashing the energy in the atom, among other major discoveries—all brought about a profound re-examination of the nature of the universe during the first half of the twentieth century. These discoveries enriched our understanding of the universe and awakened us to an *unseen* reality. Einstein's revelatory breakthroughs—especially his general theory of relativity of 1905 and his special theory of relativity of 1909—helped launch knowledge of the universe. They released modern science from its naïve presumption that the universe is fundamentally materialistic, mechanistic, and monistic. Ultimately, his discoveries were confirmed. Energy is convertible to matter and matter to energy. Einstein's discoveries awakened human consciousness to the mystery that energy and the inchoate energy inherent in matter constitute the foundation of the universe. The vast source of energy in the universe is hidden, much of it in solid matter.

From the revelation of Einstein's theory of relativity in 1905 to the splitting of the atom in 1945, consciousness has been enlightened by the fact that mass disappears when the atom is split and converts to energy.[52] Science has played an important part in unraveling the mystery of life's origin and in disclosing important aspects of the universe that ensued. Paradoxically, science has shattered the complacency of those who hold a materialist assumption of the nature of the universe. Science reaffirms the fact that factual happenings in history are immersed in and are the upshot of another world: a universe in which the foundation of human life entails energy and spirit.

Twentieth-century science found itself captivated by a paradox. Focused on the material reality of the universe, the physical sciences not only shattered but invalidated their materialist presumption. Planck's quantum theory, Bohr's atomic theory, and Einstein's theory of relativity were major factors in bringing about a serious re-examination of the epistemology of the scientific enterprise—the philosophy concerning the nature and scope of knowledge.

Physicist Werner Heisenberg weighed in on the revolution going on in the physical sciences. He questioned the validity of the primacy of matter and the assumption of a mechanistic, materialistic, and monistic universe. He acknowledged that in the rigid framework of natural science in the nineteenth century, "mind would be introduced into the general picture only as a kind of mirror of the material world; and when one studied properties of this mirror in the science of psychology, the scientists were always tempted . . . to pay more attention to its mechanical than to its optical properties." Heisenberg contended that contemporary physics had brought about the most important change by its dissolution of the rigid frame of concepts of classical physics—space, time, matter, and causality—especially causality.[53] By the end of the twentieth century, some scientists had a message for the scientific community, especially concerning the field of biochemistry in which science plays an important role. Heisenberg had seriously challenged scientism: belief in the universal applicability of the scientific method as the most authoritative worldview that excluded other perspectives.

II

The first attempt to cobble together a synthesis of the various domains of knowledge was carried out by Pierre Teilhard de Chardin (1881–1955). This was followed by the work of Gerald L. Schroeder, an MIT physical scientist schooled in molecular biology and Old Testament theology. Some seven decades after Teilhard's work appeared, Schroeder fills in some of the gaps in Teilhard's analysis. Schroeder contends that a "single consciousness, an all-encompassing wisdom, pervades the universe." The discoveries of science, Schroeder claimed—those that research the quantum nature of subatomic matter, those that explore the molecular complexity of biology, and those that probe the brain and mind interface—"have moved us to the brink of a startling realization: all existence is the expression of this wisdom."[54] Surprisingly, I could not find in Schroeder's three major works concerning religion and science written in the twenty-first century any mention of Teilhard's works published some seventy-five years earlier. In the remainder of this chapter, Teilhard's contribution to knowledge will be reviewed, and Schroeder's will be discussed further in the next chapter.

Teilhard's major work, *The Phenomenon of Man*, written while in Peking from 1938 to 1940, with *"Summing Up or Postscript"* and *"Appendix"* dated October 28, 1948, did not appear in print until much later. The Catholic Church withheld Teilhard's book from publication until his death in 1955. Teilhard regards the theory of evolution to be a light dawning and at last "revealing the irreversible coherence of all that exists."[55]

As Galileo ruptured the ancient geocentric view and expanded man's vision to the boundless universe, Teilhard claimed that Darwin and other nineteenth-century evolutionists nudged consciousness to envisage "the sweep of a movement whose orbit infinitely transcends the natural sciences and has successively invaded and conquered the surrounding territory— chemistry, physics, sociology and even mathematics and the history of religions."[56] Nevertheless, Teilhard recognized the shortcoming of Darwinism and claimed that "evolution is still only transformism, and transformism is only an old Darwinian hypothesis as local and as dated as Laplace's conception of the solar system or Wegener's Theory of Continental Drift."[57] Teilhard regarded the evolutionists, including the more current scientists, as being halfway to the truth.

Teilhard's *Phenomenon of Man* received an enthusiastic and passionate welcome in multidisciplinary faculty seminars at Michigan State University in the 1960s. We mulled over and debated his idea that evolution of the universe itself gave birth to life and consciousness on the planet. Teilhard embraced the view that sets him apart from the evolutionists, even though he realized their contributions. The "long animal heredity," he chided evolutionists, "might well have formed our limbs, but our mind was always above the play of the realities it enumerated."[58] He sustained the view that the basic aspects of the universe—matter, biology, morphology, and physiology—engender a qualitative attribute that the within of our lives alone is able to fathom. Concerning our spiritual nature, he was in substantial agreement with the religious existentialists of the nineteenth century who included, among others, Søren Kierkegaard, Vladimir Solovyev, Fyodor Dostoevsky, and Nicholas Berdyaev.

Teilhard maintained the idea of the *complexio oppositorum* (a union of opposites) of psyche and matter as the basic stuff of the universe underlying cosmogenesis and planetary evolution. He presumed the stuff of the universe—from its minutest corpuscles to its macrostructures—contains in itself both psychic and material attributes. His hypothesis challenged the presumption of abiogenesis, the spontaneous origin of living organisms directly from lifeless matter. "The history of consciousness and its place in the world remain incomprehensible to anyone who has not seen first of all that the cosmos in which man finds himself caught up constitutes, by reason of the unimpeachable wholeness of its whole, a *system*, a *totum* and a *quantum*: a system by its plurality, a *totum* by its unity, a quantum by its energy; all three within a boundless contour."[59]

Teilhard identified "two energies—of mind and matter—spread respectively through the two layers of the world (the within and the without)." He also presumed that they "are constantly associated and in some way pass into each other." The full significance of this fact is a simple truth: "To think, we must eat."[60] Spiritual power presupposes the capacity to think. Consciousness, thought, and spirit are intimately intertwined with biophysical reality. Although all energy is physical in nature, what appears as physical from the without of matter comprises two distinct energy forms carrying out two differing functions—one tangential and the other radial. The tangential (which scientists are able to quantify; e.g., eating and digesting food) links elements together (food and life behavior); radial energy (a force for synthesis; e.g., consciousness, thought, spirit) underlies complexification, convergence, and the emergence of the new (that is, the creation of civilizations, weapons of mass destruction, etc.). This second form of energy, radial energy, eludes scientific analysis, even though it is the source from which scientific analysis stems. Teilhard alleged that radial energy is knowable only through reflective consciousness, grasped through our intuitive intelligence. It is absent in the equations of scientific analysis and in any endeavor to validate its findings in empirical reality and mathematics. Radial energy underlies what he referred to as the law of complexification, the synthesizing power of evolution that gives rise to convergence and the emergence into new branches on the tree of life.

In his writings, Teilhard described the two energies as follows: "*a tangential energy* which links the elements with all others of the same order (that is to say, of the same complexity and the same centricity) as itself in the universe; and a *radial energy* which draws it toward ever greater complexity and centricity—in other words forwards."[61] In so far as radial energy within remained undisclosed or disclosed itself mathematically—as quantum opposed to quality—radial energy remained hidden in evolution. It disclosed itself to the human mind and was of profound importance in understanding the limitation of Darwinism. What is important and understandable scientifically is the fact that there is no detection of measurable new energy in physical-chemical analysis. Teilhard noted that in "no case does the energy required for synthesis appear to be provided by an influx of fresh capital, but by expenditure. What is gained on one side is lost on the other. Nothing is constructed except at the price of an equivalent destruction."[62] The second law of thermodynamics disclosed that "a fraction of the available energy is irrecoverably 'entropised,' lost, that is to say, in the form of heat . . . something is finally burned in the course of every synthesis in order to pay for the synthesis."[63] Two principles are working complementarily: conservation and dissipation.

III

On the human scale, Teilhard used the analogy "to think, we must eat" to elucidate the fact that a simple correspondence between tangential and radial energy is impossible. He clarified this complex correspondence between the two forms of energy: "what a variety of thoughts we get out of one slice of bread! Like the letters of the alphabet, which can equally well be assembled into nonsense as into the most beautiful poem, the same calories seem as indifferent as they are necessary to the spiritual values they nourish. . . . On the one hand, only a minute fraction of 'physical' energy is used up in the highest exercise of spiritual energy: on the other, the minute fraction once absorbed results on the internal scale in the most extraordinary oscillations."[64] Teilhard alleged that Darwinism's chance and natural selection contain only half the truth. This has driven scientists to account for the other half—the greatest of mysteries—the transition from the chemical-inorganic reality to cellular life on the planet.

Religion itself, in its various cultural forms, is a revelation of transcendent energy, spirit, and freedom. The natural-social-cultural world is an objectification and embodiment of energy and spirit. Humans carry within themselves the power of freedom and creativity. In scriptural symbols, human beings are born in the image and likeness of God—the eternal. For Teilhard, no theory of evolution in the sense of transformism in a material sense can evade the truth of the existence of this primary energy and spirit. Thus, his synthesis of religion and science disregarded the materialist views of evolutionists blind to the fact that "their scientific intelligence had anything to do in itself with evolution."[65] According to Teilhard, this means that reflective consciousness emergent in *Homo sapiens* is at the root of scientific methodology. Evolution engenders, consequently, something beyond and above natural selection as an adaptive mechanism. The idea of evolution is much more than a theory, a system, or a hypothesis. It is "a general condition to which all theories, all hypotheses, all systems must bow and which they must satisfy henceforward if they are to be thinkable and true. Evolution is a light illuminating all facts, a curve that all lines must follow."[66] "The consciousness of each of us is evolution looking at itself and reflecting."[67]

Human convergence, Teilhard maintained, is based on the concept of the law of an all-pervading cosmic tendency taking place in cosmogenesis—the evolution of the cosmos and the universe. The big bang theory presupposes the birth of the universe with its development still unfolding. It is the evolution of an increasingly elaborate organization in which the mineral world and the world of life appear as antithetical creations on the intermediary scale of human life. But on a closer examination and far back along the scale of time, he contended, "when we force our way right down to the microscopic level and beyond to the infinitesimal . . . they [the mineral world and the world of life] seem quite otherwise—a single mass gradually melting in on itself."[68] He noted the supreme mystery underlying biogenesis: the transition from physio-chemical to cellular life that eludes human consciousness, except in symbolic systems whether mystical or mathematical.

Teilhard introduced a revolutionary idea concerning the advent of life. Such substances classified as dead, "would be incomprehensible if they did not possess already, deep down in themselves, some sort of rudimentary psyche." Even though "each being has and must have a cosmic embryogenesis" (i.e., a point of birth in the cosmos), this "in no way invalidates the reality of its historic birth."[69] In every domain in the passage from subatomic units to atoms, from atoms to inorganic molecules, to subcellular living units or self-replicating assemblages of molecules, to cells, to multicellular individuals, to cephalized metazoa with brains, to primitive man, and beyond—"when anything exceeds a certain measurement, it suddenly changes its aspect, condition or nature."[70]

Teilhard assumed something akin to a sacred marriage of the material and psychic components immanent in the stuff of the universe, from the level of corpuscles to the human scale of reality. He took for granted that any attempt to grasp the moment of transition from supposed dead to the advent of enlivened matter will remain a mystery. In a provocative way, he insisted that the materialist assumption of abiogenesis (matter giving birth to life) is invalid, let alone unprovable scientifically. "No amount of historical research will ever reveal the details of this story. Unless the science of tomorrow is able to reconstruct the process in the laboratory, we shall probably never find any material vestige of this emergence of the microscopic from the molecular, of the organic from the chemical, of the living from the pre-living."[71]

What then was Teilhard's hypothesis in light of Pasteur's discovery that life in a laboratory never appears in a medium in which all germs were eliminated through sterilization? This procedure established that protoplasm, the material of which living cells are made, was no longer formed directly from the inorganic substances of the earth. Teilhard claimed that Pasteur's experiments of sterilization may be "capable of destroying not only the living germs, whose elimination is desired, but also 'pre-living germs' from which alone life might emerge." For Teilhard, the most convincing proof "that life was produced once and once only on earth is furnished by the profound structural unity of the tree of life."[72] He presupposed that the evolution from the atom to the molecule might have occurred through a critical singular point, an unparalleled moment on the curve of terrestrial evolution. This might have been the point of germination, a critical point in earth's evolution in which protoplasm "was formed once and once only on earth, just as nuclei and electrons were formed once and once only in the cosmos."[73] The unique point of germination in evolution would explain the outcome of Pasteur's experiments: "why we never at any point find the formation of the least living thing which is not there as the result of generation."[74] After that moment in the evolution of the universe, life only germinates from life.

What if there is a "next pulsation" brewing around us? Although Teilhard assumed this as an academic question, he also foresaw this as a fundamental similarity in all organic beings. The truly curious fact is that "all molecules of living substances are asymmetrical *in the same way*, and contain precisely the same vitamins." He disclosed moreover that "the more complex organisms become, the more evident becomes their inherent kinship" which "manifests itself in the absolute and universal uniformity of the basic cellular pattern, particularly in animals."[75] He distinguished identical solutions "for various problems of perception, nutrition, and reproduction—everywhere we find vascular and nervous systems, everywhere some form of blood, everywhere gonads and everywhere eyes." Finally, he realized the similarity which crops up again in "the general laws of development . . . which give to the living world, considered as a whole, the coherence of a single upthrust."[76]

In questioning Pasteur's discovery, Teilhard alluded to the fact that "the origin of organized bodies is linked with a chemical transformation unprecedented and unrepeated in the history of the world." In other words, life "was born and propagates itself on the earth as a solitary pulsation," and "it is the propagation of that unique wave that we must now follow, right up to man and if possible beyond him."[77]

In his book *Science and Christ*, Teilhard took a bold stance before molecular biology developed new technologies to shed light on his position. He contended something unquestionable about scientific methodology: it validates theory by factual evidence. So that at every level of scientific analysis, any footprint or clue of a nonmaterial ordering principle, such as an invisible energy source immanent in the phenomenon studied, eludes observations and scientific calculation. The tangible, visible component of the phenomenon being examined itself becomes conceptualized mistakenly as the primary reality. Thereby, the ordered reality (exclusive of its nonvisible ordering principle) appears as a stable nature susceptible of analysis and reducible to its sub-elements.[78]

A simple example brings home this idea. Try as one may, no clue of the energy source can be found in a scientific assessment of the material components in an automobile. Yet, we know its creation emanates from human thought and human energy, which are not visible in the components of a car. And such is the limit of science, even in its mathematical quest. And as mentioned throughout this book, this is true of the natural world we are born into, including its human-created reality. This is also the admission of Roger Penrose in his reassessment of modern physics: quality forever eludes quantitative analysis, even in using matrix calculus and algorithms (calculational procedures concerning mental activity which carry out some well-defined sequence of operations).[79]

IV

Teilhard's evolutionary stance shed light on the emergence of new species in the process of evolution, as the psychic-biologic-material stuff of the universe gropes its way toward complexification. Challenging the dogma of Darwinism, Teilhard held that the energy driving cosmogenesis is a single, undifferentiated force of psyche-drenched matter groping toward higher levels of convergence, as though it has a will to live and evolve. This process of increasing complexification gives rise to large-scale evolutionary change from which new species emerge in an essentially single evolutionary leap, through a major mutation of unknown causes. The organizing principle—the intrinsic, nonvisible psychic component—is doing the synthesizing in the process of complexification and convergence, and mysteriously gives rise to the new. Teilhard therefrom proposed the elemental movements of life—the spontaneous ramification of the living mass and what ultimately emerges on the tree of life—involve more than transformation, more than mere procreation or the redistribution of existing stuff of the universe; they embody creativeness. Something new has entered geogenesis, an evolving psychic system. In other words, "evolution has a precise *orientation* and a privileged *axis*."[80]

Teilhard assumed a cosmic energy differentiated by "elementary consciousness . . . originally imprisoned in the matter of earth." He ignored the assumption of a fecundating power entering the planetary system, offered by some scientists, as quite useless. He presumed that an external fecundating "hypothesis disfigures, without explaining, the wonderful phenomenon of life, with its noble corollary, the phenomenon of man."[81] He put forth the idea that the early earth in its chemical composition is itself the complex germ we are seeking. He thereby presumed that pre-life was congenitally carried within the early womb of Earth. About the within of matter he suggested that "we are logically forced to assume the existence in rudimentary form (in a microscopic, i.e., an infinitely diffuse, state) of some sort of psyche in every corpuscle, even in those (the mega-molecules and below) whose complexity is of such a low or modest order as to render it (the psyche) imperceptible—just as the physicist assumes and can calculate those changes of mass (utterly imperceptible to direct observations) occasioned by slow movement."[82] In his *Hidden Face of God* discussed in the next chapter, Gerald Schroeder will have more to say about the idea of some sort of rudimentary psyche in every corpuscle, as disclosed in contemporary molecular biology.

With the emergence of *Homo sapiens* on the tree of life, evolution arrives at the threshold of reflection, in what Teilhard claimed the "hominisation of the individual." Unlike other purely materialist evolutionists, he envisioned matter as an outcome brought about by spirit and consciousness. Moreover, he drew a crucial distinction with respect to the manifestation of the psychic element in the animal world. In contrast to all other living creatures, for Teilhard, the pivotal phenomenon of man on the planet is his power of reflection, not manifested in insect and animal life. He defined reflection as the power of "consciousness to turn on itself; to take possession of itself *as of an object* endowed with its own particular consistence and value: no longer merely to know, but to know oneself; no longer merely to know, but to know that one knows."[83] The fact of this psychical transformation, this emergence of *Homo sapiens* on the tree of life, is of such immense consequence as any fact recorded in physics and astronomy, even though materialist evolutionists tend to challenge "the validity of such a breach of continuity" in evolution.[84]

Unlike the limited psychic element in insects and animals, reflection is a creative attribute that allows the human being "to raise himself into a new sphere. In reality, another world is born." Teilhard listed the outcome of reflection and human intelligence, in contradistinction to the psychic element in lower forms of life: humans have the power of "abstraction, logic, reasoned choice and inventions, mathematics, art, calculation of space and time, anxieties and dreams of love—all these activities of inner life are nothing else than the effervescence of the newly-formed centre as it explodes onto itself."[85] He attests to an undeniable fact: knowledge is an inner event in human life that enriches life and being on the planet. It is the reflective, creative capacity of consciousness—humanity's spiritual capacity and intelligence. Reflexive consciousness, Teilhard concluded, "constitutes a radical advance on all forms of life that have gone before."[86]

With the onset of reflective consciousness in human beings, a threshold in evolution was crossed. Teilhard agreed with evolutionists of a material persuasion that human beings were just one further stage in a series of animal forms. "From the cell to the thinking animal, as from the atom to the cell, a single process (a psychical kindling or concentration) goes on without interruption and always in the same direction."[87] There is a mystery here in which a spiritual explanation (the transcendence of humans over the rest of nature) in opposition to a materialist explanation (a human being is just one further species in a series of animal forms) discloses discontinuity in continuity. The threshold or critical point of "hominisation" or evolutionary transformation took place; it is not transformism in the sense that a "special intervention" or the actualization of a creative principle enters into the evolutionary process. "Psychogenesis has led to man. Now it effaces itself, relieved or absorbed by another and a higher function—the engendering and subsequent development of all the stages of mind, in one word, *noogenesis*. When for the first time in a living creature instinct perceived itself in its own mirror, the whole world took a pace forward."[88] The onset of reflective consciousness initiated on the planet a new era in evolution: the era of noogenesis (a mindsphere), constituting the era of *Homo sapiens*. It brought into being noogenesis in addition to geogenesis, biogenesis, and psychogenesis in planetary life. This "hominisation" or spiritualization, Teilhard alleged, is not as the evolutionists would have it, mere metamorphosis or outward change in form; it is rather in reality a revolutionary transformation—a leap on the tree of life. It gave rise to noogenesis reaching the borders of intuitive intelligence and ultimately laying claim to the transcendence of humans over the rest of nature and planetary life.

From the organic-biological perspective of metamorphosis, the emphasis is placed on a better brain. This is no doubt necessary biologically in cerebral functioning. Yet, for Teilhard, as well as evolutionists generally, a whole series of other conditions converged in conjunction: two-footedness, freeing of the hands, and eyes brought together—all affected the growth of the size of the brain. Ultimately, the conjunction of conditions in the birth of intelligence represents more than a bigger brain, more than the evolving of the nervous system; it represents a creature in which the psychical was turning in upon itself and giving rise to an inner transfiguration of the whole being. The grain of matter has evolved into the grain of life, and the grain of life has evolved into a grain of thought. "The cell has become someone."[89] The genus *Homo* had acquired another degree, another order of complexity. The genus had acquired a spiritual element. Some five or six millennia ago, it gave birth to the crystallization of the spiritual life and world of the spirit recorded in symbolic systems of writing and transmitting a record of spiritual evolution to future generations—all of which is the outpouring of reflective and reflexive consciousness. But from its advent difficulties arose, extreme confusion prevailed, varied groups forming humankind divided into diverse categories of races, tribes, states, nations, civilizations, cultures, and other artificial categories.

Thus, out of this evolutionary process, the mystery of noogenesis, complexity, and heterogeneous units gave birth to a noosphere: a repository, so to speak, of the output of human mental life and creations, surviving and transcending the natural death of individuals and cultures, that blankets the world and establishes an invisible world of thought. The noosphere is the domain of reality that provides the human species with a record of human and spiritual evolution. It is the human specie's exterior memory of past performance and recorded wisdom—the embodiments of the human spirit that enrich and aid humanity in its spiritual evolution.

Noogenesis is the dividing line in evolution between blind emergent evolution groping for billions of years and the creative evolution driven by *Homo sapiens*. It is the threshold after which planetary life is transformed and becomes ever more complex. According to Teilhard, it is also the threshold in which human consciousness is impelled toward the awakening to Omega—the invisible pulling force of the creative power underlying all life. Teilhard went deeper than, but would agree in part with, J. B. S. Haldane and Julian Huxley: "The one great difference between man and all other animals is that for them evolution must always be a blind force, of which they are quite unconscious; whereas man has, in some measure at least, the possibility of consciously controlling evolution according to his wishes."[90]

V

Given the fact of our freedom to create universally from the natural world, we would be remiss in failing to recognize the truth that everything human beings bring or have brought forth on the planet embodies human thought. We would also be remiss in not recognizing the fact that the outward manifestation of human creations discloses to the observer neither the thought embodied in nor the creative source of the observed phenomena. The natural world—including humanity's recorded thoughts and creations—is therefore visibly, audibly, and tactilely voiceless concerning its creative source. The primary reality of the universe, grounded in energy and spirit, remains perceptually and sensuously silent, closed off to our five senses in the phenomenal reality it has created. "It was only in the Neolithic age," Teilhard reminds us, "that the great cementing of human elements began which was never thenceforward to stop. The Neolithic age, disdained by pre-historians because its phases cannot be exactly dated, was nevertheless a critical age and one of solemn importance among all the epochs of the past, for in it Civilisation was born."[91]

The question Teilhard put off answering is this: how does the law of complexification, convergence, and emergence occur in light of entropy? How does evolution defy entropy, bringing into being new life-forms? That the evolving tree of life gave birth to the human being with a reflective power defies entropy. Yet, there remains a tendency toward disorder manifesting itself in all of life's endeavors. Especially obvious is the fact of deterioration in everything we humans create. Our human creations run down, deteriorate, unless tended to by an influx of energy and spirit. If one builds a house and leaves it unattended over a long period, it starts to disintegrate, then decomposes, and ultimately reverts to nature. It's as if nature reclaims its energy sources when its created entities are left shorn of continual infusions of energy. This is readily observable in rundown neighborhoods where buildings stand abandoned for years. And the same thing is true of human institutions. We are living in a time when anarchy and turmoil are on the increase throughout the planet, calling out to the human spirit to reverse the process.

Teilhard alleged that "something in the cosmos escapes from entropy, and does so more and more."[92] This remains a great mystery that eludes scientific analysis: an anti-entropic energy that suffuses the whole of reality, from the microcosm to the macrocosm. It can be grasped existentially through reflective consciousness in human life. This hidden energy in evolution, Teilhard claimed is love: "the affinity of being with being."[93] This has to do with the attributes he called the Omega Point: after falling into and being captivated by illusion, humanity and modern thought are on the verge of becoming acclimated to the idea of the creative value of synthesis rooted in love. Teilhard enumerated Omega's energy, spirit, and affinity, from the corpuscular to the human level: "there is definitely more in the molecule than in the atom, more in the cell than in the molecule, more in society than in the individual, and more in mathematical construction than in calculations and theorems."[94] This energy is not peculiar to humans but "a general property of all life."[95] In its various modalities and degrees, immanent in all forms of organized matter, this affinity of being with being is present. Love promotes the creative value of synthesis in the evolutionary process. Love, as far as mammals are concerned, manifests itself in the modalities of sexual passion, parental instinct, and social solidarity. When we look farther down on the tree of life, below the animal level to the plant level, love manifests itself in the within of things more obscurely until it becomes so faint it's imperceptible to humans.

Evolution is therefore an ascent toward consciousness that is advancing toward some sort of supreme consciousness—toward a spiritual awakening, toward superconsciousness. Teilhard's allusion to a possible critical mass awakening to the spiritual reality is a leap forward: "a new step in the genesis of mind." He put this question to us: "In the direction of thought, could the universe terminate with anything less than the measureless— any more than it could the direction of time and space?"[96] His idea of the measureless refers to the hidden, creative source underlying life and being. "One thing is sure," Teilhard maintained, "from the moment we adopt a thoroughly realistic view of the noosphere and of the hyper-organic nature of social bonds, the present situation of the world becomes clearer; we find a very simple meaning for the profound troubles which disturb the layer of mankind at this moment."[97] Teilhard was alluding to the significance of the noosphere and its human-historical record as a goldmine for human survival given the crisis the world is facing.

Superconsciousness, consciousness rooted in the eternal rather than in the socio-temporal world, is a crucial point in spiritual evolution beyond egoism, which confuses individuality with personality. Superconsciousness breaks the bonds of a false orientation of the spirit afflicted by modern forms of totalitarianism (whether fascism, communism, or devitalized democracy plagued by corporate industrial capitalism). Arriving at the critical point on the planet, superconsciousness is, in Teilhard's words, becoming "super-humanised" and "hyper-personal." It is becoming spiritually literate, awakening to the significance of the spiritual reality and the law of love; anti-entropic forces shielding and safeguarding life on the planet. "The Future-Universal," Teilhard noted, "could not be anything else but the Hyper-Personal."[98] Such a transitional stage in human and planetary life-forms, if it were to occur, is revealed in the noosphere. It would reverse the worldwide entropic forces of death, destruction, and demolition among warring nations oblivious to planetary life and creating ever more powerful weapons of mass destruction. Unless humanity awakens to love and spirituality, giving rise to a harmonized collectivity of consciousness equivalent to a mass awakening to the superconscious, planetary life is bound to succumb to an irreversible entropic plight.

VI

Crossing the threshold beyond the contemporary global crisis in humanity to the realm of spiritual literacy is to prepare the way for entry into the Era of the Spirit. This is what Berdyaev characterized as the third revelation beyond the Era of the Law and the Era of Redemption—the Era of the Spirit, biblically unscripted. This has been presaged by mystics and farsighted people through the ages of spiritual evolution. The new era in spiritual evolution, an Era of the Spirit, will hopefully moderate the growing terror of postmodernity, encourage widespread instruction of our youth in spiritual literacy, and fulfill our yearning for union with the transcendent power of life and love in its various forms—empathy, compassion, and forgiveness. Our evolution toward the epoch of the spirit heralds the possibility of resolving the devastation and ongoing violence gripping the contemporary world. In the words of Teilhard, a "new domain of psychical expansion—that is what we lack. And it is staring us in the face if we would only raise our heads to look at it."[99] Spiritual literacy will facilitate the union of faith and knowledge with the freedom of the human spirit. "After all half a million years, perhaps even a million," Teilhard observed, "were required for life to pass from the pre-hominids to modern man. Should we now start wringing our hands because, less than two centuries after glimpsing a higher state, modern man is still at loggerheads with himself?"[100]

Alluding to communism and fascism, "the most ghastly fetters," Teilhard claimed, we ended up with "the crystal instead of the cell; the ant-hill instead of brotherhood. Instead of the upsurge of consciousness which we expected, it is mechanization that seems to emerge inevitably from totalisation."[101] Yet change and movement come about: "our reaction should not be one of despair but of a determination to re-examine ourselves. When an energy runs amok, the engineer far from questioning the power itself simply works out his calculations afresh to see how it can be brought better under control." Teilhard maintained hope that "the great human machine is designed to work and must work—by producing a super-abundance of mind. If it does not work, or rather if it produces only matter, this means that it has gone into reverse."[102] Ultimately, he came back to love as energy. "It is the general property of all life and as such it embraces, in its varieties and degrees, all the forms successively adopted by organized matter."[103] "Love alone is capable of uniting living beings in such a way as to complete and fulfill them, for it alone takes them and joins them by what is deepest in themselves." He maintained hope and trust in humanity: "the spirit of the earth: the synthesis of individuals and peoples, the paradoxical conciliation of the element with the whole, and of unity with multitude—all these are called Utopian and yet they are biologically necessary. And for them to be incarnated in the world all we may well need is to imagine our power of loving developing until it embraces the total of men and of the earth."[104]

The emergence of superconsciousness is an outcome of spiritual evolution, culminating in consciousness passing through the movement of synthesis leading to the discovery of Omega. This synthesis gravitating against the tide of probability is a thrust toward a divine focus of mind that draws it upward. "Thus something in the cosmos escapes from entropy, and does so more and more."[105] What escapes are the four attributes of Omega (the energy-complex of the universe): "autonomy, actuality, irreversibility, and thus finally transcendence."[106] In contrast to entropy, "the Great Stability is not at the bottom in the infra-elementary sphere, but at the top in the ultra-synthetic sphere." Once a reflected center formed in humanity, a persistent march toward greater consciousness led to the expansion of the noosphere. In Teilhard's words, we come to escape from entropy by turning back to Omega. . . . The universe is a collector and conservator, not of mechanical energy, as we supposed, but of persons. All round us, one by one, like a continual exhalation, 'souls' break away, carrying upwards their incommunicable load of consciousness. One by one, yet not in isolation.

Since, for each of them, by the very nature of Omega, there can only be one possible point of definitive emersion—that point at which, under the synthesizing action of personalizing union, the noosphere . . . will reach collectively its point of convergence—at the 'end of the world.'[107]

Teilhard's allusion to the apocalyptic event, "the end of the world," has two meanings, one positive and life sustaining, the other adverse and life depleting. The life-affirming meaning of "the end of the world" takes place when the self realizes that it has access to knowledge of the world embodied in the noosphere. The self awakens to the spiritual reality, and consciousness is elevated to superconsciousness—to the third era in spiritual evolution, the Era of the Spirit. "All life paths may be a movement toward the soul. In which cases, our death may be the final and most integrating of our life's experiences." This is what Christianity calls the resurrection of the body, a self-transformation that entails awakening to spiritual truth.

As to Teilhard's first meaning of the end of the world, spiritual awakening, he wrote: "No one would dare to picture to himself what the noosphere will be like in its final guise, no one, that is, who has glimpsed however faintly the incredible potential of unexpectedness accumulated in the spirit of the earth."[108] Teilhard considered the second meaning of the end of the world, an adverse outcome to today's global crisis in humanity in which societies have developed weapons of mass destruction and weapons of mind control. "With age and increasing complication we are ever more threatened by internal dangers at the core of both the biosphere and the noosphere. Onslaughts of microbes, organic counter-evolutions, sterility, war, revolutions—there are so many ways of coming to an end."[109] Our creative vocation grounded in freedom is challenged. If we manage a positive outcome to the global crisis in humanity, our planet has, David Bodanis maintained, another five billion years to go according to his calculation of the vast energy of the sun.[110]

The noosphere transmits to us knowledge of the eras of spiritual evolution. We can grasp from this knowledge the tragic nature of freedom to do good or evil with the possibility of destructive power escalating in the future. A radical transformation of the stuff of the universe with the entry of human reflective thought has brought about both modern physics and molecular biology. The materialist-reductionist theory of evolution based on chance and random changes over billions of years has given way to its opposite: to the realization of an eternal creative source of life and being active in matter itself.

The eternal manifests itself in various forms: mystical religious revelations, rational disclosures of philosophers, partial truths of science, and literary and artistic revelations in the liberal arts. All these embodiments of human creativity are an outpouring of human consciousness. Spiritual literacy is the power of consciousness to read, decipher, and apprehend the meaning of these various spiritual embodiments. Whether of the sciences, religion, philosophy, or the liberal arts (history, mathematics, and the humanities), this transdisciplinary synthesis embodies revelations of the eternal energy and spirit at the core of human life.

CHAPTER 3

Revelations of Life's Origin and Complexity

I

Science continues to advance in many fields: biochemistry, molecular biology, and the human genome—the genetic material of an organism. Yet, viewing science from the perspective of twentieth-century discoveries, we find some interesting ironies. The American anthropologist-philosopher Loren Eiseley is one among many thinkers who called to mind the paradox of science. In excluding faith from scientific endeavors, Eiseley disclosed the fact that modern science "owes its origins to an act of faith," namely that "the universe can be rationally interpreted."[111] Origins are unrepeatable events and therefore neither empirically testable nor falsifiable by science.

Seven decades after Teilhard's revelations of the eternal, the molecular biologist and religious scholar Gerald L. Schroeder professed in his groundbreaking book, *The Hidden Face of God: How Science Reveals the Ultimate Truth*, that humans are the universe come alive. "A single consciousness, an all-encompassing wisdom, pervades the universe." Scientific technologies that study the quantum nature of subatomic matter and probe the periphery of the brain reveal the molecular complexity of biology. These findings moved science to the brink of a startling realization: "all existence is the expression of this wisdom."[112] Schroeder validated Teilhard's assumption of a psychic element intrinsic in matter. "This emergence of wisdom in the material world appears as if it is de novo only if we fail to realize that an aspect of mind is 'inherent in every atom.'"[113] Schroeder catalogued the numerous contributions of science in helping us understand religious revelations. "Only when we understand those hidden wisdoms will we be able to read between the prophetic lines and fully understand the message. With the help of science, we are learning to read between the lines."[114]

Schroeder filled in some of the gaps in Teilhard's work, without mentioning Teilhard. Schroeder contended, as did Teilhard, that human beings possess a spiritual nature, signifying that all existence is an expression of wisdom and that a psychic component is at the root of matter in the form of energy. In effect, this is a return to the pre-modern religious perspective that human beings are a microcosm of the macrocosm. Schroeder claims that humans "are the embodiment of a synchronous mystery."[115] Neither science nor religion acting alone can provide the necessary synthesis to reverse the global crisis in humanity that humanity confronts. "Neither by itself can achieve the goal of peace on earth and good will toward all."[116] Given freedom, humans are still prone to generate irrational and dreadful behavior.

Consistent with Teilhard's theory underlying complexification, Schroeder's fundamental contention is that the twentieth-century discipline of physics—beginning with Einstein's theory of relativity, quantum mechanics, and Heisenberg's uncertainty principle—has replaced classical physics. Schroeder presents us with the fundamental assumption that energy and spirit constitute the primary reality of life and being. In the interim of seventy years after the publication of Teilhard's *Phenomenon of Man*, scientific understanding of the physiology of the cell and the complexity of the brain with the aid of cutting-edge scientific instruments had greatly increased. Advanced technologies in molecular biology have enhanced the capacity to enter the infrastructure of biological matter. Scientists thereby have been able to explore the underlying complexity of the simplest organic processes. What molecular biology has accomplished for the life sciences, quantum mechanics has accomplished for the physical sciences. Both have established the impossibility of randomness and chance as the driving force behind life's origin and life processes. Decades after Teilhard's *Phenomenon of Man*, scientists have come to accept the reality that the chemistry of human life, with its power of creativity and freedom, are just as extraordinary and well-tuned as the universe.

II

Confirming Teilhard's presumption of a psychic element intrinsic in matter, including the atom and molecule, Schroeder established that "Every particle, every being, from atom to human, appears to have within it a level of information, of conscious wisdom."[117] Teilhard would be in full agreement. And so would mystics throughout the ages. Furthermore, Schroeder made known that the "mystery of life's origins and its ordered complexity is not simply one more scientific roadblock waiting for a physical explanation. Life, and certainly conscious life, is no more apparent in the primordial ball of energy produced in the creation, than . . . the information stored in the genetic code common to all life, DNA"—a molecule that carries most of the genetic instructions used in the growth, development, functioning, and reproduction of all known living organisms. Neither is the mystery of life's origin and its ordered complexity "implied by the biological building blocks of DNA." (Schroeder clarified the relationship between the brain and the mind.) "Nor is consciousness implied in the structure of the brain."[118] These phenomena (life, DNA, consciousness) imply a wisdom that precedes energy and matter. "Within the brain we perceive the consciousness of the mind, and via the mind we can touch a consciousness that pervades the universe. At those treasured moments our individual self dissolves into an eternal unity within which our universe is embedded. This is the message both of physics and of metaphysics."[119] As complex and as difficult to explain as the brain is, science has as yet no explanation of its "control panel"—the mind.

For Schroeder, a puzzling factor is that "information just appears as a given, with no causal agent evident, as if it were an intrinsic facet of nature."[120] In contrast to Teilhard's nonvisible pulling force Omega, Schroeder sustained the view of wisdom within wisdom within wisdom, from the atom, to the molecule, to the cell, and on to the cosmos. Both Teilhard and Schroeder accepted the hypothesis of the big bang theory and a creative power outside the universe that is eternal and infinite. Life beats the odds of chaos (deterioration and disorder) not by defeating entropy but by the hidden power underlying the universe (an orderly systematic universe embodying a creative source of energy).

Schroeder held to the existence of a wisdom that pervades all matter, from the atom, the molecule, the cell, and on up through all the orders of reality. Life wins by outwitting entropy, the second law of thermodynamics: "*Nothing*, no-thingness, does that." He awakened scientists to think more deeply: "When, as reductionists, we study individual atoms, we find a sense of choice but no limit of cleverness. Yet somehow, the dust spewed into space by the nuclear furnace of a bygone supernova has become a human brain that learned to make nuclear reactors here on earth."[121] A spiritual unity underlies physical reality; the natural reality is the outer physical expression of some-*thing* nonvisible. Scientific tools have allowed scientists to gain insight into the some-*thing* (energy and spirit) underlying the natural reality. Schroeder maintained that a search for the consciousness of the mind must start first with the study of the biology of the brain, for "the path leading from thought to the act, millions of cells and billions of atoms acting on command were required to accomplish that mundane fate."[122]

Scientists now standing at the threshold of something that transcends the temporal-spatial reality have stumbled onto what previously had been alluded to as something strictly mystical, religious, or merely a matter of faith. But the threshold beyond which scientific methodology is barred from crossing has brought scientists face to face with the presence of an unseen creative source of existence. Some scientists are willing to admit to the possibility of the spiritual reality and the world of the spirit. A recognition is dawning that metaphysical and metahistorical spiritual entities are knowable only in the realm of human subjectivity. Schroeder claims that some-*thing* eternal predates the universe. "This whatever-it-is has no bodily parts, is totally nonmaterial, is eternal, and though being absolutely nothing physically has the infinite potential to produce vast universes."[123]

For Schroeder, "some-thing" eternally and invisibly present eludes the sciences, including physics, molecular biology, and cosmology. It is clear that there is a hidden presence "of wisdom, of ordered complex information that is nowhere hinted at in the governing laws of nature or in the particles of matter that form the brain that lies below the mind's thought." Schroeder is at one with mystics and biblical prophets, Teilhard among them. Schroeder maintained that the some-*thing* is "Kind of like the biblical description of God. In fact it is the biblical description of God with one significant difference. A 'potential field' doesn't give a hoot about the universes it spins off. The Bible, however, claims the Creator is intimately interested and involved in its creations."[124]

In his earlier book, Schroeder returned to the Old and New Testament Scriptures, which attests to the fact that the entire physical structure is a concretization of wisdom, spiritual knowledge of the eternal—the Creative Source of life and being. According to Jewish mysticism an ancient source on biblical interpretation, infinite reality interacts with the finite creation; wisdom is conceived to be more fundamental than energy. 'With wisdom God created the heavens and earth.' 'By the word of the Eternal the heavens were made.' (Psalm 33:6); and a thousand years later, 'In the beginning was the word.' (John 1:1)"[125] Schroeder took scientists like Stephen Hawkins and likeminded thinkers to task for espousing a shortsighted and mistaken view of religion. They admit to unity operating throughout the laws of nature but believe scientific laws entail the ultimate reality. To them, timeless reality (the eternal) is merely these physical laws.

Schroeder assessed the scientific significance of the big bang theory and the laws of physics. He correlated the scientific perspective with the study of theology in order to answer the question: why turn to theology? Schroeder takes the reader on a scientific journey, disclosing the correspondence between his research in molecular biology and physical laws. Strange as it may seem, he concluded that physical laws eternally pre-existed the physical material reality. "But it is the only solution that we scientists can offer."[126]

III

Details of the big bang theory, Schroeder regarded as uncertain, "but the concept that our universe started hot and dense and is expanding finds ever more supporting data."[127] About the beginning of the universe, which is also the beginning of time-space, he concluded, "Whatever brought the universe into existence must of course predate the universe, which in turn means that whatever brought the universe into existence must predate time. That which predates time is not bound by time. Not inside of time. In other words, it is eternal. If the laws of physics, or at least some aspect of the laws of physics, did the job of creation, those laws by necessity are eternal."[128]

Schroeder's reasoning appears at first glance tautological, but considered spiritually, there is something not immediately accessible to our consciousness unless we stop to think for a moment. Where do the laws of physics come from? From the human mind. It can be argued that these laws are reflected in the facts themselves—objective and verifiable reality of the universe—picked up by human consciousness; or, it can be judiciously argued that consciousness has a spiritual potential. Using scientific methodology, scientists think that they can discern a reality that exists; they have discovered science's physical laws.

Today, when we consider any creation within time and space (the natural environment born to our five senses), we have no trouble reasoning that it has a nonvisible component. And this is what Schroeder was endeavoring to teach us in his many examples in molecular biology. "But how does someone label or even think about that which is not part of our physical world? Confining the metaphysical to a physical description totally misses the 'meta' aspect."[129]

All conjectures about beginnings—Schroeder informs us—have in common "that something, or more accurately stated some non-thing, an eternal whatever" that predates our universe.[130] Schroeder clarified Einstein's discovery of the basis of all matter, solid, liquid, and gas, everywhere in the universe: it is an ethereal energy. And this ethereal energy can give rise to that which appears to be solid matter. Einstein's discovery of the relativity of time, Schroeder noted, "was the first of the steps that moved physics into the realm of metaphysics."[131] Einstein cast a shadow of doubt on the scientific dogma that rejects out of hand a metaphysical realm of being as the primary reality. Einstein noted that the "scientist is possessed by the sense of universal causation."[132] Admitting to the possibility of a metaphysical reality would of course open the door to the idea of a special creation beyond the universe. Moreover, it would put to rest modern science's non-verifiable presupposition that reality is a materialistic, mechanistic, and monistic chain of causation. Ultimately, Schroeder mused over the possibility of information being inherent in the primary reality that provides the basis from which energy precedes.

IV

Schroeder disclosed the consistent emergence of wisdom that dispels any childlike view that everything proceeds from a random, chance, and meaningless beginning by taking the reader on an extraordinary journey in molecular biology. He reveals a degree of freedom in the atom itself. The second discovery was the enormously complex creative activity taking place within the cell. These two facts defy once and for all the premise of randomness and chance because there is order within both. Schroeder regarded today's vocal atheists to be atavistic. Richard Dawkins, Christopher Hitchens, and Sam Harris, among others, are out of touch with significant discoveries in twentieth- and twenty-first-century physics and molecular biology. This is not to imply that their voices do not sort through and pick over the childlike chaff manifest in fundamentalism and authoritarian religious institutions. Unfortunately, atheists fail to recognize the profound meaning underlying spiritual revelations. Too often they remain, as is the case with religious fundamentalists, on the literalistic level in interpreting religious revelations. Many have very little truck therefore with making sense of the philosophical minds of a Kierkegaard, Solovyev, Dostoevsky, Tolstoy, and Ibsen, among others, who rose above secular humanism in the nineteenth century. Atheists are generally oblivious to the truth embodied in spiritual literacy that transcends crude materialism and crude individualism. Their mockery of religion appears to derive from their misguided and misconceived understanding of the limitation of scientific epistemology—the study of the origin, structure, and validity of knowledge—as it applies to both scientific methodology and the symbolic, mythological, and mystical grammar underlying religious revelations. More to the point, today's atheists cannot provide an answer to Schroeder's discoveries in both modern biology and particle physics.

Deeping our spiritual literacy, the ideas embodied in Schroeder's molecular observations of the extraordinary goings-on within cells are illuminating. The activity he described is as continuous, creative, and ordered as one would find observing the life activity in a beehive. Continuously in every second, in every cell and cell group, millions of atoms are joining together and acting on command. Each and every cell in our body is selecting at every moment approximately five hundred thousand amino acids consisting of some ten million atoms. It organizes them into preselected strings, joining, forming, and reforming them together. Each string is folded into specific shapes, and the newly formed protein is shipped off to sites—inside and outside the cell when a need is signaled for specific proteins. The membrane of the cell wall allows good stuff in and keeps bad stuff out. It contains "myriad portals" to open and allow entrance using several means: "subtle changes in voltage difference across the membranes;" others open "when a molecular key comes and unlocks them." The activity comes from cues "within the cell if it's a call for the building blocks needed in protein replication, and from outside if, for example, it's a nerve cell coaxing a neighboring cell into action. A vast number of assumptions are woven into the simple act of singling a membrane port to open."[133]

Schroeder disclosed that this "wonderland of activity" underlying the natural world is permeated with wisdom by some nonvisible means. "We are so immersed in consciousness, juggling thoughts even when day dreaming, that we project consciousness onto these chemical messages that control portals." The question needs posing: where does all this ordered activity get its "smarts"? "Since when do carbon, nitrogen, oxygen, hydrogen, sulfur, phosphorous—the preliminary building blocks of biology—have ideas of their own, or any ideas at all? They are just atoms strung together to make molecules."[134] On and on Schroeder records his observations of nature filled with wisdom: thousands of receptor and transporter molecules; activity in muscle cells; the release of doses of adrenaline into the blood as a response to fight or flight; the machinery to take glucose from the food we eat, combusting it and storing the released energy; the path of an ingested bit of carbohydrate; the unity brought about by the regulatory system DNA-RNA team organizing individual-lifeless raw materials "into living, thinking, choosing beings," and so forth.[135]

Schroeder noted that "one has to bend over backward to accept that all of these necessary and interwoven steps have evolved randomly. There are only two forms of reproduction. There are no intermediate forms visible in nature. . . . In human reproduction mitosis [responsible for reproducing somatic cells] gives way to meiosis [responsible for reproducing germ cells]." Schroeder describes the mystery in enormous detail, too complex to go into here. "Don't lose sight," he informs us, "of the fact that it is all molecules at work. There is no brain on site." Whether the fetal development is observed in utero or in vitro, it is identical "through four days post-fertility with human eggs and sperm, and in other vertebrates for much larger fractions of total gestation. Somehow the egg knows what it must become."[136]

Schroeder's analysis is supported by three Americans—James E. Rothman, Randy W. Schekman, and Thomas C. Sudhof—who recently won the Nobel Prize in physiology for discovering the machinery that "regulates how cells transport major molecules in a cargo system that delivers them to the right place at the right time in cells." They discovered that the "molecules are moved around cells in small packages called vesicles." Each scientist "discovered different facets that are needed to ensure that the right cargo is shipped to the correct destination at precisely the right time." Their research also revealed that the "tiny vesicles, which have a covering known as membranes, shuttle the cargo between different compartments or fuse with the membrane. The transport system activates nerves. It also controls the release of hormones." The combined efforts of these scientists also disclosed that disturbances "in this exquisitely precise control system cause serious damage that, in turn, can contribute to conditions like neurological diseases, diabetes and immunological disorders."[137]

Molecular biology has given scientists a view of the human body as a finely tuned machine: "a magnificent metropolis in which, as its inhabitants, each of the 75 trillion cells, composed of 10 to the 27th atoms, move in symbiotic precision."[138] Molecular biologists have found consistently at every level of complexity that "the information that emerges from a structure exceeds the information inherent in the components of that structure. This is true from subatomic electrons, the lightest of known particles, to the human brain, the most complex structure yet encountered in our universe."[139]

Molecular biology and particle science provide a significant contribution to our understanding of the phenomenon of consciousness made known to us and to the very existence of the universe and its eternal attributes. With the 2013 discovery of a new elementary particle called the Higgs boson, or Higgs particle, physicists have entered deeper into the elements contained in the atom and, hence, into the infrastructure of matter. The deeper science penetrates the microstructure of matter, and the farther out it discerns attributes of the macrostructure of the universe, the more humanity realizes that the phenomenon of consciousness is a divine attribute commensurate with the spiritual foundation of the universe.

Schroeder answers the question: to what extent is life and being written into the fabric of the universe? "Being written into the fabric of the universe implies something other than merely having the created laws of nature amenable to the flourishing of life. Being written into the law of the universe tells us that we are made of the stuff of the big bang. We were present at the creation."[140] Schroeder's molecular biological validation of the divine inheritance of the human being, consistent with that of Teilhard de Chardin, was foreshadowed and worked out in Judeo-Christianity's mystical revelations. Beyond the discoveries of Teilhard and Schroeder, the scientific community now finds itself awakening to a possibility of a creator beyond the universe, as we will discuss in the next chapter.

The scientific debate of life's origin is no mere academic dispute. A judgment of plausibility of the special creation by a creator beyond the cosmos, beyond time and space out of nothing, will have a profound influence on planetary life, on knowledge of the life and world of the spirit, and on introducing spiritual literacy to children at an early age in formal education. A scientific admission of plausibility of creative energy and spirit beyond the cosmos challenges the reigning dogma of abiogenesis—the mechanistic, materialistic, and monistic theory prevailing in science textbooks today. Already, a materialist bias has surreptitiously captured the subconscious mind of a substantial number of people worldwide, including, ironically, many who sustain a religious perspective. Fragmentation of consciousness is an affliction that does not escape the educated. The global crisis in humanity demands clarification concerning the predominant materialist bias still dogging modern science, despite its enormous contributions to the integration of the various cognitive domains—the religious, spiritual, philosophical, as well as the liberal arts and humanities.

V

About the time of publication of Teilhard's *Phenomenon of Man*, three discerning thinkers, among others—Nicholas Berdyaev, Reinhold Niebuhr, and C. S. Lewis—had called our attention to the divine, cosmic character of human beings, the life and world of the spirit, and the eternal reality.

Their thinking, along with Teilhard's, was substantiated by Schroeder's molecular biological analysis.

Berdyaev addressed the issue of the divine plan and the divine idea of human beings as spiritual beings. The spirituality of human beings "must be disclosed, the spirituality which may hitherto have been in an unawakened and merely potential state." Consistent with Teilhard and Schroeder, Berdyaev contended that our divine nature is the "realization of personality"—the realization of the human being's divine character. "But the awakening of the spiritual nature takes place in secret ways. It is not subject to an objectified and external hierarchical principle." This awakening has nothing in common with individualism; it pertains to our communal nature and presumes the self undergoing a cosmic transfiguration. "Behind empirical and phenomenal man stands transcendental man. . . . There is a divine element in man and it is crushed not only by man's lower nature to which he falls a slave; it is crushed also by religious thought which reflects the slavery of man, by religious sanction of this slavery. This is evident from the extreme importance which authoritarian Christian thought has attached to obedience to authority."[141] The Era of the Spirit will be an era which gives rise to a sense of community and an era in which the self will undergo a social, cosmic, and personal transfiguration devoid of master and slave, free from the degrading relations, in which free people and free relations will endure.

Reinhold Niebuhr considered in depth the kingdom of truth which transcends the phenomenal reality, our world alienated from its true character. "The kingdom of truth is . . . not the kingdom of some other world. It is the picture of what this world ought to be. This kingdom is thus not of this world, inasfar as the world is constantly denying the fundamental laws of human existence. Yet it is of this world. It is not some realm of eternal perfection which has nothing to do with historical existence. It constantly impinges upon man's every decision and is involved in every action."[142]

Niebuhr proclaimed that "the only kingdom which can defy and conquer the world is one which is not of this world." Those awakened to the eternal, those "who are of the truth" recognize that "pure justice indicts injustice; the law of love reveals their selfishness; and the vision of God reveals their true centre and source of existence." Niebuhr maintained that those of truth "may continue to be disobedient to the heavenly vision; but they can never be as they have been."[143]

The end and meaning of history, Niebuhr declared, "must begin with a distinction between two dimensions of the relation of eternity to time. Eternity stands over time on the one hand and the end of time on the other. It stands over time in the sense that it is the ultimate source and power of all derived and dependent existence." He clarified the fact that despite the importance of culture for human existence, it is a derived and dependent existence and not the fundamental reality. Thus the eternal "is not a separate order of existence. . . . The eternal is the ground and source of the temporal." The phenomenal world, including culture and civilization, are derivative of the spiritual reality. "The divine consciousness gives meaning to the mere succession of natural events by comprehending them simultaneously, even as human consciousness gives meaning to segments of natural sequence by comprehending them simultaneously in memory and foresight."[144] Niebuhr summoned our attention to the fact that eternity cannot be conceived of having an end. "Eternity outlasts time, though we know nothing about either an abrupt ending of the world or of the gradual dissipation of its natural energies. Our efforts to picture the relation in spatial terms always lead us astray and project a particular point in future time which will also be the end of time."[145]

Although his work was published a few years before Teilhard's, C. S. Lewis helped clarify another facet of spiritual evolution. It "is not mere improvement but Transformation." Lewis likened spiritual evolution to a transformation akin to the chrysalis found in the insect world; although he made clear that the transformation is a spiritual chrysalis, not morphological as is the chrysalis from the caterpillar to the butterfly. The radiant beauty in human transformation occurs as a fundamental change in the direction, structure, and content of consciousness. Lewis envisioned the "Next Step" to be a sharp bend away from the assumption evolutionists and neurologists likely imagine—developing bigger and bigger brains and gaining greater mastery over nature.

The "Next Step," C. S. Lewis suggested, will be really new and "go off in a direction you could never have dreamed of"—a transformation that is anthropogenic. It would be not merely a difference "but a new kind of difference," even "a new method of producing the change." He explained that "the Christian view is precisely that the Next Step has already appeared." Instead of being "a change from brainy men to brainier men," it is "a change from being creatures of God to being sons of God."[146] The chrysalis, so to speak, is an anthropogenic unfolding within Man's eternal spiritual nature: the death of being absorbed in the natural world of time and a rebirth of God in Man and the rebirth of Man in God. It is a transition in the sense of death, or the end of our idolatry of this-worldly consciousness and our rebirth (our divine birth) to the otherworldly reality—an awakening to our transcendental inheritance. It is the end of the direction and structure of consciousness, which entails a transition beyond being immersed in our conscious and unconscious minds. That is to say, it is a breakthrough of conscience—imprisoned in and held in bondage to historical forces—now awakened to the superconscious. In C. S. Lewis's words, "the change is not 'Evolution' at all, because it is not something arising out of the natural process of events but something coming into nature from outside."[147] That is, it springs from the otherworld, from the great mystery of freedom and creativity. "But the new step, the step from being creatures to being sons, is voluntary. At least voluntary in one sense. It is not voluntary in the sense that we of ourselves could have chosen to take it or could even have imagined it; but it is voluntary in the sense that when it is offered to us we can refuse it. We can, if we please, shrink back; we can dig in our heels and let the new Humanity go on without us."[148]

Lewis's outlook is cautiously optimistic. "Already the new men are dotted here and there all over the earth. Some . . . are still hardly recognizable: but others can be recognized. Every now and then one meets them. Their very voices and faces are different from ours; stronger, quieter, happier, and more radiant. They begin where most of us leave off. . . . They will not be very like the idea of 'religious' people which you have formed from your general reading."[149] Lewis warned about and addressed the question of the "last man": the recognition of growing human forces to control and condition human beings—mentally, emotionally, socially, and biologically. In this possibility lies "the abolition of man." Lewis affirmed the fact that human freedom is not free of the possibility of a tragic outcome. "The last men, far from being the heirs of power, will be of all men most subject to the dead hand of the great planners and conditioners and will themselves exercise least power upon the future."[150]

VI

Professor Harold Saxton Burr of the Yale School of Medicine discovered a reality that cast a new light on the clash between religion and science. With electronic instruments and techniques he developed, Burr studied the electrical patterns of life that measure the electromagnetic field of an organism. His studies revealed that human beings and all forms of life "are ordered and controlled by electro-dynamic fields, measurable and mapped with precision." He found that "like fields of physics, they [electromagnetic fields] are part of the organization of the Universe and are influenced by the vast forces of space. Akin to fields of physics, too, they have organizing and directing qualities which have been revealed by many thousands of experiments." As a scientist, Burr was not reluctant to declare that his discovery assures us that our life is not rooted in chance or accident: "Organization and direction, the direct opposite of chance, imply purpose." These electromagnetic fields provide electronic-instrumental evidence clarifying our integral relation to the universe. He affirmed that "man is no accident. On the contrary, he is an integral part of the Cosmos, embedded in its all-powerful fields, subject to its inflexible laws and a participant in the destiny and purpose of the Universe."[151]

Though these electromagnetic fields are invisible and intangible, they established human beings' symbiotic relationship not only to planetary life but to the universe itself. Professor Burr was able to study the human body and the electronic patterns of the life of molecules and cells in constant regeneration. He discovered that "molecules and cells in the body are constantly being torn apart and rebuilt with fresh material from the food we eat. But, thanks to the controlling L-field [the electro-dynamic life field], the new molecules and cells are rebuilt as before [in a matrix formation] and arrange themselves in the same pattern as the old ones." His research "revealed that the materials of our bodies and brains are renewed much more often than was previously realized. All the protein in the body, for example, is 'turned over' every six months and, in some organs such as the liver, the protein is renewed more frequently." After six months, there is not one molecule in the face of a friend which was there when we last saw him. "But, thanks to the controlling L-field, the new molecules have fallen into the old, familiar pattern and we recognize his face." Biologists were at a loss to explain how bodies keep in shape "until modern instruments revealed the existence of controlling L-fields." Moreover, "the mystery has been solved, the electro-dynamic field of the body serves as a matrix or mould, which preserves 'shape' or arrangement of any material poured into it, however often the material may be changed."[152]

Burr's voltage measurements were not challenged by the scientific community, yet it all but ignored them. Today, an interface is developing among biological-materials, micro-nano-electronics, and biomedical engineering. The emerging field of bioelectronics enters into the infrastructure of biology in conjunction with electronics in a wider context, including and encompassing biology, fuel cells, bionics, and biomaterials for information processing, info storage, and electronic components. A whole world has opened since Burr's discovery, giving rise to biomedical engineering that includes tissue engineering, genetic engineering, neural engineering, and pharmaceutical engineering. Biomedical engineering combines the design and problem-solving skills of engineering, medical sciences, and biological sciences to advance healthcare through new diagnostics, monitoring, and therapy. We have all heard about or encountered diagnoses of human ailments through the use of MRIs (magnetic resonance imaging), NMRIs (nuclear magnetic resonance imaging), MRTs (magnetic resonance tomography), and TSMs (transcranial magnetic stimulation). These have all come about since Burr's discoveries.

For a full recognition of the cosmic character of human life, one more fact is necessary: the fact of the spiritual character of our lives—our freedom to create and our creative vocation as a planetary creature. We possess a unique cosmic attribute, the power to create universally from the natural reality. As members of the animal kingdom, humans are not merely animals. Animals create in a fixed, instinctual manner according to the nature of their particular species. Any change or disruption of this pattern comes from human influence on animal species or from changes in climatic conditions. Human evolution, from the hunting and foraging stages to the agricultural stage—including the recorded history of all subsequent civilizations—has been a testament to the ability of the human species remarkable creative potential.

Many today hold the belief that the mind is nothing more than the brain: a biological entity from which and through which ideas come into being. Human creativity is assumed to be nothing more than the outpourings of our brain matter—severed from any transcendent cosmic inheritance. It is true that the size and complexity of the human brain is a necessary attribute explaining the human phenomenon of creativity and spirituality; it is not, however, a sufficient explanation. The brain is part of the body. The baby's body gestates in the mother's womb as the mother ingests the fruits of the earth, which supply organic and inorganic elements necessary for the baby to grow and survive. In order for a fully formed human being to function, there must be synchronized relatedness to the five spheres of reality—the atmosphere, biosphere, geosphere, hydrosphere, and noosphere. Nourished by the light and energy of the sun, the earth is a small part of a larger galaxy.

The consciousness of human beings is a phenomenon revealing the fundamental cosmic order and structure of reality. The size and complexity of the human brain play essential parts in the actualization of consciousness. In contrast to animals, human beings possess the unique power of creative freedom, will, and spirit, which give us the capacity to change planetary life. Where does this spiritual power come from to create and to bring into being something that never existed before? From the visible side of reality, new creations come out of nothing—*no-thing-ness*. They derive from our imperceptible creative faculty.

CHAPTER 4

Scientific Studies of the Mystery of Life's Origin

I

This chapter reviews scientific studies that provide valuable and compelling evidence concerning the mystery of life's origin. Scientific developments in the twentieth and twenty-first centuries, especially the contributions arising from the theory of relativity and quantum physics, cast serious doubt on the presumption of abiogenesis; that is, the natural generation of life from nonliving matter. A team of scientists in particular—Charles Thaxton (chemist), Walter Bradley (material scientist), and Roger Olsen (geochemist)—questioned the evolution of life from nonliving matter and sought to clarify the origin of life. The fundamental question these scientists posed and examined was the evolution of life from chemical matter as a result of chance, randomness, and accident. Chemical evolution is conceived as the pre-biological phase of evolution.

Radiocarbon dating of organic materials has now been cross-validated, calling into question abiogenesis. Since the mid-twentieth century, archaeological, paleontological, and geological discoveries have been based on the physical or chemical properties of artifacts and natural formations. By measuring the proportion of carbon-14 in organic material, scientists have been able to calculate the dates of organic matter embedded in artifacts and fossils. This resulted in a sharp increase in the length of time estimated for abiogenesis to have taken place; that is, for life-forms to evolve by random and accidental changes from chemical matter, estimated to take billions of years. The oldest known star in the Milky Way is estimated to be some 15 billion years old, probably formed shortly after the big bang. Earth is dated at about 5 billion years. The evidence in the dating of microscopic organisms puts life-forms on the planet at about 3.5–3.8 billion years. In geological time, this means the evidence of molecular fossils and microfossils dates the origin of life as nearly contemporaneous with the cooling of the surface of the planet. Chemical evolution of life's origin from random chance and accident thus appears more and more moot and outdated.

The debate regarding the mystery of life's origin in a divided scientific community is a fascinating story, rich in scientific and philosophical analyses. Both sides in the debate tout physical laws, marshal facts, and crunch data, mathematically and statistically. The science behind it is complex, given that life's origin is a unique, non-repeatable event that can neither be validated nor falsified scientifically. Yet, scientists have a lot to offer despite the fact that neither empirical evidence nor mathematical-statistical computations can validate a non-repeatable event. A staggering number of scientific experiments simulating the presumed prebiotic conditions of the planet have been made based on probability theory backed by the laws of thermodynamics applied to living systems.

Both Teilhard de Chardin and Gerald Schroeder admitted to the possibility of an evolutionary thrust beyond spontaneous, physicochemical evolution of life. They presumed the existence of a creative source of energy and spirit beyond the universe. Carbon dating has divided the scientific community. Some scientists now doubt the possibility of abiogenesis—the presumption that the evolution of life is merely the rearrangement of the elements of a closed universe, devoid of an ordering principle and a creative source of energy beyond the cosmos and universe.

What makes this mystery intriguing is the fact that two groups of scientists, working diligently for the past half century or so, are aligned like two groups of lawyers examining scientific and philosophical data of life's origin, an event similar to resolving a murder mystery without eyewitnesses—as Thaxton, Bradley, and Olsen put it—using probability theory, experimental findings, and mathematics as circumstantial evidence. Needless to say, scientific methodology requires replicating facts to validate or falsify an event based on the presumption that life's origin has spontaneously, randomly, and accidently evolved from chemical matter.

The presumption that life springs from life is taken for granted. But something deeper has asserted itself within the ongoing debate in the scientific community: Can scientists experimentally simulate spontaneous creation of life from minerals in laboratory studies or provide a plausible philosophical argument that takes us beyond probability? Charles Thaxton (chemist), Walter Bradley (material scientists) and Roger Olsen (geochemist) pointed out that there are two conflicting issues that have to be resolved. The question concerning the resolution of scientific methodology and the dating of life's origin on the planet? The question concerns whether scientific methodology can render a judgment regarding the existence of a creative source of energy and spirit underlying the cosmos. The scientific, religious, and metaphysical analyses put forward by Teilhard and Schroeder have posited a judgment in favor of such a possibility. The outcome of the debate among the two groups of scientists hinges on an examination of four theories (discussed below) that assess life's origins. A final judgment of a jury of philosophers, theologians, scientists, and the spiritually literate is called for.

Fortunately, since the late 1960s, scientists empowered by computers have been able to use probability theory to establish the mathematical odds of a chance formation, given the highly complex molecular structures necessary for the formation of life. The discovery of the structure of DNA (the hereditary code embedded in life-forms) was apparently found to contradict the theory of spontaneous chemical evolution. This demanded a review of the neo-Darwinian synthesis that advanced the presumption of natural selection; that is, the process in nature by which organisms that are better adapted to their environment tend to survive longer and transmit more of their genetic characteristics than those that are less adapted.

Thaxton, et al.'s theories of life's origin was based on a vast array of scientific simulation studies. Some theories sought to validate, and others to falsify, the chemical theory of evolution. Thaxton, et al. reviewed these studies based, in substantial part, on the two laws of thermodynamics: the law of conservation of energy and the law of entropy. The enormous number of scientific studies seeking to make sense of the mystery of life's origin led Thaxton, et al. to review the data and assess the plausibility of the theories they advanced.

Their efforts were of vital significance. Since the 1970s, authors of textbooks on evolution have jumped the gun by advancing "biochemical predestination," claiming scientific affirmation of the theory of chemical evolution. But Thaxton et al. plausibly alleged that such a view is metaphysical and presumptive. Biochemical predestination claimed life's origin to be materialistic, mechanistic, and monistic. *Materialistic* in so far as natural processes alone brought about life-forms, apart from any mysterious divine or creative intervention. Scientific dogma assumes the rearrangement of the stuff of the world takes place in a closed universe, absent a creative source of energy. *Mechanistic* in so far as the intrinsic properties of matter are the singular underlying cause of increasing complexity that brought about abiogenesis. *Monistic* in so far as chance, randomness, and accident acted as the primary causation of increasing order in the development of chemical compounds. These presuppositions of the origin of life—materialistic, mechanistic, and monistic—are metaphysical and therefore not scientifically verifiable factually, theoretically, mathematically, or statistically.

Though averse to metaphysical presumptions, the scientific community became seriously conflicted about the scientific studies of life's origin. The data implied the possibility of something beyond naturalistic-materialistic forces operating both at the moment of creation of the universe and at the moment of transition from the mineral reality to the cell—the presumed origin of life on the planet some 3.5–3.8 billion years ago. Scientists sought to determine what precisely underlies the naturalistic forces that gave birth to life on Earth. Some scientists, including Thaxton et al. were hesitant and uneasy about the unverifiable bias of chance and accident. They disagreed with the timeline of the major stages of chemical evolution in its transition to the origin of life, based on the laws of physics and the presumptions made about the state of the atmosphere of the prebiotic earth. They also questioned the assumption underlying scientific reasoning that excludes "psychic elements" of varying magnitudes of the "within"—of atoms and molecules in cellular formation. The data and theories concerning chemical evolution put forth disclosed "that reasonable doubt exists concerning whether simple chemicals on a primitive earth did spontaneously evolve (or organize themselves) into the first life."[153]

II

The scientific definition of life presumes that life-forms require "regions of order which use energy to maintain their organization against the disruptive force of entropy"—the second law of thermodynamics.[154] Entropy informs us that without an energy input a system runs downs: it goes from order to disorder. The higher the order of the system (including a living system), the more energy input is needed to stave off decomposition. For example, all human creations are subject to wind, sun, rain, and electric storms that bring about deterioration, decomposition, and disintegration (entropy) without an adequate input of energy. Entropy is a measure of the probability of the weakening and disintegrating of a given arrangement of mass and its internal energy, including life systems.

Having examined the evidence for and against chemical evolution (abiogenesis), Charles Thaxton, Walter Bradley, & Roger Olsen sought to evaluate four scientific theories that presume a materialistic-mechanistic view of life's origin. The first put forth by some scientists concerned the possibility that new laws in the fields of physics and chemistry might yet be discovered that would "reconcile statistical and thermodynamic constraints," contradicting the natural "formation of living systems."[155] A continuous flow of energy alone, though necessary, was not a sufficient condition to sustain life systems in so far as they require an additional crucial factor: "a means of converting this energy into the necessary useful work to build and maintain complex living systems."[156]

Thaxton et al. used the example of an automobile's internal combustion engine as an analogy to man's digestive system. In order to move, the automobile requires more than the combustion of gasoline within the engine. The transmission and drive chain in an automobile are necessary mechanisms in converting the energy of burning gasoline in the engine to move the vehicle forward or backward. "The additional crucial factor is a means of converting this energy. . . . Without such an 'energy converter,' however, obtaining transportation from gasoline would be impossible. Similarly, food would do little for a man whose stomach, intestines, liver, or pancreas were removed. Without these, he would surely die even though he continued to eat."[157] Thus, new physical and chemical laws would have to disclose how negative entropy (that is, an ordering thrust counteracting decomposition) in living systems must be coupled with an energy converter to continually restore the system against the forces of disintegration (entropy).

Thaxton et al. found that chemical evolution (abiogenesis) "a reasonable explanation for doing the chemical and *thermal entropy work*, but clearly inadequate to account for the *configuration entropy work* of coding (not to mention the sorting and selecting work)."[158] They understood that *configurational energy* "measures randomness in the distribution of matter in much the same way that thermal entropy measures randomness in the distribution of energy."[159] Thus scientific studies can account for entropy (the loss of energy and the movement toward disorder) in the linking of like elements. But what scientific studies cannot account for is *configurational energy* in the process of synthesis, namely the energy source drawing together "neighboring" elements. The energy doing the synthesis in the hierarchical progression of evolution does not manifest itself. Thaxton et al. were puzzled by the fact that synthesis, which requires an input of energy, does not manifest itself in the movement toward complexification.

In his analysis, Teilhard de Chardin attributed synthesis to two energy forces: a radial (internal) energy and a tangential (external) energy. He presumed that these two forms of energy are of mind and matter "spread respectively through the two layers of the world (the within and the without)."[160] Teilhard further maintained that the "tangential energy" links the element with all others of the same order (that is to say, of the same complexity and the same centricity). The "radial energy," on the other hand, draws elements toward "ever greater complexity and centricity—in other words forward."[161] The tangential energy is doing the linking; the radial energy is bringing about the movement toward higher levels of complexity, providing an evolutionary thrust.

Akin to Teilhard's assumption, an inner groping trend within the inorganic and organic world could provide the synthesizing momentum. The evolutionary thrust, the emergence of higher elements could not have taken place without a coupling mechanism as a "way to convert the negative entropy taking place in complexification of matter and emergence.... Is it reasonable to believe such a 'hidden' coupling mechanism will be found in the future that can play this crucial role of a template, metabolic motor, etc., directing the flow of energy in such a way as to create new information?"[162] Thaxton et al., in accordance with Teilhard's study, assumed that energy contained both in the inorganic and organic elements comprises a rudimentary psychic element that becomes more and more obvious with increased levels of complexification and consciousness. Schroeder presented a similar view: wisdom is contained within the simplest particles and an ever-mystifying amount of wisdom is present as life becomes more complex. Thaxton, Bradley, and Olsen's study appeared before Schroeder's books were published. In retrospect, they would agree with Schroeder. "Intelligent contrivances harness a portion of the energy flow for work in the human world. How some energy converting/coupling means might arise without intelligence in the inorganic world before life is difficult to say."[163]

What is clear is that scientific methodology—at the threshold between the quantitative and qualitative reality—bars science's entry into the qualitative realm. Yet, Thaxton et al. sustained a premonition of and saw the possibility that some form of intelligence underlies the materialistic-naturalistic reality. The same premonition might be said of the moment of the big bang that gave rise to the universe. As Schroeder put it, rudimentary freedom is inherent in the atom and wisdom in the cell. Yet many scientists refuse to admit that freedom and wisdom (rudimentary forms of intelligence) are inherent in the evolutionary process. They hold to their view that some new law of physics may one day be discovered, safeguarding their materialistic, mechanistic, and monistic presumption of the origin of life in the universe.

<h1 align="center">III</h1>

Beyond assessing the response to scientists who contended that new scientific laws may be discovered, Thaxton et al. examined a second view put forward by some scientists: the theory of panspermia. This theory proposed that microscopic life-forms survived the effects of traveling through space from other planets, becoming active in the process of evolution on earth. The theory of panspermia established that sperms or spores offering the possibility of life gave rise to the origin of life on earth. This theory gained renewed interest in recent years by some scientists who have an interest in space travel and presumed that life spores were driven to earth from somewhere else in the universe. Thaxton et al.'s theory of panspermia is not really an account of life's origin on the planet. They merely considered the possibility that particles (including the size of most living cells) could have reached the earth and did not burn up upon entry into the earth's atmosphere, nor were they obliterated upon impact (i.e., made "soft" landings). The hypothesis of panspermia, according to Thaxton et al., has no relevance in scientific inquiry. It offers no theory of life's origin and fails to resolve the issue, merely pushing the question of chemical evolution to some other milieu in the universe where conditions were presumed to be more favorable than on earth.

In their geochemical assessment of the atmosphere and the various water basins of primitive earth, Thaxton, Bradley, & Olsen conjectured that many destructive interactions would have so vastly diminished, if not altogether consumed, essential precursor chemicals that chemical evolution rates would have been negligible. The prebiotic soup would have been too dilute for direct polymerization to occur; that is, for a chemical process to have transpired by which two or more molecules combined to form larger molecules, providing the reduplication of parts of an organism. "Furthermore, no geological evidence indicates an organic soup . . . ever existed." "Space-incident organic molecules do little to solve the mystery of life's origin. . . In spite of the problems with Panspermia, the number of scientists ready to defend it is growing."[164]

Thaxton et al. evaluated some of the speculations that extraterrestrials may have intended to make earth a "wilderness zoo," or perhaps a "cosmic dump site," or that life spores were carelessly left on earth "on some ancient astronaut's boot." When Thaxton et al. examined directed panspermia in some depth too complex to discuss herein, they found such speculations had little or no credible scientific significance. "The doctrine of cosmic Panspermia can only be conceived if one accepts the idea of the carriage of life germs by foreign astronauts. This is a facile hypothesis, a subterfuge which seeks to avoid the fundamental problem of the origin of life."[165]

The fact remains that the theory of directed panspermia, like the theory of panspermia, provides no credible account of the origin of life. "It merely assumes that spontaneous generation must have occurred in some favored environment somewhere in the cosmos. Directed Panspermia is primarily a suggested mechanism to get life safely to earth."[166]

IV

As Darwin understood, a fair account and probable result can be attained only by balancing the arguments on both the scientific and metaphysical sides of the theory of life's origin. The falsifiability of the chemical theory (abiogenesis) is not possible in so far as one can always argue that new scientific laws may be discovered to give credence to the theory that the origin of life derives from spontaneous evolution, which is materialistic and naturalistic. Scientists on both sides are thus left arguing the plausibility of metaphysical assumptions underlying the mystery of the origin of life.

After a thorough examination of the scientific literature, Thaxton, Bradley, and Olsen held to a plausible argument of a special creation involving intelligence. In opposition to the theories of a prebiotic soup and chemical evolution, they adduced several analogies that concern some rudimentary form of intelligence as the precipitating cause. For example, "in numerous cases certain effects always have intelligent causes, such as dictionaries, sculptures, machines, and paintings. . . . We would similarly conclude the presence of intelligent activity were we to come upon an elephant-shaped topiary in a cedar forest."[167] They went on to ask: "Why then doesn't the message sequence on the DNA molecule also constitute *prima facie* evidence for an intelligent source? After all, DNA information is not just analogous to a message such as the Morse code, it is such a message sequence."[168]

In previous chapters I have established that objects in our natural environment do not manifest an underlying intelligence merely when observed empirically. For example, houses, bridges, dams, cities, canals, civilizations, and all other created things that become part of our natural environment all embody human creativity and intelligence; they are the embodiment of human spirit and energy. The important point Thaxton et al. brought to light beyond analogies, such as DNA, RNA, and genes as codes, concerned evidence of nonrandom complex syntheses taking place. These discoveries questioned the presumption of a chance hypothesis for chemical evolution. Despite the fact that scientists themselves utilize intelligence to carry out their scientific study of reality, they fail to awaken to, or fail to break their dogmatic adherence concerning the limitations of scientific methodology. Their consciousness becomes too clouded and dimmed by the materialistic, mechanistic, and monistic presumption of modern science to admit to the fact that they employ qualitative, subjective characteristics of consciousness and intelligence in their studies of the empirical reality. Counterintuitively, they tend to sustain a faith that the empirical reality and its materiality constitute the primary reality. This leads them to ignore the limitation of modern science, namely that only facts in repeatable events can validate or falsify hypotheses.

According to Thaxton, Bradley, & Olsen another meaningful mystery reveals itself: a *special creation by a creator* as life's origin. Was the special creation by a creator *within* the cosmos or was the creation by a creator *beyond* the cosmos? In so far as origin events are nonreplicable, the existence of a special creation falls outside the domain of modern science. This is the domain of metahistorical and metaphysical events, as occurred in the discovery of agriculture in the Neolithic Revolution. Origin events, revelations of a transcendental aspect of reality, have been universal since the Neolithic Revolution. They emanate from the creative potential of human consciousness and intelligence, whether they are borne of a satori (a state of intuitive illumination) or an epiphany (an illuminating discovery). It is important to note that humans possess in their being atoms, molecules, cells, and the components of the universe.

V

The second law of thermodynamics, entropy, the tendency toward disorder—the movement from complexity to simplicity—disputes abiogenesis. We observe on the planet the progression toward increasing complexity and the emergence of higher living forms. By means of mathematical calculation of the problems of complexity, given the fact of entropy, Thaxton et al. disputed chance, randomness, and accident as the origin of the evolution of life. They arrived at an opposite conclusion to chance and natural selection as a plausible hypothesis, asserting scientific studies do not support "the scenario of chemical evolution (abiogenesis). In fact, what has emerged over the last three decades . . . is an alternative scenario which is characterized by destruction, and not the synthesis of life."[169] After considerable assessment and discussion of the theories of life's origin, Thaxton et al. reasoned that a "Special Creation by a Creator beyond the cosmos is a plausible view of origin science."[170] They suggested that "the lion of positivism has made its last roar and we can learn from advances in philosophy and science since the time of Darwin. If we can learn from our mistakes, we may expect more productive interchanges in the future. Toward that end we reach."[171]

To substantiate their position, Thaxton et al. distinguished two theories of a special creation by a creator: one theory posits that a creative intelligence exists within the cosmos; the second presumes that the creative source of life and being exists beyond the cosmos. The discussions are complex and require too extensive an understanding of biology, chemistry, and statistical analysis to provide a full account of their reasoning herein. However, their views can be summarized as follows: "Special Creation by a Creator beyond the cosmos holds there was once a time when matter was in a simple arrangement, inert and lifeless. Then at a later time matter was in the state of biological specificity sufficient for bearing and sustaining life." They note further that "Special Creation (whether from within the cosmos or beyond it) differs from abiogenesis in holding that the *source which produced* life was intelligent."[172]

The issue for many scientists confronted with the idea of a special creation by a creator is that it implies the entry of metaphysical reflection in the debate concerning the origin of life. This refutes the naturalistic presumption of modern science and puts in question "spontaneous generation." A creative act disrupts modern science's vision of a seamless web of universal causation. Thaxton, Bradley, and Olson quoted Einstein, among others, who conceive scientists as being possessed by the sense of universal causation.[173] These diehard scientists are described as holding to their belief in chemical evolution as "a nice theory" without a shred of scientific evidence. "What exists is only the scientist's wish *not to admit a discontinuity in nature* and not to assume a creative act, forever beyond comprehension."[174]

Nevertheless, Thaxton et al. realized that the grand edifice of classical science was uprooted and shaken to its foundation with respect to non-repeatable events such as origins. Science's contributions reside in and are of utmost importance with respect to the spatial-temporal reality and the patterns of recurring events subject to verification and falsification. Yet, human beings are able to discern, distinguish, analyze, synthesize, and draw conclusions, having, in addition to scientific knowledge of the natural reality, spiritual awareness. We can imagine flying above the earth's surface and observing a huge mound of bricks. Ten years later, we fly over the exact location and find a huge brick structure in its place. We conclude that a nonvisible some-*thing*, an energy source, configured the bricks. Years later, we find the brick structure well maintained. According to the second law of thermodynamics, entropy (disorder) would have left the brick structure prone to natural forces. The state of the brick structure reveals that some configurational work had taken place to counteract entropy: a creative source of energy maintained the structure. We would reason that some unseen energy input had been taking place, counteracting the tendency toward decomposition and deterioration of the brick structure.

VI

Scientists applying the laws of thermodynamics to life systems point analogously to the fact that had simple organic forms evolved from chemical matter, their linking together—their chemical reaction in which two or more molecules are combined to form larger molecules (i.e., their polymerization into complex molecules)—would require some energy input. In the words of Belgium physical chemist and Nobel Laureate Ilya Prigogine and colleagues, the "probability that at ordinary temperatures a macroscopic number of molecules is assembled to give rise to the highly ordered structures and to coordinated functions characterizing living organisms is vanishingly small. The idea of spontaneous genesis of life in its present form is therefore highly improbable, even on the scale of billions of years during which prebiotic evolution occurred."[175]

When we consider the changing of the planet over time, we recognize something important about life-forms, from the plant level (life), to the animal (life plus consciousness), and to the human level (life, plus consciousness, plus, what E. F. Schumacher called, the mysterious power of self-awareness or spirit). Schumacher noted that this power of self-awareness has undoubtedly a great deal to do with the fact that human beings are not only able to think but are also able to be aware of the fact of their thinking. "Consciousness and intelligence, as it were, recoil upon themselves. There is not merely a conscious being, but a being capable of being conscious of its consciousness, not merely a thinker, but a thinker capable of watching and studying his own thinking. . . . This power . . . consciousness recoiling upon itself, opens up unlimited possibilities of purposeful learning, investigation, exploring, and of formulating and accumulating knowledge."[176] What Schumacher called the mysterious power *self-awareness*, religion calls the revelatory power of consciousness *spirit*: consciousness opening to conscience, wisdom intrinsic in the infinite eternal.

All life-forms evolve from some seminal entity. We know the seed contains within itself potential life that interacts with the soil, a medium that supports life. Soil contains organic matter that improves soil structure and soil moisture retention, macronutrients such as carbon, hydrogen, oxygen, phosphorous, etc. Soil also contains micronutrients such as traces of iron, boron, copper, etc. It contains a range of microorganisms that supports plant growth. Through photosynthesis, plants use light and energy to drive the chemical factory that converts carbon dioxide into sugars, which leads to other life-supporting reactions. Thus, plant life needs various forms of energy input to create and sustain life. As energy sources diminish, entropy increases, and ultimately the plant dies and returns to its natural elements.

When we keep an eye on the chain of being, we discover at the animal level that plants and other animals become their prey for nutrients. An animal as a living system requires a continual input of energy to stave off increases in entropy and ultimately death and decay. At the highest level in the chain of being, human beings use plant and animal life as their energy source. It is at this level, in contrast to the animal level, that human beings possess something in addition to consciousness—self-consciousness—an intellectual property that advances and values discoveries, and that promotes discovery going on in the natural reality: a spiritual property.

During different periods in the planet's history, we discover historical facts of fundamental changes in life-forms (plants), animal forms, and human forms of existence. With respect to humans, recorded history discloses the existence of settled communities evolving into cities and into civilizations, to destroyed cities, and on to renewed civilizations. The planet is in a continual state of metamorphosis. One momentous factor missing in the history of the past is knowledge of the energy source that was and is causing all this change—the configurational work. What is the energy source of the configurational work that counteracts the second law of thermodynamics—entropy—and keeps plant life, animal life, human life, and huge complexes of human settlements from decomposing into randomness and chaos? It is precisely here that modern science by virtue of its methodology meets a quantitative wall that has no threshold into the qualitative. From the abundance of all kinds of seeds on the planet, from plant seeds to animal seeds to human seeds, the configurational work counteracting entropy goes on—outside the materialistic and mechanistic view of scientific reality. The human seeds, ovum and sperm, contain within themselves the potential of creative freedom within the constraints of DNA.

Thaxton, Bradley, and Olsen claimed that the time span from the birth of the planet (about 4.54 billion years) to the emergence of simple life-forms on the planet (about 3.5–3.8 billion years) discloses the probability of chemical evolution at approximately zero. They concluded that "the undirected flow of energy through a primordial atmosphere and ocean is at present a woefully inadequate explanation for the incredible complexity associated with even simple living systems, and is probably wrong." Yet, despite this and in answer to the persistence of many scientists to embrace the theory of spontaneous chemical evolution, they responded: "One would be irrational to adhere to a falsified hypothesis. We have only presented a case that chemical evolution is highly implausible. By the nature of the case that is all one can do." They followed this up with their admission of the limitation of science, which is incapable of rendering a metaphysical presumption. "In a strict, technical sense, chemical evolution cannot be falsified because it is not falsifiable. Chemical evolution is a speculative reconstruction of a unique past event, and cannot therefore be tested against recurring nature."[177]

Nonetheless, many scientists refuse to abandon their presumption of chemical evolution. Thaxton et al. noted that "the speculative nature of chemical evolution does not mean that it is without value."[178] Through an adversarial approach about the truth or falsity of chemical evolution as life's origin, they suggested proponents from both sides of the debate can continue to examine and weigh the evidence, thereby keeping the debate open. "To be sure, the case for the origin of life via chemical evolution as usually presented sounds plausible, and has been accepted very widely, if not generally, by the scientific community. Furthermore, popularizations have carried the case to millions in a persuasive manner. Because of the fact that chemical evolution cannot be falsified, however, its apparent plausibility can easily be exaggerated beyond its true status as speculation and be regarded instead as knowledge."[179] Despite the danger with speculative approaches, Thaxton, Bradley, and Olsen believed "reasonable doubt exists concerning whether simple chemicals on a primitive earth did spontaneously evolve (or organize themselves) in the first life."[180] From the perspective of science, it can only be left to the jury of peers to decide.

VII

A startling example helps clarify the limitations of science and its capacity to grasp the qualitative reality, even though scientific inquiry exercises consciousness and intelligence. An ordinary life situation, a married professor and his inspired graduate assistant drawn passionately to one another, throws light on the underlying, nonvisible (yet experiential) cause of behavior. Owing to obvious circumstances of age and marital commitment, as well as social decorum, the professor and student's mutual love is naturally closely guarded and disguised. Their rapture and delight bind them together but also torment them, as disclosure bodes ill, given the professor's marital status, his violation of trust, and the age of his graduate assistant. They contrive a furtive pattern of communication to bring about what would appear to the casual observer as an accidental or incidental rendezvous. Needless to say, their fear, intimately allied to their passionate love, creates an enigmatic pattern of empirical data.

The question is this: can science detect the reality (the ordering principle of their behavior) that binds them in a relationship full of intensity and love in the subjective (qualitative) domain, but baffling, if not bizarre, behavior in the visible, objective (quantitative) domain of reality? Supposing further that their role playing is worthy of superior theater and their feigned propriety lacks the least trace of duplicity, would it be possible for a renowned, international team of social, biological, and medical scientists to discern, through scientific methodology the inward, concealed, rich, and qualitative depth of their experience (the nonvisible ordering component) that orders their outward demeanor?

What could possibly be discovered about the real "energy" underlying their relationship? In spite of the prodigious wealth of scientific instruments providing an effluvium of abstractions—changing pulse rates, blood pressure levels, personality test scores, social interactive patterns, role conflict theory assessments, Marxist and Freudian analysis, MRIs, etc.—all these could not possibly unveil what can only be known qualitatively. Should their cells and tissues be examined under the most rigorous medical conditions using state-of-the-art technology, these scientific efforts would be fruitless. The quality of being, the moving power of love that is ordering their behavior, could not possibly be detected. The internal and external patterns of observable behavior—the ordered, tangible elements—would represent expressions and signs that are a function of the intangible power of love—a nonvisible, qualitative reality. What is causing the events or occurrences would elude science, which is based on deductive and inductive reasoning, as it is the qualitative that is the essential reality bringing about the observable "events."

This is where science stands today: it has provided us with marvelous discoveries but stops short at the threshold of the metaphysical. Science is a significant, monumental, and marvelous achievement of human consciousness. But as Roger Penrose, the gifted mathematician-physicist, correctly stated the case, the "reality of the physical world itself seems more nebulous than it had seemed before the advent of the SUPERB theories of relativity and quantum mechanics. The very precision of these theories has provided an almost abstract mathematical existence for actual physical reality. Is this in any way a paradox? How can concrete reality become abstract and mathematical?"[181] Here Penrose reinforces Thaxton and his colleagues' conclusion of the plausibility of intelligence and a special creation by a creator beyond the cosmos. As Penrose asserts, consciousness appears to be such an important phenomenon that it simply cannot be something just "'accidentally' conjured up by a complicated computation. It is the phenomenon whereby the universe's very existence is made known. It is only the phenomenon of consciousness that can conjure a putative 'theoretical' into actual existence."[182]

The ongoing scientific debate about life's origin is no mere academic dispute. Thaxton et al.'s judgment of plausibility of a special creation by a creator beyond the cosmos, beyond time and space, out of nothing (no-*thing*-ness), will have a profound influence on knowledge of planetary life, on knowledge of the life and world of the spirit, and on the necessity of introducing spiritual literacy in formal education, starting in the early life of our children. A scientific admission of the plausibility of creative energy and spirit beyond the cosmos would challenge the reigning dogma of the materialistic, mechanistic, and monistic theory of abiogenesis prevailing in science textbooks today. A materialist bias has surreptitiously captured the subconscious mind of a substantial number of people worldwide including, ironically, many who sustain a religious perspective. Fragmentation of consciousness is an affliction that does not spare the educated. The global crisis in humanity demands clarification of this presumption.

One more clarification that Thaxton, Bradley, & Olsen accounted for needs to be considered, and that is the profound difference between the two origin theories: the special creation by a creator *within* the cosmos and a special creation by a creator *beyond* the cosmos. An example can put the difference in its proper light. In so far as the creator is *within* the cosmos, the ordered reality created would reveal the creator's presence. Take, for example, Frank Lloyd Wright, an architect who created beautiful structures. Many of his creations dating from the end of the nineteenth century and into the twentieth form a marvelous collection of beautiful architectural structures scattered throughout the American landscape. But nowhere will Frank Lloyd Wright, the creator, be found within his creations. The creator always stands beyond the cosmos—the ordered reality created.

For human consciousness to grasp a special creation by a creator *beyond* the cosmos, consciousness must transcend the psychological realm and awaken to the spiritual realm of reality. This is true of all domains of knowledge, including the sciences, religion, philosophy, and other branches of the liberal arts and humanities. To enter into the spiritual realm means to awaken to the embodiment of the spirit in these cognitive domains. The creator always remains an imageless source of life and being *beyond* the cosmos—the eternal—manifesting itself within the realm of the human spirit.

CHAPTER 5

The Crisis in Humanism

I

From the fifteenth to the end of the nineteenth century, Western thought confronted philosophical and scientific breakthroughs that included, in principle at any rate, the gradual expansion of freedom in the lives of human beings. This thrust toward freedom gave rise to divisions in the Catholic Church during the Reformation of the sixteenth century, resulting in the freeing of reason and thought during the Enlightenment of the seventeenth and eighteenth centuries. In the vast cultural turmoil of the Thirty Years' War (1618–1648) and the Peace of Westphalia (1648), the feudalism of the ninth to the fifteenth century finally succumbed to a gradual transition to the nation-state system of the modern world. An ensuing series of wars were some of the most destructive conflicts in European history. What began as a war between Protestants and Catholics gradually extended into a general conflict among Europeans.

As early as the last half of the nineteenth century, philosophical, religious, scientific, and literary thinkers critiqued and sought to clarify Christian dogma and theology. The intellectual class openly scorned the literal interpretation of religious revelations of the eternal. Among them were Søren Kierkegaard, Vladimir Solovyev, Leo Tolstoy, Karl Marx, Fyodor Dostoevsky, Friedrich Nietzsche, Henrik Ibsen, and Sigmund Freud. These thinkers were the forerunners of the twentieth and twenty-first centuries. Many of their philosophical insights grew out of their inner state of despair, depression, and anxiety as they confronted nihilism in its many forms with a deep sense of dread. Facing the crisis in humanism, they sought to clarify for themselves the human essence and the capacity for self-determination. Many came to the realization that human beings are not self-sufficient, as their lives are duty bound to the law of love. Freedom must thereby be self-constrained in order to safeguard the harmonious relations necessary for human survival. The concept of a wisdom inherent in the universe appeared as a common thread in their writings and anticipated the later examinations of the subject discussed herein. To make concrete this transitional stage in consciousness, this chapter reviews the life journey of Leo Tolstoy (1828–1910), a Russian writer regarded as one of the greatest authors of all time. The next chapter reviews the lives and contributions of Fyodor Dostoevsky and Friedrich Nietzsche.

II

At an early age, Leo Tolstoy's thinking became wedded to secular humanism, rejecting belief in the revelations of Orthodox Christianity. He could not abide the hypocrisy of religion and its dogma. Among his literary and philosophical writings is one of the great novels in Western literature, *War and Peace*, in which he examined the absurdity, hypocrisy, and shallowness of aristocratic society, a world of hereditary nobility. Tolstoy's life was one of enormous success and worldwide acclaim. He had increased not only his personal wealth and material security but also his standing among members of the Russian aristocracy. His life was filled with literary creativity, and he enjoyed robust health. In his thirties, he began to experience premonitions of despair but was able to shrug it off with the anticipation of his oncoming marriage and the hope it occasioned. During his youth and on into his adulthood, his view was locked in the finite world of time and space, of history and progress, of humanism and social justice. He was concerned with the psychological, social, and cultural aspects of human life, experience, and its tragic nature. Despite all his achievements and worldly renown, he fell into the bleak throes of depression, despair, and a sense of meaninglessness in his forty-seventh year. His spiritual journey in search of truth is disclosed in his autobiography, *Confession*, which provides us an opportunity to observe a person of genius in the clutches of nineteenth-century humanism undergoing a spiritual trial of death and rebirth.

Tolstoy characterized his state of anguish as follows: My life came to a stop. I could breathe, eat, drink, and sleep; indeed, I could not help but breathe, eat, drink, and sleep. But there was no life in me because I had no desires whose satisfaction I would have found reasonable. . . . I did not even want to discover truth anymore because I had guessed what it was. The truth was that life is meaningless. . . . I came to the precipice, and I clearly saw that there was nothing ahead except ruin. And there was no stopping, no turning back, no closing my eyes so I would not see that there was nothing ahead except the deception of life and of happiness and the reality of suffering and death, of complete annihilation. . . . The thought of suicide came to me as naturally then as the thought of improving life had come to me before."[183]

Tolstoy fell into a state of *ontic despair*: he found himself caught in the psychological state of fate, necessity, and chance with respect to the relative conditions of life and a tormenting awareness of an ultimate end, death. Ontic despair concerns the self's relationship to the various orders of reality—the natural, social, cultural, cosmic, and divine. Ontic despair arose in spite of Tolstoy's worldly success. A loss of hope at the height of his literary achievements reflected an ambitiousness that had extended to the very *limit of necessity*—he had every-*thing* one could possibly wish for. Given his privileged life, he was oblivious to his obligations to others, the community, and the eternal. Instead of expressing his gratitude, he was abusive to his serfs on whom his life depended. He centered his ambitions on increased privileges and the expansion of wealth for himself and his family.

Tolstoy confessed to his "pathetic" and "instructive" ten years of youthful indiscretion. "Every time I tried to express my most heartfelt desires to be morally good I met with contempt and ridicule; and as soon as I would give in to vile passions I was praised and encouraged. Ambition, love of power, self-interest, lechery, pride, anger, vengeance—all of it was highly esteemed. As I gave myself over to these passions I became like my elders, and I felt that they were pleased with me."[184]

Akin to Tolstoy, many today find themselves similarly caught in ontic despair, in a psychological state between fate (the completion of oneself within the constraints of freedom) and death (suffering despite the material and social success that presumably constitutes fulfillment). Unless and until the self experiences ontic despair, the cause of any momentary anguish and despondency remains hidden from consciousness. The self remains in darkness as long as it retains the illusion that greater success will fulfill its yearning. Possessed of a hedonistic predisposition, the self becomes enchanted by the possibility of a future of greater wealth, a wished-for elixir that provides a reprieve from its woeful existence. Success and social status insulate the self from pangs of conscience. Success forms an impregnable barrier to self-awakening; freedom becomes waylaid by a yearning for greater achievements to fill an inner void, as slavish necessity is mistaken for the path to life fulfillment. Truth lies hidden from consciousness. The root of ontic despair is the failure of spirit to fathom from life experiences even a modicum of awareness of self-alienation. The suffering of despair calls attention to something fundamentally amiss. It is a mental alarm calling into play reflective and reflexive consciousness. At first the self is confused as to the root of its ailment, so wedded is it to the dreamlike conformity of its social class—until, that is, the self is struck with despair (a spiritual disorder) and depression (a psychological disorder).

Ontic despair becomes muffled, sidetracked, or assuaged as the self busily seeks to cull from life ever-greater worldly success. Tolstoy had arrived at a point in which he could no longer abide such an illusory life despite—or precisely because of—his worldly success. His conscience was bound to and embedded in aristocratic class values and a materialistic existence of status and social acceptance. "I described my spiritual condition to myself in this way: my life is some kind of stupid and evil practical joke that someone is playing on me. In spite of the fact that I did not acknowledge the existence of any 'Someone' who might have created me, the notion that someone brought me into the world as a stupid and evil joke seemed to be the most natural way to describe my condition."[185]

Upon later reflection, Tolstoy clarified what he had discovered: What, indeed, had I done in all my thirty years of conscious life? Not only had I failed to live my life for the sake of all, but I had not even lived it for myself. I had lived as a parasite, and once I had asked myself why I lived, the answer I received was for nothing. If the meaning of human life lies in the way it is lived, then how could I, who had spent thirty years not living life but ruining it for myself and others, receive any reply other than this, that my life was meaningless and evil. It was indeed meaningless and evil.[186]

Tolstoy eventually confirmed the source of his state of ontic despair. In his infringement and violation of the natural, social, cosmic, and eternal reality, he had surrendered his conscience to his social class. He deemed that human beings "should earn their lives exactly the same way the animals do but with one difference": the human being "will perish if he does it alone—he must live his life not for himself but for all."[187] His state of despair had taught him that he had failed to take into consideration his blessings and his literary and creative contributions. No doubt he exaggerated to some extent his lack of creative contributions to human welfare.

Ontic despair calls our attention to the violation of the limits of truth and reality; that is, our interdependence with others, the chain of being, and the cosmic reality—from the mineral, to the plant and animal, and to the human level. In violating the limits of the nature and structure of being and life, conscience becomes troubled. The self is called to self-judgment and summoned to reflect on the path and quality of the choices made. Traditional knowledge is our historical inheritance of the logic and grammar of spiritual literacy that instruct us in our cosmic nature. In despair, the self's socially accepted moral values must be submitted to self-scrutiny. Conscience, mistaking the social-cultural reality for the ultimate reality, is called to attention by the anguish of despair. Despair, therefore, is a defining moment that kindles the self's freedom to assess the meaning of its life experience. In pain, the self seeks to open up to and beseech help. Redemption encompasses repenting and seeking forgiveness. Belief and faith in a transcendent reality are vital. The lack of this mental and emotional state of being is precisely what is at the root of ontic despair.

Later, Tolstoy realized the delusion that had veiled his despair and the limits he had transgressed. He clarified this state with a metaphor of being caught between a beast (time, necessity, and the unbearable suffering of the loss of hope, living in self-deception) and a dragon (death, suffering that confronts us). His life was akin to being caught between escaping a raging wild beast and jumping into a pit in order to avoid death. But at the bottom of the pit, a dragon (death) awaited him. His response was to grab on to the branch of time to escape the dragon, while trying to lick a bit of honey on the branch to sustain life. But he saw the branch being eaten away by the white and black mice of time—day and night. "The former delusion of the happiness of life that had concealed from me the horror of the dragon [death] no longer deceives me. No matter how much I tell myself that I cannot understand the meaning of life, that I should live without thinking about it, I cannot do this because I have done it for too long already." Why had he failed to recognize the despair hidden from him earlier? "It is possible to live only as long as life intoxicates us; once we are sober we cannot help seeing that it is all a delusion, a stupid delusion!"[188]

The Danish philosopher and theologian Søren Kierkegaard scoured the source of despair, having experienced it in his life. He branded it the sickness unto death, the suffering that must be endured or escaped until the self awakens to the eternal. Despair is the bearer of the psychological force that rallies the spirit to break the self's enslavement to necessity, thereby freeing its creative vocation. Despair is a painful nudge to consciousness to seek a way out of the dungeon of death; it prefigures the possible rebirth of the self to its creative inheritance. In despair, the self is stripped of belief and faith and must find, by its own creative efforts, union with the eternal. The crisis in humanism presents a traumatic choice in so far as the self stands spiritually bruised—indicted by freedom to make a decision. The self must strive for communion with the various orders of reality—social, communal, cosmic, and eternal—through a free act of love. Despair is the self's abandonment of its freedom while in a state of severe suffering and loss of hope. Kierkegaard maintained that as soon as despair makes its presence known, the self recognizes that it has always been in despair. "For in case the condition comes about which brings him to despair, it is at that same moment manifest that he has been in despair throughout the whole of his previous life."[189]

What is the psycho-social source that blindly obstructs despair until suffering becomes intolerable? Precisely the running after this and that illusory *thing* to appease the restlessness of our inner life when we have transgressed the limit of truth and reality—metaphorically, being taken by surprise by a wild beast pursuing us (despair) and in being enthralled to a degrading form of egoism that thwarts consciousness from realizing the complex reality sustaining us. Despair, still not conscious to us, is akin to pulling the electrical cord of a water pump from its electrical source in a state of terrible thirst while trying to draw water from a well. We wait in vain, for in freedom we have turned off the source of energy. Our egocentric self justifies this state of alienation by suppressing and sublimating the pain of our inner depths through restless daily activity. Thus unrecognized, ontic despair puts us in flight mode, resulting in mimicking social trends without reflecting on the value of our choices.

For this reason, we are destined to break through self-suppression or repression only in so far as our ego is no longer able to offer the tyrant self-will any-*thing* more to appease it. This is akin to a person who, in ignorance, believes the atmosphere has little to do with one's personal life. But the moment the supply of needed oxygen is cut off even for a minute or two, the self struggles frantically to gain this *sine qua non*. At this moment, the person becomes aware of how precious the atmosphere and oxygen are in sustaining life. Such is the case with our psychological life as we seek a way out of despair in a state of spiritual illiteracy. The positive aspect of this suffering, as St. John of the Cross taught, is the driving force that opens up our spiritual portal to its creative endowment. Paradoxically, suffering emboldens us to undergo a terrible ordeal in our passing from psychological death to rebirth and on to eternal life.

The violation of intellectual, moral, and biophysical limits is mounting as our world grows more complex and we grow more self-indulgent. Spiritual literacy becomes imperative in ameliorating psychological and spiritual suffering. It awakens us to the meaning of despair, enabling us in freedom to turn from selfishness to responsibility, from self-indulgence to obligation to others and the natural reality, from crude individualism to personal communion with the creative source and power of life. Despair is the state in which the soul lives in the darkness of night. No some-*thing* as an ersatz fulfillment can be willed to assuage the inner void.

Biochemical palliatives to relieve despair (a spiritual malady) and depression (psychological anguish) not only abound, new forms of psychotropic drugs are being discovered and dispensed to replace those that no longer alleviate mental and emotional anguish. The state of being is psychological, the illness is spiritual, and the resolution must ultimately be spiritual. Used wisely, psychotropic drugs accompanied by some form of psycho-spiritual therapy can help ease ontic despair.

III

Tolstoy's despair was exacerbated by his daily feelings of emptiness despite carrying on his literary work and family life. His emptiness upon awakening each morning impelled him toward suicide and spurred him to grab on to any glimmer of hope before going under. He set out to examine the various knowledge domains that might disclose a means of reducing his suffering.

In contrast to ontic despair, *spiritual despair* is the point in life when the self has arrived at the loss of hope of ever discovering the meaning and purpose of life. Ontic despair concerns the self's violation of the limit of its relationship to others, the natural world, the cosmos, and the sacred gift of life. It has to do with the direction of the self's will and its creative efforts. Spiritual despair is arriving at the limit in which the self can no longer conceive a way out of despair; it entails the loss of hope that the self can ever fulfill the gift of life or arrive at joyful living. Ontic despair has to do with the way we relate to the natural-social reality. Spiritual despair focuses on our problematic future and our ability to think and reason our way out. It concerns our potential to reflect on and envision a means of bringing about a positive, life-affirming outcome. Spiritual despair is akin to the self trapped in the psychological vise between moment-to-moment emptiness in carrying out its daily activity and the belief in the futility and ultimate meaninglessness of life. Despite carrying out his literary work daily, Tolstoy felt the utter futility and haunting sense of the meaningless-ness of life.

To fend off his self-destructive impulses, Tolstoy immersed himself in the knowledge claims of various fields of study. These included the "exper-imental sciences" (mathematics, the natural sciences, the life sciences), the "speculative sciences" (the liberal and fine arts, including religion and philosophy), and the "half-sciences" (the social, historical, and juridical sciences). Tolstoy found modern science to be concerned with empirical reality, which "reveals the greatness of the human intellect whenever its investigations do not enter into ultimate causes."[190] Conversely, he found that the liberal arts reveal the great achievement of the human intellect, but this was so only in so far as they remove from discourse "all questions concerning the sequence of causal phenomena."[191]

Tolstoy understood that neither science nor speculative, philosophical knowledge (the liberal arts) could provide an answer to the question of the meaning of life. The clearer the knowledge (e.g., scientific knowledge), the less it is able to give a plausible answer to life's meaning. The liberal arts, on the other hand, provide a negative answer—that nothing would come of our lives. From one branch of human knowledge, he received an endless number of precise answers to questions he had not asked, "answers concerning the chemical composition of the stars, the movement of the sun toward the constellation Hercules, the origin of the species and of man, the forms of infinitely small atoms, and the vibration of infinitely small and imponderable particles of ether." Modern science, he claimed, taught that he was nothing more than "a temporary, random conglomeration of particles . . . the mutual interaction and alteration of these particles. . . . You are a little lump of something randomly stuck together. The lump decomposes. The decomposition of the lump is known as your life."[192]

The liberal arts, he reasoned, dealt with questions about the meaning of life; yet he could find in them no release from his insignificant and futile existence. "I saw that in spite of—or rather precisely because of—the fact that this knowledge was designed to answer my question, there could be no answer other than the one I had given myself: What is the meaning of my life? It has none. Or: What will come of life? Nothing. Or: Why does everything that is exist, and why do I exist? Because it exists."[193] The liberal arts, he concluded, provided no way to bridge the finite world of time, space, and history with the infinite world of timeless and abiding reality. Imbued with a secular humanist bias, he discounted the path of religious belief and faith.

Tolstoy's attempt to work through spiritual despair brought him both very close to, and very far from, grasping the answer that continued to pop up in his contemplation: meaning resides in *nothingness*. Obviously, the answer he was searching for resides in no-*thing*-ness in so far as it cannot manifest itself empirically as some-*thing*. Meaning can no more manifest itself in time and space than the way to repair a defective carburetor on an internal combustion engine can manifest itself to an individual ignorant of its functioning. Yet, unlike knowledge of ultimate reality, a carburetor is a *thing*: it has visible components even though knowledge of its functioning and its rightful relationship to the internal combustion engine is hidden from view. But one can acquire knowledge of the carburetor if inspired to do so; it is objectified spirit—the embodiment of creativity that brought it into being. Similarly, in many instances of biological ailments, the no-*thing*-ness of medical knowledge can also be sought and acquired.

In spiritual despair, self-revelation must emanate from within by way of a mystical breakthrough. Help is derivable from awakening to meaning transmitted in revelations embodied in traditional knowledge. In the state of spiritual despair, it is distinctly because the soul is lost in the temporal-spatial reality anchored exclusively to "this world" that the self falls into emptiness and meaninglessness. Both reason and emotions—mind and heart—become wedded to the world of necessity. Spiritual despair, therefore, is precisely being devoid of faith and belief in the transcendent, "otherworldly" reality. Spiritual despair can lead (as it ultimately did for Tolstoy) to an end of false consciousness that heralds a transfiguration of consciousness, thereby a self-awakening to knowledge of truth and reality. For this to occur, consciousness must turn, *in freedom*, to belief and faith. The cleaved soul, with its consciousness focused on the material reality, must redirect its spirit to its inward life as it interacts with the outer world. Its creative potential must turn to the collective wisdom of traditional knowledge that provides the instruction manual for treating spiritual despair. The self living without the will or inclination to turn to traditional knowledge enables it to penetrate the obscure meaning of symbols and religious dogmas. Humanism is a state of being in which the self takes religious symbols and dogmas literally.

In so far as Tolstoy rejected belief and faith out of hand, his troubled conscience left him with the certainty that life was meaningless. He remained self-imprisoned, closed off to the collective wisdom of traditional knowledge. A mystical awakening to religious revelations is necessary to enter the pathway to the self's inward transfiguration. The direction, structure, and content of consciousness thus become severed from their attachments to "this-worldly" reality. Only then the human personality gains a glimpse of the "otherworld"; only then "this world" takes on the symbolic splendor of the "otherworld." Still living in a state of spiritual despair, Tolstoy turned his inquiry to nonacademic philosophers and sages—Socrates, Schopenhauer, Solomon, and Buddha.

In this venture, he found himself even more perplexed, drawing from them a view that life is rooted in nothingness. From Socrates, he learned that the "life of the body is an evil and a lie." From Schopenhauer: "Life is what it should not be, an evil; and a passage into nothingness is the only blessing that life has to offer." From Solomon: "Everything in the world—folly and wisdom, wealth and poverty, joy and sorrow—all is vanity and emptiness." From Buddha: "It is not possible to live, knowing that suffering, decrepitude, old age and death are inevitable; we must free ourselves from life and from all possibilities of life."[194] Tolstoy took literally the paradoxical thought of these thinkers and thereby became convinced that he was neither in error nor sick of mind. "On the contrary, this knowledge confirmed the fact that I had been thinking correctly and had been in agreement with the most powerful minds known to humanity."[195]

Tolstoy mistook the collective wisdom of traditional knowledge in which death is symbolically characterized as the end of consciousness wedded to worldly reality. He failed to avail himself of the path he must take in freedom, to undergo a transfiguration of consciousness and rebirth in the "otherworld" that is, the eternal realty. The meaning of no*thing*ness, or *death*, symbolically expresses the inner mystery that must be apprehended in preparation for overcoming the dark night of the soul. Spiritual despair is an outcome of the tragic loss of faith. As philosopher Martin Buber explained, faith "is not a feeling in the soul of man, but an entrance into reality, an entrance in the whole reality without reduction and curtailment."[196] Faith provides an entrance by turning one's soul in freedom to the inward reality; that is, to spiritual life, the primary reality.

Tolstoy began to doubt the validity of his perceptions of reality. Now I see that if I did not kill myself, it was because I had some vague notion that my ideas were all wrong. . . . My doubt was expressed in this way: I, that is, my reason declared that life is irrational. If there is nothing higher than reason (and there is no way to prove that there is) . . . then for me there would be no life. So how can this reason deny life when it is itself the creator of life? Or to put it differently: if there were no life, my reason would not exist either. Therefore, reason is the offspring of life. Life is all. Reason is the fruit of life and yet this reason denies that very life. I felt that something was wrong here.[197]

IV

Still oblivious to the path of faith, Tolstoy was nevertheless struck by the apparent complacency and smug self-satisfaction of the majority of his aristocratic contemporaries and the clergy living in material comfort—excluding the monks who attracted his attention. Moreover, despite his anguish, he marveled at what he saw of the mass of serfs living in apparent contentment and faith despite being ill-treated and exploited. This intensified the ache of guilt he felt for his past treatment of his serfs. It aroused his conscience. He began to explore another dimension of despair—*moral despair*: the self caught in the throes of guilt and wrongdoing, on the one hand, and self-condemnation and self-rejection, on the other. As opposed to spiritual despair, moral despair awakened in him self-judgment concerning choices he made during his lifetime. Whereas spiritual despair arouses our mental life and imagination to look forward to a way out of meaninglessness, moral despair is backward looking. The self suffers terrible pangs of guilt and shame when it dwells on memories of past wrongdoing. Tolstoy condemned his lack of compassion and empathy for those whom he had exploited or injured.

Tolstoy recognized that before the onset of despair his life had mirrored the same smug self-satisfaction of most members of his privileged class. Now apparent, his former hypocrisy hit him like a bolt of lightning, magnifying his guilt and self-condemnation. His former moral complacency stung his conscience. He envisioned his life being one of ignorance steeped in the conventional falsities of religion and science, family life and society, culture and civilization. He had yet to grasp the fact that fallacy and misconception poison the mind, heart, and soul. Fallacy dwelled in the self as an attribute of his former power, position, and privilege. With his growing awareness of guilt and self-condemnation, he could no longer find diversion from his suffering as did his fellow aristocrats. In hindsight, he began to fathom that his former epicurean life had staved off despair temporarily, allowing him to sustain a dullness of imagination. He viewed his former life, and that of members of his class, as a state of moral ignorance. Their epicurean life served as an escape from the inevitable approach of the grim reaper. "The situation in which they find themselves is such that it affords them more of the good things in life than the bad ... they forget that for every man with a thousand wives there are a thousand men without wives, that for every palace there are a thousand men who built it by the sweat of their brows . . . the dullness of the imagination of these people enables them to forget . . . the inevitability of sickness, old age, and death."[198]

Tolstoy turned to others of his class who, unlike himself, had taken the pathway of "strength"—that of suicide when they reached, in self-condemnation, the belief that life is meaningless. Strength "consists of destroying life once one has realized that life is evil and meaningless." Others took the path he now accused himself of taking, that of weakness: when one has knowledge of the meaninglessness of life while hanging on to life without the strength to take the final step. Weakness "consists of continuing to drag out a life that is evil and meaningless, knowing beforehand that nothing can come of it. The people in this category know that death is better than life, but they do not have the strength to act rationally and quickly to put an end to the delusion by killing themselves; instead they seem to be waiting for something to happen."[199]

Tolstoy reviled himself for his perceived lack of courage to put an end to his life. This state of despair concerning the self's sense of weakness, Kierkegaard disclosed, "does not reach any metamorphosis in which the consciousness of the eternal in the self breaks through, so that the battle might begin which either potentiates despair to a higher power or leads to faith."[200] Tolstoy's moral despair brought him to self-condemnation. Yet, he had not reached any semblance of a positive change in consciousness that would prepare him to turn to faith and to the spiritual reality. Self-condemnation due to his presumed weakness permitted him momentarily to dwell on his lack of courage to muster the strength of will to put an end to his life, rather than awaken him to the meaning of despair that would in turn awaken him to faith. Kierkegaard clearly understood the error in a person's moral reasoning at this point of admitting to one's weakness. "The despairer understands that it is weakness to take the earthly so much to heart, that it is weakness to despair. But then, instead of veering sharply away from despair to faith, humbling himself before God for his weakness, he is more deeply absorbed in despair and despairs over his weakness."[201] In this lies Tolstoy's agonizing self-condemnation and self-rejection: the moral despair that lingers until suicide or until the self gains a glimpse of the light of faith and undergoes an inner transfiguration of consciousness.

V

Tolstoy's awakening came from the least expected source. Despite his intense suicidality, he was tenacious and left no stone unturned to make sense of the depth of his suffering. His determination attests to his underlying moral strength, notwithstanding his self-judgment to the contrary. In desperation, he turned to the humble masses, inquisitive to gain a modicum of insight into their life of deprivation and suffering. The servile feudal class had been the very source of his physical sustenance. In his self-condemnation, he realized that he had repaid them with scorn and abuse. A perplexing question struck a chord in his self-reflection: how on earth could these maltreated millions live in faith in God without doubting the meaning of life, given their bitter lot of drudgery and dearth? Considering their suffering, Tolstoy hit upon and gained a glimmer of hope in the direction his life must take. Yet, he remained skeptical about the possibility of a personal transfiguration of consciousness and self-transformation.

Tolstoy acknowledged that faith is an irrational knowledge, the one thing that he could not accept. "This was God who is both one and three." He admitted to his incredulity apropos the creation in six days, the array of symbols of angels and the devil, and the existence of a supernatural reality. "I knew that I could find nothing in the way of rational knowledge except a denial of life, and in faith I could find nothing except a denial of reason, and this was even more impossible than a denial of life." As far as rational knowledge was concerned, he was convinced it led to one answer: "life is evil." But when he turned to the idea of faith, he found it perplexing. "According to faith, it followed that in order to understand the meaning of life I would have to turn away from reason, the very thing for which meaning was necessary."[202]

His fall into skepticism and disbelief at an early age had led him, and all who follow this vision, to a life of despair. He grasped at the same time that he could no longer be diverted in his suffering by pleasure and worldly success, or the weakness of pursuing what he now believed to be a meaningless existence. Members of the feudal class lived in a state of belief and faith, and this befuddled him. He turned to examining the reality of faith, and over a protracted period, he gradually awakened to the gift of life, the fact of his freedom, and the realization of the pitiful path he had chosen. "I realized that I had lost my way and how I had lost my way. My straying had resulted not so much from wrong thinking as *from bad living*." He admitted to his moral misconduct and transgression: his separation and alienation from communal life and from the natural world. "I realized that the truth had been hidden from me not so much because my thoughts were in error as because my life itself had been squandered in the satisfaction of lusts, spent under the exceptional condition of Epicureanism . . . . 'What is my life?' . . . 'An evil,' I was entirely correct."[203] He had been in error in projecting his meaningless life onto life in general. Eventually he turned cautiously toward the path of faith.

Tolstoy arrived at the juncture in life when the self approaches the possibility of crossing the divide from spiritual death to resurrection that sets one on the path to rebirth. This crossing can be sharp and instantaneous, an awakening to the ultimate demand of freedom; an awakening to personal guilt that releases one from the demands of the external world of necessity in which the self discerns the meaning of the transcendent reality. This sharp, instantaneous break is biblically exemplified in the path befallen one of the two thieves crucified beside Christ. At the critical moment of crucifixion and physical death, one thief disdained once and for all his past life and identity and answered the call of conscience. This instantaneous awakening is also the experience of Saul on the road to Damascus that brought about St. Paul's transfiguration and transformation.

More frequently, the path to salvation is protracted, as was Tolstoy's. Through a period of suffering and self-reflection, he gradually awakened to the spiritual source of his anguish. The inner darkness of spiritual blindness lit up from within. The scales dropped from the inner eye, his soul. His conversion, deliverance, redemption, and rebirth was a self-awakening to the gift, mystery, and struggle of life. He sought to go further: to self-validate and clarify the error of rational knowledge severed from the irrational—belief and faith. Tolstoy discovered that belief and faith could not bring about a full spiritual awakening that gives rise to resurrection and rebirth. He saw many of his countrymen living in belief and faith who became afflicted with a form of transcendental egoism. Others became susceptible to a host of superstitions, lacking in spiritual acumen. Their transfiguration of consciousness was temporary and dependent on religious rituals. He gained firsthand insight into the synthesis of rational and irrational knowledge. "I realized that if I want to understand life and its meaning, I would have to live not the life of a parasite but the genuine life, and once I have accepted the meaning that is given to life by the real humanity that makes up life, I would have to test it out."[204]

Tolstoy focused on the central spiritual pivot on the path to salvation: the relation between faith and meaning. Something transcendent, he recognized, is not rational but issues from intuitive intelligence—emotions, volitions, and lived experience. It is not reason, nor thoughts, nor ideas themselves that quelled his feelings of dread, loneliness, and forlornness. "No matter what answers a given faith might provide for us, every answer of faith gives infinite meaning to finite existence that is not destroyed by suffering, deprivation, and death."[205] Through belief and faith, the self awakens to the kingdom of meaning. Consciousness enters the realm of superconsciousness; conscience severed from the herd mentality. Tolstoy's conversion—a fundamental change in the direction, structure, and content of consciousness—was his gradual awakening to the meaning of "nothingness" affirmed by nonacademic philosophers.

Kierkegaard explains self-revelation as the mystery of the self's awakening to the world of the spirit. Consciousness turning toward faith on the suffering path recognizes and apprehends the self's relationship to both the finite and the infinite reality. Ultimately, the self awakens to "the conscious synthesis of infinitude and finitude which relates itself to itself, whose task is to become itself, a task which can be performed only by means of a relation to God."[206] The self in freedom must escape the trap of fundamentalism (the literalization of religious revelations) as well as the trap of scientism (the belief in the universal applicability of the scientific method to the exclusion of other viewpoints). Kierkegaard brought to light the path to awakening: "to become oneself is to be concrete. But to become concrete means neither to become finite nor infinite, for that which is to become concrete is a synthesis."[207]

VI

The transcultural world represents the universal foundation of all cultures and civilizations. It embodies the intimate bond between the human spirit and the eternal reality. This was the experience of both Kierkegaard and Tolstoy. Through suffering and transcending despair, they imparted something profound regarding the prophetic prospect looming on our horizon: less about the crisis in humanism of the nineteenth century but more about the global crisis in humanity emerging during the twentieth century and on into the twenty-first. Both Kierkegaard and Tolstoy sustained the prospect of preparing humanity to awaken to the Era of the Spirit, beyond the Era of the Law and the Era of the Resurrection. They thereby enabled humanity to cope with the tragic nature of freedom in ruling and directing our personal lives. The Era of the Spirit inspires the self's awakening to the meaning of life's trials and tribulations, setting humanity on the path to overcoming psychological and spiritual futility.

Kierkegaard rightly regarded awakening to meaning—knowledge of truth and goodness in the living moment—a "moment of eternity." In the kingdom of meaning, the self finds itself in its spiritual home and recognizes, in freedom and gratitude, the spiritual nature of its arduous journey in the inscrutable world of time and space. In the kingdom of meaning, the self is destined to understand that the phenomenal world is the embodiment of the spirit in which light from the transcendent world filters through the opaque spatial-temporal reality. The self awakens to its creative vocation and its transcendental mission. Neither the historical-natural antecedents (the finite world) nor the divinely given potential of creative freedom (the eternal) remain unrecognized. Belief and faith thereby serve as the preparatory stage in the self's entry into the Era of the Spirit. The spatial-temporal world (the phenomenal world) stands in stark contrast to the spiritual world (the kingdom of meaning).

Religious revelations and dogmas are symbolic embodiments of mystical insights into the realm of the spiritual. Spiritual meanings are neither apparent to our senses nor obvious to our intelligence. At the root of revelations are the mystical experiences of prophets and saints who, in communion with the eternal, convey their insights in a symbolic and metaphorical grammar. For those lacking spiritual literacy, belief and faith can cleverly rule over consciousness for good or ill. Paradoxically, belief and faith are capable of keeping the self locked out of the inner drama of the life of the spirit. Belief and faith, as necessary as they are, can give rise to zeal, fanaticism, and self-submission to a cult in which the self lives in a mirage of sanctity and righteousness. To be rescued from spiritual suffering, the meaning of religious dogmas and revelations must be spiritually experienced and inwardly validated.

Ultimately, Tolstoy had an enormous influence on the modern world. He commanded a revolutionary obedience to the moral law and passive resistance to evil. Tolstoy contributed to the understanding of human nature beyond the impact of academic philosophers and learned psychologists and sociologists by the end of the nineteenth century and into the twentieth.

CHAPTER 6

The Last Man, the Man-God, and the God-Man

I

Our evolving transcultural world shines a light on the crisis in humanism that not only confronted Tolstoy but other farsighted thinkers in the nineteenth century. Among them were Fyodor Dostoevsky (1821–1881) and Friedrich Nietzsche (1844–1900) who sought to rise above the crisis in humanism of the nineteenth century. Both foresaw that freedom could lead humanity to succumb to the worst state of being, the "ant heap" (as Dostoevsky maintained) or the "last man" (as Nietzsche claimed). Both foresaw a possible future characterized by a social order in which tyranny prevailed. A society in which, Dostoevsky alleged, Caesar would triumph over Christ, and, Nietzsche declared, the masses would lack knowledge of the eternal reality.

Whereas Dostoevsky sought to rescue the truth, freedom, and revelations of Christianity and humanity's creative nature, safeguarded in the life, death, and resurrection of Jesus, Nietzsche regarded Christianity as undermining humanity's creative calling, thereby enfeebling the masses. According to Nietzsche, God was dead and humanity was being swallowed up in a righteous void. Nietzsche wrestled with a means of reviving and restoring the creative calling of humanity in an age of nihilism deprived of consciousness of the eternal. In opposition to Dostoevsky, Nietzsche failed to fathom the possibility of redemption inspired by religious faith. Nietzsche's creative endeavor was to cultivate leaders with the will-to-power over themselves—the Übermensch (Superman)—capable of leadership over the submissive masses whom he deemed incapable of achieving knowledge of the eternal. In contrast to Christ as the God-man, Nietzsche conceived the man-god.

At the heart of Dostoevsky's belief, faith, and creative endeavor was the awakening of humanity to the tragic nature of freedom in Christianity, its meaning revealed in the life of Christ, the God-man; a religion of self-deliverance and spiritual maturity grounded in truth, goodness, and beauty. Dostoevsky's endeavor was to revive and spread the religion of the resurrection of body and soul. As a gifted literary artist and psychologist, his novels sought to expose and clarify distinctions in human behavior, differentiating the character of Nietzsche's man-god (Übermensch) and the God-man (Christ). Dostoevsky sought to confirm the truth embodied in Christianity and its fundamental importance in enhancing personal and moral virtues.

The forewarning of the onslaught of the global crisis in humanity of the twentieth and twenty-first centuries was not recognizable on the mental horizon of nineteenth-century thinkers, nor is it recognizable today among many pundits and intellectuals. The dreadful possibility that confronts humanity today is the outcome of twentieth-century scientific weapons of mass destruction and scientific means of mental control of the masses. The contemporary world is torn asunder by its virulent religious sectarianism, its scientific invention of weapons of mass destruction, its breakdown of social institutions, its growing anarchy, and its demise of nations with their powerful oligarchies in a world becoming ever more interconnected and interdependent.

II

Dostoevsky conceived his psychological and philosophical ideas through the characters in his artistic works. He was mindful of the readers' freedom and the importance of stirring their psychological, moral, and spiritual understanding, using the psychological and emotional states of his characters and their actions in his novels in lieu of an abstract psychological or philosophical analysis. He sought to awaken the sacredness of freedom inherent in the universe, embodied in human existence, beneficial to spiritual understanding. He fervently believed that spiritual development is the outcome of the fate of freedom. Human beings suffer from their sinfulness due to their human-divine nature—being creatures with both a natural and a spiritual character. His psychological and philosophical endeavor was to establish the truth that a world without evil would be deprived of human freedom and humanity's creative vocation. There would be no advance in human evolution and no quest for redemption. No psychological, social, and spiritual evolution; no history; no stewardship of the earth's ecosystem would be realized without the freedom intrinsic in the universe and in human beings. Lodged in freedom, evil, suffering, and redemption, human life reflects the spiritual essence underlying the cosmos and universe. According to Berdyaev, Dostoevsky "believed firmly in the redemptive and regenerative power of suffering: life is the expiation of sin by suffering. Freedom has opened the path of evil to man, it is a proof of freedom, and man must pay the price. The price is suffering, and by it the freedom that has been spoiled and turned into its contrary is reborn and given back to man. Therefore is Christ the Saviour freedom itself."[208]

Dostoevsky's first major novel, *Crime and Punishment* (1866) established the psychological, moral, and social theme of the state of the man-god—Raskolnikov. At the core of Raskolnikov's psyche is the obsession and intention, in the interest of humanitarianism, to take the life of another he deemed to be despicable. Raskolnikov's inner conflict, moral conscience, torment, and ultimately his redemption exemplify a person torn between sympathy, pity, and humanitarian feelings, on the one hand, and a prideful, egoistic self-image, on the other. He experiences contempt for those of a herd mentality and slave morality. Several of Dostoevsky's novels dealt with different aspects of the theme of the man-god wherein the reader gets a glimpse into the mystery of the man-god's idealistic state, leading to homicidal, patricidal, suicidal, or other horrid crimes. In the case of *Crime and Punishment* and the novel *Possessed*, Dostoevsky examined the inner life of the self in a state of monomaniacal obsession. Dostoevsky's final novel, *The Brothers Karamazov*, published a year before his death, is a work of genius in which he distinguished the character of the man-god and the God-man, Christ.

Dostoevsky sought to reveal that an obsessed person is no longer free. Freedom is assailed, on the one hand, by a crude egoism fostered by the rising political economy of the personal and moral virtues at the root of Adam Smith's *Wealth of Nations*, and on the other, by the philosophical thought of Karl Marx in his dialectic of capitalism-socialism and individ-ualism-communism. Dostoevsky was suspicious of the political economy evolving, despite the fact that Russia had emancipated the serfs in 1861, five years before the publication of *Crime and Punishment.*

III

In his *Brothers Karamazov,* Dostoevsky synthesized all his partial endeav-ors to work out the conflict between reason and Christian faith—between the man-god and the God-man—in the never-ending dispute concerning humanity's destiny grounded in the eternal. In his final novel, Dostoevsky conceived *The Legend of The Grand Inquisitor,* which juxtaposes the Grand Inquisitor (the man-god, the Anti-Christ) and the God-man (Christ). "The Grand Inquisitor" is a poem conceived by the secular intellectual brother, Ivan Karamazov, one of four brothers implicated in the murder of their father. The poem sought to cast doubt on the life choice of his youngest brother, Alyosha, bent on entering the religious life of a monk. In the leg-end, Christ returns to earth during the Inquisition of the sixteenth century, as flames were crackling around heretics being burned at the stake by the Church in the name of truth, justice, and love. Christ, Ivan Karamazov charges in his poem, "deigned to appear for a moment to the people, to the tortured, suffering people, sunk in iniquity, but loving Him like children." The crowd recognizes Christ, surrounds Him, and flocks to Him. Christ "moves silently in their midst with a gentle smile of infinite compassion. The sun of love burns in His heart, light and power shine from His eyes, and their radiance, shed on the people, stirs their hearts with responsive love. Christ holds out his hand to them, blesses them, and a healing virtue comes from contact with Him. . . . The crowd weeps, and kisses the earth under His feet." The Grand Inquisitor, in his old monk's cassock, watches Christ from afar and bids the guards to arrest Christ. Such is the power of the Grand Inquisitor, "so completely are the people cowed into submission and trembling obedience to him, that the crowd immediately makes way for the guards."[209]

The following day, the imprisoned Christ is interrogated by the Grand Inquisitor. The Grand Inquisitor sets himself against the Son of God to safeguard the welfare of weak humanity, paradoxically in the name of the

Son of God. Dostoevsky here disclosed two universal principles—freedom and compulsion: belief and faith in the meaning and purpose of life exemplified in the life of Christ, on the one hand; disbelief, humanism, and humanitarian pity, on the other, exemplified by the Grand Inquisitor, whose secret is that he does not believe in God and an eternal reality, and consequently, he does not believe that humanity's destiny lies in freedom. The Grand Inquisitor charges Christ: "For centuries we have been wrestling with Thy freedom, but now it is ended and over for good. Dost Thou not believe that it is over for Good? . . . But let me tell you that now, today, people are more persuaded than ever that they have perfect freedom, yet they have brought their freedom to us and laid it humbly at our feet. But that has been our doing."[210]

The Grand Inquisitor claims that the Church has taken the sword of Caesar and proclaimed itself sole ruler of the earth, as a means of ruling the masses and planning their universal happiness. The God-man Christ has been supplanted by the man-god, cloaked in the vestment and dogmas of the Church. The Grand Inquisitor chides Christ's naïveté: "Thou wouldst have accomplished all that man seeks on earth—that is, someone to worship, someone to keep his conscience, and some means of uniting all in one unanimous and harmonious ant heap, because the craving for universal unity is the third and last anguish of men. Mankind as a whole has always striven to organize a universal state."[211]

Dostoevsky understood that the sword of Caesar as opposed to the love and freedom of Christ appeals to both the political left and the political right. It involves the three powers that cloud the mind of human beings, which Christ rejected: to control the masses by the use of miracles, mystery, and authority. Dostoevsky stood firmly in his conception of the God-man as the fundamental, universal characteristic of freedom that leads to the awakening of the self to the spiritual reality and the achievement of spiritual literacy. In contrast, the Grand Inquisitor, appealing to the political left and right, sustained the enslavement of humanity by a division of those few who arrogate to themselves unlimited personal freedom and rights over the masses, with the flock-like sheep indoctrinated with a herd mentality and slave morality.

In addition to humanitarian pity for the masses living in an ant heap, the legend of *"The Grand Inquisitor"* upholds the view that the vast majority of humanity is incapable of rising to the exalted heights of spiritual literacy. The masses are led to worship a kingdom of this world and to live deprived of freedom and truth. The Grand Inquisitor rebukes Christ for the unrest, confusion, and unhappiness humans suffer, despite the agony Christ bore for their freedom. "Thou didst crave for the free love and not the base raptures of the slave. . . . But Thou didst think too highly of men therein, for they are slaves, of course, though rebellious by nature. Look round and judge . . . centuries have passed, look upon them. Whom hast Thou raised up to thyself? I swear, man is weaker and baser by nature than Thou hast believed him!"[212]

In the justification put forth by the Grand Inquisitor, Dostoevsky endeavors to contrast the man-god and the God-man's ability to discern the truth. Did Christ come for the elect alone? How are the weak to blame, unable to receive such a terrible burden as the gift of freedom? The Grand Inquisitor, the man-god, justifies questioning Christ. "Canst Thou have simply come to the elect and for the elect?"[213] The Grand Inquisitor represents the view of the proponents of authoritarian religion. In response to the universal freedom of Christ, the authoritarian elect claim for themselves a humanitarian response to the overpowering burden of freedom of the millions upon millions among the suffering masses. How are the masses to survive with the heavy burden of the absolute freedom of Christ? It is only we, the Grand Inquisitor contends self-righteously, who guard the mystery and who shall be unhappy and who have taken upon ourselves "the curse of knowledge of good and evil." The thousands of millions among the masses, living in ignorance under the guidance of the elect, will live and die peacefully in the name of Christ. Beyond the grave they will find nothing but death. "But we shall keep the secret . . . for their happiness." The authoritarian elect in control of the religious institution will "allure them with the reward of heaven and eternity. Though if there were anything in the other world, it certainly would not be for such as they."[214]

Dostoevsky's Grand Inquisitor, a democrat and socialist presumably full of pity for man, Berdyaev maintained, is "a new principle, refined, attractive, looking like goodness, and the superficial likeness between the evil antichristian principle and the good Christian principle." But it "is a source of great danger." Humanity finds itself imbued at the "end time" of the modern epoch, as Dostoevsky envisioned, at an obscure threshold separating truth from falsehood. According to Berdyaev, "The image of good begins to be 'divided,' Christ's image fades away and is merged with that of Antichrist. Men appear with divided minds. . . . Dostoevsky foresaw this state of mind and his description of it was prophetical. When he has reached an extremity of inner division and is psychologically unbalanced, with all the customary landmarks wiped out and no new ones in sight, then man hears the call of the Antichrist."[215] This antithesis between the man-god (the Grand Inquisitor) and God-man (Christ) preoccupied religious philosophers of the nineteenth century including Søren Kierkegaard and Vladimir Solovyev, as well as Friedrich Nietzsche. Having rejected Christianity as the religion of the Antichrist, Nietzsche sought to reveal what he took to be the hidden nature of the God-man, the Übermensch—the superman.

IV

Dostoevsky's *"The Grand Inquisitor"* put at the core of the crisis in humanism during the unfolding of the "end time" of the modern epoch the dialectic of the man-god and the God-man. Yet, Dostoevsky also considered in this novel a positive pathway to the deliverance of humanity through the teachings of the humble monk Father Zossima. Dostoevsky maintained that no power wielded by humanitarian pity for suffering humanity by those who arrogate to themselves the will-to-power to remedy the human plight is compatible with the moving power of love grounded in the freedom and creative vocation of human beings, exemplified in the crucifixion and resurrection of Christ. Dostoevsky thereby endeavored to put in perspective the distortion and misrepresentation of the man-god (the Grand Inquisitor) by setting forth the teachings of Father Zossima.

The humble monk, Father Zossima, reveals the outcome of the loss of traditional knowledge rooted in the moral and personal virtues rapidly being replaced in the nineteenth century by the rising ideology of utilitarian egoism. Human beings, Father Zossima claims, "all have been given rights, but have not been shown the means of satisfying their wants." In the words of Father Zossima, Dostoevsky proclaims that despite the "the reign of freedom, especially of late," we have gotten nothing "but slavery and self destruction! For the world says: "You have desires and so satisfy them, for you have the same rights as the most rich and powerful. Don't be afraid of satisfying them and even multiply your desires.". . . And what follows from the right of multiplication of desires? In the rich, isolation and spiritual suicide; in the poor envy and murder. For they all have been given rights, but have not been shown the means of satisfying their wants. They maintain that the world is getting ever more united, more and more bound together in brotherly community, as it overcomes distance and sets thoughts flying through the air.[216]

Dostoevsky saw freedom being degraded to the level of material reality, to utilitarianism, to the distortion of human nature. In accumulating a mass of objects as the realization of freedom and self-fulfillment, Dostoevsky recognizes the loss of freedom of the spirit and spiritual joy, and attacked modern science: "in science there is nothing but what is the object of sense. The spiritual world, the higher part of man's being, is rejected altogether, dismissed with a sort of triumph, even with hatred."[217] "What is hell?" Father Zossima asks: "I maintain it is the suffering of being unable to love. . . . They talk of hell fire in the material sense. I don't go into that mystery and I shun it . . . for I imagine that in material agony, their still greater spiritual agony would be forgotten for a moment. Moreover, spiritual agony cannot be taken from them, for that suffering is not external but within them. . . . Oh, there are some who remain proud and fierce even in hell, in spite of their certain knowledge and contemplation of the absolute truth."[218] For some who have given themselves fully to their spiritual agony, they "live upon their vindictive pride like a starving man in the desert sucking blood out of his own body. But they are never satisfied, and they refuse forgiveness. . . . They cannot behold the living God without hatred."[219]

Dostoevsky provides a vision of faith and self-transcendence in the words of Father Zossima: "you cannot be a judge of anyone. For no one can judge a criminal, until he recognizes that he is just such a criminal . . . and that he perhaps is more than all men to blame for that crime. . . . If you can take upon yourself the crime of the criminal your heart is judging, take it at once, suffer for him yourself, and let him go without reproach. And even if the law makes you his judge, act in the same spirit so far as possible, for he will go away and condemns himself more bitterly than you have done."[220] Father Zossima sets forth a positive litany for the love of life in freedom: "When you are left alone pray. Love to throw yourself on the earth and kiss it. Kiss the earth and love it with an unceasing, consuming love. Love all men. Love everything. Seek that rapture and ecstasy. Water the earth with the tears of your joy and love those tears. Don't be ashamed of that ecstasy, prize it, for it is a gift of God and a great one; it is not given to many but only to the elect."[221]

Dostoevsky provides us finally with the spiritual awakening of Alyosha, the monk and youngest Karamazov brother. At Father Zossima's Requiem, the Elegy contemplating Christ's first miracle arouses Alyosha and soothes his consternation apropos "The Grand Inquisitor." Alyosha realizes the meaning of Christ's first miracle, the changing of the water into wine to extend the gladness of the guests at the wedding feast of Cana in Galilee. He grasps at that moment the joy of Christ: "He who loves men loves their gladness too."[222] Alyosha remembers Father Zossima's words: "We are drinking the new wine, the wine of new, great gladness." Dostoevsky poetically expressed Alyosha's spiritual awakening: his transfiguration of consciousness beyond worldly knowledge. "Something glowed in Alyosha's heart. Something filled it until it ached. Tears of rapture rose from his soul. . . . And never, never, all his life, did Alyosha forget that minute."[223]

V

Dostoevsky placed the ethical stance of the Grand Inquisitor (the man-god) face to face with the spiritual affirmations of Father Zossima concerning Christ (the God-man). For human beings in the contemporary world, the global crisis in humanity must open to the anticipated era in spiritual evolution beyond the eras of the law and redemption if humanity is to avoid a planetary catastrophe. People worldwide must rise above belief and faith if they are to awaken to the imperative of spiritual literacy in a world torn apart into myriad religions, philosophies, scientific discoveries, and artistic embodiments of truth and reality. Dostoevsky lit up the pathway to the opposite outcome of the "anthill" and the "last man" syndrome wherein the man-gods are driven by their will-to-power—disoriented, bewildered, and wanting in truth and knowledge of the eternal. Today, faith and belief alone, whether with respect to the religious or the secular world, cannot stem the false conception of complex notions about the ethical reality, especially utilitarian philosophy rooted in materialism—the principle of the greatest happiness for the greatest number. That principle has become the principal guide to morals, public policy, legal administration, political reform, and economic theory as well as the solution to social problems.[224]

Human beings are becoming ever more forlorn in an ever-fragmenting community, from the local to the international level. The confusion of the man-gods, Dostoevsky understood, no longer could fathom humanity's stumbling path into the future, ill-informed of truth and knowledge of the eternal. All sociopolitical philosophies have failed postmodern people: fascism, socialism, communism, democracy, libertarianism, and free-enterprise ideology. The man-gods can find nowhere to turn to stave off the spiritual agony spreading in contemporary society.

Dostoevsky's prophetic assessment of the nineteenth-century crisis in humanism helps jog the memory of humanity concerning the importance of traditional knowledge bequeathed to the postmodern world. But the world of the twenty-first century, more complex and globally interdependent, requires spiritual literacy be made possible in our transcultural world to light the way forward. Today's masses and man-gods generally—those in political positions of power devoid of spiritual literacy—have become absorbed in materialism and overwhelming state power. Social institutions are deteriorating before their eyes; the self has become blinded by the complex thought and the scourge of sectarian religions. The transcultural world—yet to make its debut in the halls of higher learning—demands spiritual literacy be transmitted through public education, from kindergarten to higher learning, and advanced side-by-side with worldly literacy to bring about a renaissance of the spirit.

We must avert the danger inherent in the postmodern world subject to the possibility of an era of dehumanization and widespread alienation in which the welfare of humanity becomes merely an appendage to the process of production and consumption. Propagators of continuous arms production in a world caught up in an unceasing arms race must face the fact that democracy may ultimately forfeit the qualities of a society called "democratic" and "free." Lacking truth and knowledge of the spiritual reality, humanity may find itself powerless and unqualified to fulfill Dostoevsky's road to Truth and the Good, and incapable of seizing the possibility of guiding humanity through the darkness and horror of cata-strophic division and onto the pathway of veritable freedom.

VI

Friedrich Nietzsche had foreseen, from the perspective of the nineteenth century, a continued degeneration and decline in modern life, deprived of absolute value, with the onset of nihilism camouflaged by the "holiest of names." In his judgment, "Christianity has been humanity's greatest mis-fortune hitherto." It stood opposed "to everything happily constituted in the mind,—it can make use only of morbid reason as Christian reason; it takes the side of everything idiotic, it utters a curse upon 'intellect,' upon the superbia of the healthy intellect."[225] Nietzsche placed the final value not in the human but in the superhuman. He regarded Man as a shame-ful and pitiable creature who must be overcome. Human beings must strive for something which is higher than themselves, the *Übermensch*, the superman—the man-god. As the French existentialist Gabriel Marcel maintained, Nietzsche's "kind of humanism . . . sought to transfer to man certain attributes that formerly belonged to a God now declared to be dead."[226] Berdyaev maintained that "the motives of Nietzsche's criticism of Christian morality are profound . . . creatively daring but religiously blind."[227] Nietzsche was concerned with historical Christianity which, in many respects, represented an inversion of Christian truth. Despite this irony, Nietzsche turned out to be "the sacrificial forerunner of a new moral epoch."[228] His daring compelled Christianity—involved in a tragic betrayal of Christ historically—to re-evaluate its moral and religious stance.

Nietzsche finished his philosophical autobiography, *Ecce Homo: One Becomes What One Is*, in the year of his mental collapse—1888. In it, he identified his significance as a philosopher and literary artist. He provided a keen commentary on his major works. One discovers a scholar who vacil-lates between pride and humility, bluster and gentleness, compulsiveness and composure, as he reviews his philosophical works, peppering his com-ments with sarcasm, philosophical mischievousness, and a sense of humor. From the work of his early years, beginning with his first book at the age of twenty-four, one becomes aware of an exceptional mind exuding confi-dence, a thinker brimming with freedom of thought and penetrating insight into religion, philosophy, science, history, and literature. Not shackled by the dogmas of faith, he fixed his sight on historical Christianity in an effort to do battle and slay the dragon, what he took to be the corroding influence of belief and faith in dogmatized, literalized Christianity.

The Übermensch he conceived, the man-god Zarathustra, possesses an aristocratic morality: the superman alone, Nietzsche maintained, possesses "the meaning of the earth." Entry into the realm of meaning in mystical religious terms is referred to as entry into the kingdom of God. This signifies the self's awakening to the spiritual realm, the hidden embodiment of spirit underlying the facts of history and cultural evolution. What is Nietzsche alluding to if not the spiritual reality? He is searching for the kingdom of God, the kingdom of meaning. He replaces Christ with his literary Übermensch, Zarathustra. In his mental collapse, Nietzsche identified himself as the "crucified"!

In contrast to the herd morality, Nietzsche labored in the philosophical and spiritual burrows, seeking to excavate and clarify the depths of the psycho-social-biological and historical reality. Belief in a heavenly realm—the "otherworld" as a realm of being (some haven in the heavens)—was and is still true for many. What is puzzling for the erudition of a philosophical and psychological intellect of Nietzsche's stature is his imputing this to be the meaning of the Gospels of the New Testament. It's hard to reconcile, for example, his taking the realm of reality called "heaven" literally—e.g., Michelangelo's depiction of the creation of Adam on the ceiling of the Sistine Chapel—as the profound scriptural meaning of the Gospels. Nietzsche's failure to grasp the deep mystical revelations of Christianity is indeed not a childlike interpretation. His oversight was his failure to make a distinction between the historical practice of Christianity and the truth of Christianity. Scripturally, the "otherworldly" reality is qualitative not quantitative, inward and spiritual rather than outward and empirical, metahistorical rather than historical. His endeavor to transvalue value was a challenge to historical Christianity, an endeavor to shake up stupefied consciousness in a world tilting toward chaos and nihilism.

In rejecting the historical practice of Christianity, Nietzsche took it upon himself to start from scratch. He turned to the ancient Greeks. His was a grand intellectual and philosophical enterprise. In his attempt to transvalue value, he left the "otherworldly" reality out of his equation. His was a "humanism" that took human life to the extreme, morally, culturally, and philosophically, denuded of religious belief and faith. In doing so, he taught how the fate of human beings will pan out in the future, with life evolving at a time when religion had lost its grip on human consciousness. He envisions the creation of a leadership class, the Übermensch who have struggled through the will-to-power and thereby gained knowledge of the eternal reality, beyond good and evil. His superman stands in opposition to the humanists, those who would give rise to the "last man" and an epoch of a New Dark Age. He rejected both humanism and Christianity's God-man, the divine-human character of all human beings, as a way out of a possible dark age descending on humanity—the age of the "last man."

Nietzsche characterized the age of the "last man": "Alas, the time is coming when man will no longer give birth to a star. Alas, the time of the most despicable man is coming, he that is no longer able to despise himself. Behold, I show you the last man." "'What is love? What is creation? What is longing? What is a star?' thus asks the last man, and he blinks. . . . The earth has become small, and on it hops the last man, who makes everything small. His race is as ineradicable as the flea-beetle; the last man lives longest."[229]

Berdyaev maintained that Nietzsche sought to overcome decadent humanism. "For Nietzsche man must be overcome, he must arrive at something which is higher than man, the superman. Humanism conquers not from above through grace, but from beneath through man's own power—and this is the great achievement of Nietzsche." Berdyaev upheld firmly and emphatically that Nietzsche "is the forerunner of a new religious anthropology."[230] In this regard, Nietzsche's efforts foreshadowed spiritual literacy. But in contrast to the transcultural world of the twentieth and twenty-first centuries, Nietzsche envisioned this possibility for those on the path to the will-to-power over their conditioned selves—a possibility for the supermen alone.

In the judgment of the religious philosopher Paul Tillich, Nietzsche depicted a world in which humankind had fallen into utter meaninglessness. Having undergone a personal crisis, humanity appears to have suffered considerably from what the self understood to be an absence from, and a rejection of, a transcendent ground of reality. Nietzsche's quest was for the fundamental good beyond good and evil—that is, beyond the social construction of good and evil that gives rise to a slave morality.[231]

Reinhold Niebuhr found Nietzsche's pessimism thoroughgoing, though he concluded that Nietzsche was able, paradoxically, "to erect an ultimate optimism upon his conception of the superman, who transmutes the will-to-power into an instrument of social creativity and order."[232] This is the crux of the moral conundrum that continues to confront humanity today. Nietzsche maintained that human beings must go beyond conventional morality. Yet, the moral problem concerning the idea of his superman's will-to-power presupposes an elite class ascending spiritually and morally beyond the masses, thereby severing humanity in two: those of a creative potential with noble moral sensibility fit to be leaders, and those fit only to be led—those of a herd mentality and slave morality.

VI

Nietzsche failed to concede the possibility that all human beings possess the potential to awaken to the life and world of the spirit. His view of the life and world of the spirit parallels the historical claim about worldly literacy held from antiquity to the industrial revolution—literacy dogmatically held to be a class-related potential. He saw the world divided into two classes: the supermen possessed of the will-to-power and ordinary folk subjugated and defeated by a herd mentality. Nietzsche took a reactionary stance concerning humanity's capacity for spiritual awakening and transcultural spiritual literacy. Nearly a century since the brutality of World War I, humanity faces the same questions that Nietzsche seriously posed: To whom and to what kind of world does the future of humanity belong? Will our survival depend on the growth of a cadre of supermen with the will-to-power to lord it over a spiritually illiterate herd as a means of stemming the decline, degeneration, and nihilism still prevalent in the postmodern era? Or, will the future be a New Dark Age of the "last man," a mass society under the aegis of humanists who fail to acknowledge the spiritual and eternal reality and fail to exert over themselves the will-to-power?

For Nietzsche, the "last man" characterized those who become psychologically, socially, and biochemically self-narcotized, shorn of their creative potential and dispossessed of their will to meaning and spiritual maturity. Dostoevsky, on the other hand, imagined human survival contingent on the realization of God-human-hood: human beings spiritually enlightened and capable of begetting a social order presided over by those resurrected in body and soul. It is remarkable that Nietzsche was attracted to Dostoevsky's psychological ideas. He admitted that "Dostoevsky was the only psychologist from whom I had anything to learn; he belongs to the happiest windfalls of my life."[233]

In projecting this division of a ruling and herd class historically into the future (given the fact that it was valid concerning the past), Nietzsche's body of work put historical Christianity to the test. Nietzsche rekindled within the Christian world a re-examination of the Gospels' anthropological revelation. His philosophical and literary works not only challenged and demanded a re-examination of the corruption and literalism of Christian dogma, they sought to bring about a transvaluation of values that put nineteenth-century humanism on trial, subject to a religious, moral, and aesthetical reassessment. This was Nietzsche's philosophical contribution to those in the postmodern world.

Nevertheless, Nietzsche failed to entertain the possibility that the masses could or would ever triumph over the yoke of economic, political, and religious elites capable of manipulating consciousness by seductive ideologies. For Nietzsche, Christianity had historically "sided with everything weak, low, and botched" and against "all the self-preservative instincts of strong life," corrupting reason and the strongest intellects.[234] From his early years upon entering university until his final writings, Nietzsche vehemently condemned Christianity. In his final words written shortly before his mental collapse, Nietzsche wrote: "I call Christianity the one great curse, the one enormous and innermost perversion, the one great instinct of revenge, for which no means are too venomous, too underhand, too underground and too *petty*,—I call it the one immortal blemish of mankind."[235]

The abiding spiritual mystery conveyed by our evolving transcultural world of the twentieth and twenty-first centuries is the disclosure of humanity's transcendental spiritual nature: humanity endowed with creative freedom and the capacity to awaken to the eternal—i.e., to the human capacity to enter the kingdom of meaning—the infinite eternal embodied in the cosmos and universe. The transcultural world stands in the face of the facts of history. This disclosure of spiritual literacy has yet to reach the educated classes and yet to be transmitted in the public education of our youth. The imperative of spiritual literacy for all remains humanity's hope for a way forward beyond the horrific death, destruction, devastation, and violence gripping planetary life caught in the throes of warring nation-states, each possessing control over the masses through oligarchies mired in sectarian religious and political power.

VII

The possibility of realizing an epoch of the spirit rests upon a New Renaissance which would usher in a spiritual revolution that encourages spiritual literacy, awaking humanity to super-personal, super-cultural, and trans-national values and virtues. It presupposes a prophetic age unveiling revelations of humanity's divine character, which is universal and eternal. The uppermost question facing today's global crisis in humanity is this: is humanity approaching a possible "end time" that holds the prospect of an "end of the postmodern world" that gives birth to humanity's spiritual nature transculturally? In contrast to Nietzsche's superman (man-god, Zarathustra) stands Dostoevsky's (God-man, Christ) overcoming hell fire not in its material connotation, but hell in its true sense—suffering due to "being unable to love." According to Dostoevsky, human beings must make themselves "responsible for all men's sins. As soon as you sincerely make yourself responsible for everything and for all men, you will see at once that you have found salvation."[236]

Dostoevsky and Tolstoy, unlike Nietzsche, experienced a transfiguration of consciousness, a spiritual conversion in which they awakened to the meaning of the otherworldly reality. Nietzsche rejected outright the possibility of a religious "end of time," a conversion resulting in a mass awakening to an otherworldly reality, heralding the rebirth of consciousness on a personal and transcultural scale. Strangely, Nietzsche did not reject the existence of an eternal reality. He labored unceasingly in the vineyards of the factual-historical-cultural reality. He interpreted Christianity strictly from its historical distortion: the bearer of imperialism, state power, deception, violence, and forever anon, in his view, the humiliation of human beings—their herd mentality and slave morality. Nietzsche's thought is steeped implicitly, nevertheless, in bringing about a profound death and rebirth of consciousness, instituted by his determination to transvalue all value, a book he was planning to write.

From the perspective of the twenty-first century, our evolving transcultural world anticipates human beings appropriating globally a cosmic identity rooted in the transcendent world of the spirit. Ethnic, racial, national, creedal, and sexual characteristics must be subordinated to a trans-moral and trans-spiritual reality. More to the point, human beings worldwide will have access to the transcultural world that extends spiritual knowledge beyond its exclusive confinement in sectarian world religions prone to kindle and generate division and chaos. The nineteenth century had to face up to the onset of the crisis in humanism; the beginning of the twenty-first century is threatened by the possibility of anthropocide (the extinction of man as a species-being). The global crisis in humanity is a warning of an urgent need for an Era of the Spirit beyond the era of redemption, the moral law, and personal salvation.

VIII

In Nietzsche, there is a moral depth of understanding as well as a real audacity in his prophetic vision of the moral earthquake that was to shake the foundation of Western civilization. The disaster of World War I followed by the horror of World War II is a testimony to the outcome of humanism. Indeed, Nietzsche's judgment of a possible New Dark Age is still a haunting prophecy, given the mounting chaos, anarchy, and terrorism spreading worldwide, to include the West's meddling in the affairs of the Arab world and the terrible, haunting sectarianism in Islam.

Plato taught that without wisdom—knowledge of the Good—those taking on the mantle of power would be least likely to end up as "philosopher-kings" (Plato's term). Members of Plato's guardian class (the counterpart of Nietzsche's Übermensch) carrying out the legislative and judicial functions of government include those manifesting an impeccable character brought about by a long-term education accompanied by difficult trials and ordeals to establish a measure of their moral courage. Before entering into the guardian class, they must endure more than a decade of higher learning until the prospect of awakening to knowledge of the Good becomes an actuality. Even then, Plato reminds us, some will fail to awaken. He made clear that should society bring to power true guardians (philosopher-kings possessing wisdom), they, being human, might fail to rule according to the ideal. Whether from error in selecting guardians for the next generation, miscalculations in ruling, fate, or chance, the state could become afflicted with social ills. Plato used the ideal-type, the guardian, as a means of clarifying the process by which deviations from the ideal breeds various forms of moral and criminal behavior within the state and within personal life. "It is better for everyone, we believe, to be subject to a power of godlike wisdom residing within himself, or, failing that, imposed from without, in order that all of us, being under one guidance, may be so far as possible equal and united."[237]

Guardians are those who have presumably fashioned in their soul the virtues of temperance, courage, wisdom, and justice. They are far from abandoning the self to the irrational pleasures of the brute. They will keep the bodily frame "in tune always for the sake of the resulting concord in the soul." Traditional knowledge, the bearer of collective wisdom of the past, according to Plato, bears "a pattern set up in the heavens for one who desires to see it and, seeing it, to found one in himself. But whether it exists anywhere or ever will exist is no matter; for this is the only commonwealth in whose politics he [the person] can ever take part."[238] Plato made clear that truth lies in the self that has undergone a metanoia—a fundamental change in the structure and direction of consciousness, the self-awakening to the transcendent Good, beyond good and evil.

Today, the world's civilizations are tending toward greater chaos and tyranny. And the world's major religions are finding themselves enmeshed in fervent sectarianism. It would be a risk to planetary life of utmost folly to confine and narrow our knowledge of the eternal exclusively to the domain of religion. Moreover, absent spiritual literacy mandatory in the education of children globally, nations of the present world order tend to give birth to virulent oligarchies that appropriate for themselves absolute sovereignty that secretes the toxin of continual warfare.

CHAPTER 7

Freedom, Oppression, and the Plight of Capitalism

I

The French philosopher and political activist Simone Weil made an astute evaluation of supreme significance regarding the tragedy of freedom in the economic realm. "The form of oppression that accompanied the transition from original, prehistorical to industrialized forms of economic behavior was different not only in *degree* but in *kind*. What is surprising is not that oppression should make its appearance only after higher forms of economy have been reached, but that it should always accompany them."[239] Advances in the pattern of production also gave rise to a form of oppression which changes in its essential nature. The tragedy of history is the interplay of liberty and oppression. In the early phase of economic reality, it is nature in the hunting and foraging societies that exerted overwhelming pressure on humans owing to the immediate compulsion of natural needs. Each individual is in direct relation with the natural order. Humans find themselves in a struggle with nature for survival. They work beside one another, not only for themselves but for each other. Survival is a matter of each individual being in direct contact with, and experiencing directly, the spur of nature. There is no intervening class that stands between labor and nature; there is an absence of a directing class overseeing and managing human relations.[240]

In the early stage of human reality, there was no division of the self into subject and object. To eat was to live: to eat allows one to live in accordance with the dictates of nature. Each individual is in direct union with the resources of nature. Nature is one's mother; its resources the sustenance of one's livelihood and consequently one's consciousness, thoughts, and being. The spirit resided in the depth of being—the qualitative domain—at one with nature. The individual experiences nature and its fruits as an extension of itself, just as the child experiences the mother and her breast as an extension of itself. The spirit is at one with the impenetrable mystery of cosmic energy.

The Neolithic Revolution, with its onset of agriculture and settled community life, is the outcome of an event erupting from consciousness—from the inner qualitative depth of being. The discovery of the relation between the seed and its product is an awakening of consciousness to a fundamental character of reality. The creation of agriculture amounted to a divine-human revelation, a creative act of consciousness that brought to light a fundamental mystery of the cosmos and the universe. It was the embodiment of spirit erupting from the depths of human freedom. A double loss of liberty gradually took shape, first with respect to nature and then with respect to the domination of human beings by human beings. Before awakening to this mystery, nature itself was the oppressing force. The creation of agriculture established a form of oppression different in kind; it took place in both the outer objective and the inner subjective realm of human life. It was the beginning of the alienation of the self from itself and, at the same time, the onset of self-alienation of humans from one another.

Oppression changed in kind as it passed through stages from servitude to nature to servitude to an intervening class of rulers. The oppressive force of nature became hidden behind the spur of the dictates of humans themselves. Humans fell into a class struggle with the intervention of a ruling echelon. Simone Weil maintained that at higher stages of economic production "human action continues, as a whole, to be nothing but pure obedience to the brutal spur of an immediate necessity, only, instead of being harried by nature, man is henceforth harried by man, with respect to nature, from servitude to dominion. . . . Nature gradually loses her divine character, and divinity more and more takes on human shape."[241]

Throughout recorded history, a prestigious value of veneration was projected onto the ruling class that corrupted the heart, mind, and intuitive intelligence of the masses, as well as of the powerful who misappropriated their unearned authority and wealth. Living in a state of idolatry is to live under a spell of self-submission to the powerful that diminishes the self of workers and their social class. Hence, a death blow severed the communal relationship between the ruling echelon (the masters) and the lower classes (the oppressed). In this fallen state, accordingly, the ruling echelon appropriated a divine quality exclusively for itself, while the working masses unwittingly rendered up any sense of possessing a divine character. Their lives abided in self-submission. This constituted the first stage in economic development. It was accompanied by a shift of the creative potential humankind possesses generally to a class which became venerated within the hierarchy of the social order.

II

Contemporary economic reality had its debut in the early modern era before it was systematized in the eighteenth and nineteenth centuries into free-enterprise capitalism. Its birth in the fourteenth and fifteenth centuries issued from Florentine merchants who realized that a quick fortune could be made by not spending all their profits immediately and reinvesting them in part. They soon diverted part of their earnings from their various enterprises, investing it to gain ever more profits. Capitalism slowly evolved as serfdom receded. To understand capitalism as it evolved as a "science," however, we must start by unraveling the philosophy of free-enterprise economics set forth by the Scottish moral philosopher Adam Smith (1723–1790), the originator of modern economic thought. His ideas must be subjected to a critique, including their factual, theoretical, psychological, and ethical justifications, which have been spun into the fabric and practice of the ideology of capitalism today. Thereby, we can gain a glimpse into their spiritual embodiment—their essence, their truth. Adam Smith's ideas themselves are metaphysical and metahistorical and thus constitute a spiritual outpouring of the human mind.

Modern economic theory has its roots in Adam Smith's *Theory of Moral Sentiments* published in 1761 and in his *Inquiry into the Nature and Causes of the Wealth of Nations* in 1776. In the former, he set forth his theory of the nature of man and society; in the latter, he set forth his theory of the ethical system of personal and social interaction underlying free-market economic activity. Influenced by the Enlightenment of the eighteenth century, Smith unleashed the creativity of human beings of all classes from traditional economic restraints stifling economic progress. Setting human beings of all social classes free would rid them of the oppressive domination of the guilds, the aristocracy, and the ecclesiastical class of medieval society. The foundation of modern economics was, for Smith, the recognition of an underlying natural system of markets that would circumvent the need for the encroachment of government in carrying out two fundamental functions pertaining to all economic systems—the production and the distribution of goods and services to sustain human life. The ethical foundation of his thinking is based on the idea of enlightened self-interest, which he opposed to selfishness. Adam Smith drew on the cardinal virtues of Greek, Roman, and Christian thought. He stated the ideal throughout his *Theory of Moral Sentiments*, parts of which he later incorporated in his *Wealth of Nations*. "The wise and virtuous man is at all times willing that his own private interests should be sacrificed to the public interest of his own particular order of society [his class]—that the interests of this order of society be sacrificed to the order of the state. He should therefore be equally willing that all those inferior interests should be sacrificed to the greater interest of the universe, to the interests of that great society of all sensible and intelligent beings, of which God himself is the immediate administrator and director."[242]

A person of wisdom presumably lives in a state of consciousness in which the other cardinal virtues pertain—justice, courage, and temperance. Christianity adds three theological virtues—faith, hope, and love—as characteristic of the behavior of a wise person. According to both the philosophy of Plato and the mystical revelations of Christianity, a person of wisdom and justice possesses personal knowledge of the Good, such that the self lives in union with the transcendent character of the eternal reality.

III

Enlightened self-interest presumes encountering in one's qualitative life a personal awakening to the meaning of wisdom—the truth underlying the communal nature of economic reality. The prudent or wise person, he presumed in his *Theory of Moral Sentiments*, "is always sincere;" "is always very capable of friendship;" "is always both supported and rewarded by the entire approbation of the impartial spectator;" "is averse to enter into any party disputes, hates faction, and is not always very forward to listen to the voice even of noble and great ambition." "Prudence is combined with greater and more splendid virtues, with valour, with extensive and strong benevolence, with a sacred regard to the rule of justice, and all of these supported by a proper degree of self-command."[243]

Smith based his free-enterprise economic theory on three theoretical constructs: the nature of man, the nature of society, and the nature of the free-market system. The theory outlining the nature of man and society was set forth in depth in his *Theory of Moral Sentiments*. These theoretical constructs were at the root of his *Wealth of Nations*: his theory of an economic system "where there is perfect liberty," or where the individual "may change his trade as often as he pleases."[244] In the functioning of the free market, the "whole of the advantages and disadvantages of the different employments of labor and stock (capital)" would adjust themselves over time, with this caveat: "in a society where things were left to follow their natural course, where there was perfect liberty, and where every man was perfectly free both to chuse what occupation he thought proper, and to change it as often as he thought proper. Every man's interest would prompt him to seek the advantageous, and to shun the disadvantageous employment."[245] This caveat appears again concerning the "market price of any commodity, though it may continue long above, can seldom continue long below, its natural price. . . . This would at least be the case where there was perfect liberty."[246]

Smith's philosophy of free-enterprise rests on the presumed nature of the human being and the supreme beneficence of the natural order. Oppression is conceived as issuing from the imperfections of human institutions. By removing artificial preferences and restraints, especially those imposed by government and the state, a simple system of natural liberty would establish itself. The free market would activate human conduct according to natural motives and toward the benevolence of humankind—the communal good. Enlightened self-interest is the outcome of a system of liberty in which the moral sentiments—the attitude, thought, or judgment prompted by feeling—would bring these motives into a compensatory balance. "Nature, indeed, seems to have so happily adjusted our sentiments of approbation [approval] and disapprobation [disapproval], to the conveniency both of the individual and of the society, that after the strictest examination it will be found, I believe, that this is universally the case."[247]

Smith contends that there are six predominating psychological motives, each carefully balanced so that the benefit of one could not conflict with the good of all. The first two are self-love (self-preservation) and sympathy (love of others). "The self-love of man embraced, if I may say so, his body and all its different members, his mind and all its different faculties and powers, and desired the preservation and maintenance of them all in their best and more perfect condition."[248] He regarded self-preservation as the first task required by nature. Self-love is balanced by other motives, especially by sympathy, at the heart of the explanation of moral judgment.

Smith conceived, in addition to self-love balanced by sympathy in a free-market system, the desire to be free balanced by a sense of propriety, and a habit of labor balanced by the propensity to truck, barter, and exchange one thing for another. Given these three counterbalancing psychological motives at the root of our moral faculty, Smith claimed citizens in a free-market economic system to be the best judge of their own interests and, if left free to pursue them in their own way, capable not only of attaining their own best advantage but also of furthering the common good. This was so because Providence had made society into a system in which a natural order prevailed.

For Smith, therefore, "the great object of reformation" of the economic system is "to remove the obstructions" imposed by the state and the arrogance of those in positions of political power; "to reduce the authority of the nobility; to take away the privileges of cities and provinces, and to render both the greatest individuals and the greatest orders of the state, as incapable of opposing their commands, as the weakest and most insignificant."[249] Individuals acting by the dictates of their moral faculty "necessarily pursue the most effectual means of promoting the happiness of mankind, and may therefore be said, in some sense, to co-operate with the Deity, and to advance as far as in our power the plan of Providence."[250] Consequently, both personal welfare and the common good are a matter of sweeping away the institutional obstructions of government. Smith left to government strictly negative functions since its interventions in human affairs are generally harmful. Members of the community left to maximize their own advantage and, compelled by natural law, will contribute to the maximization of the common good. He summarized the essence of free-enterprise economics: "In pursuing his own advantage, each individual was led by an invisible hand to promote an end which was no part of his intention."[251]

The proper role of government was to be limited to defense against foreign aggression, establishment of an exact administration of justice, and the maintenance of public works and institutions, such as roads, bridges, and canals, not maintained by any individual or group for lack of adequate profits. Smith attributed social ills to past mistakes of government. Paradoxically, he proposed that to preserve competition, government intervention was deemed necessary to restrict those business firms in search of monopoly power. Smith appeared under no illusion that human beings generally, and businessmen particularly, seek privileged positions for themselves. Past history was a record of misconceived attempts by government to support sectional privilege by the powerful. Enlightened self-interest presumably results from free-enterprise economics, an outcome of "self-interest" at the center of human conduct in the pursuit of profit on the part of producers and in purchasing goods and services on the part of consumers. He differentiated "self-interest" from "selfishness," the latter he conceived as the root of oppression.

In embedding his system of free-enterprise economics in natural law and non-intervention by government to support sectional interests of any social class, Smith inadvertently endowed the business class justification for its hegemony in the state. This was the opposite of his intentions. When the business class gained substantial prominence in influencing government by the nineteenth century, it was able to solidify its dominance over the laboring masses. "Perfect liberty" was from the get-go compromised in practice, exemplifying one among a host of flaws in Smith's reasoning. The flow of history and a change of the human heart cannot be diverted in short order. His labor theory of value, to be discussed below, moreover, became a stumbling block from which economic value (the price of goods and services) derive. The ownership of the natural world, Smith held, should be fully privatized; yet history, he understood, had placed the great portion of it in the private hands of the landed aristocracy. With the rise to prominence of the business class as a dominant force in society, Smith's ideas led to government falling under the yoke and power of capitalists who stood in opposition to the interest of the laboring masses and consumers.

A fundamental error of enormous significance crept into Adam Smith's philosophy. He presumed, falsely, that the cardinal virtues would ensue from the practice of the free-enterprise system itself. In other words, he presumed that the structure of economic reality would itself ensure wisdom and justice. But as was clear to Plato and Christianity—and as Tolstoy clarified following his religious conversion and Simone Weil clarified in her philosophical assessment of oppression—self-awakening to knowledge of the eternal is a difficult creative task entailing enormous personal anguish. Moreover, these thinkers recognized, in contradistinction to Adam Smith, that there is no guarantee that a social institution—the free-enterprise system of economics—would not be perverted, given the tragic nature of freedom. Freedom presumes the prospect of doing good or ill. The fundamental error in Smith's philosophy is his presumption that free-market economics would lead ultimately to enlightened self-interest and spark a widespread awakening of the self to its self-transcendent nature.

Smith maintained that enlightened self-interest would result in a system in which individuals would be free to create and change jobs (the productive function) and free to consume (the consumption function), thereby breaking the bondage that resulted in slavery in the ancient world and oppression in serfdom in the medieval world. Economic freedom in the free-market system would bring to pass the personal practice of the cardinal virtues—the self-rising above its personal, class, or national interests.

V

Smith identified three conditions to safeguard perfect liberty in a free-market economic system. The presumption that many, many buyers and sellers in each commodity market for goods and services would safeguard any single seller or buyer from gaining influence over market conditions—that is, over prices, wages, and profits. Fluctuations may occur in the market price (value) in the short term. "When the price of any commodity is neither more nor less than what is sufficient to pay the rent of the land, the wages of the labour, and the profits of the stock (capital) employed in raising, preparing and bringing it to market, according to their natural rates, the commodity is then sold for what may be called its natural price."[252] In a state of perfect liberty, any deviation of the market price of any commodity from its natural price will adjust. "The commodity is sold precisely for what it is worth, or for what it really costs the person who brings it to market."[253] In the short term, profits can go above the actual price or below; but profits never go above or below over the long term—that is, beyond paying for the factors of production according to their natural prices: land (rent), labor (wages), capital (interest), and allowance for depreciation of capital.

For free markets to prevail, Smith assumed buyers and sellers in each commodity market would have adequate knowledge of market conditions so transactions of exchange are made on the basis of self-interest. Lack of knowledge annuls or vitiates the free conditions of the market, giving rise to selfishness and avarice—especially on the part of sellers seeking to gain market hegemony for its products. For example, advertising that manipulates the consciousness and emotions of buyers of a commodity sabotaging and undermining the buyers' knowledge of the product. Emotional appeals become persuasive, warping reason and beguiling buyers. Moreover, an unscrupulous seller of a commodity can gain profitability over the long run and come into a position of money capital to purchase for a pittance—at the disadvantage of competitors—competing enterprises during a downturn in economic conditions (recessions). This was the path to *horizontal mergers* of business firms that soon gave rise to degrees of monopoly.

In practice, entrepreneurs soon embraced the idea of *caveat emptor* (buyer beware) as the slogan of the free-enterprise market. Successful during a recession, "free marketers" looked with bulging pockets of profit to go even further—to buy out not only competitors but the stock (capital) of failing suppliers, establishing *vertical mergers*. This reaped advantages for the firm owning other firms providing its supplies. Smith could hardly grasp, given the simple productive system in his day (1776), the rapacious deal-making that would take place during the nineteenth century. Without knowledge on the part of both buyers and sellers of economic goods, there was nothing to prohibit the power gradually wielded by business firms over both laborers and consumers. Smith underestimated both the gullibility of human beings and the cunning mentality that self-interest would spawn. Selfishness and the thirst for profits brought about, by the end of the nineteenth century, a new form of merging—*conglomerate mergers*: huge business firms with enormous profits not only buying out competitors and suppliers, but wheeling and dealing by purchasing the stock of unrelated enterprises, expanding profit-making.

The Great Depression, which necessitated the creation of a moderate welfare structure to make up for the lack of effectual demand worldwide, could not curb the thirst of business enterprises seeking increased profitability and monopoly control within commodity markets. By mid-twentieth century, *conglomerate multinational mergers*, corporations expanding their reach internationally, took mergers to a new level, vitiating completely Smith's free-enterprise system. Their tentacles extended worldwide in search of greater profits to satisfy the self-interest of their absentee stockholders. Their aim was to seek the highest return beyond national borders, wherever self-advantage could increase corporate profits. Overseas investment provided multinational firms cheaper labor costs and cheaper resource costs, as well as new markets in which to sell their commodities. The owners of capital themselves were caught in a process of do or die in which, without seeking greater profits, they would find themselves incapable of surviving.

Self-interest and freedom came to be nothing more than free-floating selfishness and greed in a society whose members—consumers, owners of business firms, and workers—were more and more concerned with acquisitiveness. Freedom was severed from a sense of propriety and social justice. In practice, self-interest that was to promote enlightened self-interest through free markets—the central presumption underlying Adam Smith's thought—resulted in crude individualism, shorn of any sense of the original foundation buttressed by the cardinal virtues. Lost was the putative balance in the inner life of each person left free to pursue his or her own self-interest. The transfiguration of consciousness encouraging enlightened self-interest soon languished as the self ignored the equation underlying the "free-enterprise system." Gutted of the presumption that each person would attain not only his or her own best advantage but further the common good, laissez-faire economics became an ideology representing selfishness and greed, the opposite of Smith's meaning of self-interest bound to the cardinal virtues. The complementary principles of self-love and sympathy, of freedom and propriety, were erased from modern consciousness. Freedom and justice parted ways.

This unfortunate transformation in consciousness and economic practice brought about a seismic shift in the fundamental moral character of the production and distribution of goods in modern economics. Each individual in the enterprise was regarded as expendable, a mere cost of production, having little permanent value in the capital interest of the firm. Workers were expendable at any time according to the profitability of the firm. They became, as Marx later disclosed, alienated from the product of their labor (the commodity produced) and also alienated from the activity of labor—the creative participation in producing the product. Within the firm, therefore, a battle emerged between workers and owners. Crude individualism became the bedrock of modern economics. The goal was to seek strictly one's own personal material advantage, whether it be labor, owners of capital, or buyers of commodities.

VI

The nail in the coffin of free-market economics came with the inversion of the assumption of knowledge on the part of buyers and sellers. Consumers were upended as the directing force of what commodities were to be produced and services offered. For "perfect freedom" to prevail, capital—property and money capital from which income derives—presumably flowed to the production of goods and services according to consumer demand for the various competing goods and services offered in the market system. The consumer, according to Smith, was presumed to be king—the directing force of free-enterprise economics. Consumer self-interest was regarded as the commanding force in channeling the investment of capital on the part of self-interested entrepreneurs. This presumption was central to safeguarding economic freedom. Monopoly power in the market derived, in part, from the power of the business firm to influence the minds of consumers through advertising and marketing. If the purchase of goods and services were established on the basis of self-interest, not only would the consumer become king, but no producer or owner of land or capital could presumably exploit the masses as had been done heretofore in the ancient and medieval worlds. Business firms, it would follow, were to be under the yoke of the self-interest of consumers.

Clever is the mind that inverts this presumption in the name of free markets. By the middle of the twentieth century, with the advent of the communications revolution coupled with the advent of the electronic media, the academic "disciplines" of advertising, marketing, human relations, and public relations were born. A cadre of psychologists and social scientists brought their behavioral studies to bear on the mind and behavior of consumers. Academia proved to be a fertile arena for scientific studies of human behavior. By the late 1950s, courses in the psychology of advertising were developed, and consumer behavior was dissected and examined in various experiments. In one particular experiment, volunteers were placed in a large booth to observe the layout of advertisements for a product. As each volunteer was engaged in watching ads projected onto a screen, his or her eye movements were being furtively plotted, graphed, and later studied. Unknown to these "subjects" watching the ads, those recording the pathways of their eye movements noted the time the subject dwelled on variables and the pattern of responses to color, the narrative of the ad, and other visual elements. The reactions of males versus females were also noted. From this data, many hidden, unconscious behavioral responses were elicited that helped the advertising and marketing of goods and services.

The psychology of advertising and marketing made consumers more and more pliable and flexible in their demand for products, while minimizing the business firm's potential loss of profits. The consumer had been substantially dethroned from kingship in directing the flow of capital investments. The irony of this inversion of human freedom centered on the fact that the costs of these studies optimizing the product's design, advertising, packaging, and marketing included the cost of the product paid by the consumer. Moreover, these costs, already ponied up by the consumer in the purchase price of the product, were deductible from the firm's profits in paying its taxes.

From the perspective of the twenty-first century, Smith's theory of the free-enterprise system appears nothing short of utopian. Its assumptions defy credulity in today's world. Despite the fact that it failed to characterize human behavior historically, Smith's philosophy has been turned into an abstruse ideology, on the one hand, and into a complex mathematical ideal that measures the degree of monopoly in economic matters. Any resemblance to Adam Smith's free-enterprise system of economics rooted in the cardinal virtues had become an admixture of flashes of truth amidst distortions, misrepresentations, and falsifications.

By the close of the twentieth century, it was clear that literacy had become universal for all social classes and had spread throughout nations worldwide. Yet literacy was trumped by corporate capitalism. Literacy became paradoxically a means by which corporate capitalism swayed consciousness and directed, if not distorted, the mental life and soul of the masses for the ends of profit-making.

VII

Adam Smith's *labor theory of value* presumably established prices of goods and services. With the breakdown of the medieval order of serfdom and its theory of value based on the just price established by the medieval guilds, three economic theories concerning economic value rose to prominence in the eighteenth century—those of the *mercantilists*, the *physiocrats*, and the *industrial class*. As the guilds disintegrated and industrial processes of manufacturing expanded, the trading mercantilist class came into prominence. The mercantilists contended that wealth was produced by all laboring efforts, but the key factor in establishing the value of commodities depended on the commercial class. The trading, commercial class touted the fact that they as a class constituted natural wealth and national power, rather than the landed aristocracy, which owned the land, and the industrial class, which manufactured goods and services.

Opposition to the mercantilists came from the physiocrats—theorists who took an anti-mercantilist stance. They claimed that wealth came ultimately from the land, owned by the landed aristocracy, as opposed to the commerce of the mercantile class and the manufacturing industrial class. Manufacturing labor could only change the wealth derived from nature; commerce could only change its location. The workers under the direction of the landed aristocracy produced the food necessary for human life. Adam Smith disagreed with the mercantilists, the physiocrats, and the industrial class coming into prominence. Concerning the value of goods and services, he agreed with the *economic liberals*. They maintained that the value of goods and services resided in no particular class exclusively—whether the trading, agricultural, or the up-and-coming industrial class. Value, they insisted, lies in human labor in all productive endeavors.

The economic liberals of the eighteenth century thereby took a more comprehensive view. Adam Smith agreed with them. "The real value of any commodity to the person who possesses it and who means not to use or consume it himself, but exchange it for other commodities is *equal to the quantity of labour* which enables him to purchase or command. Labour, therefore, is the real measure of the exchangeable value of all commodities."[254] In contrast to the position of the mercantilists, physiocrats, or industrialists, Adam Smith claimed that what "is bought with money or with goods is purchased by labour, as much as what we acquire by the toil of our body. . . . They [the products] contain the value of a certain quantity of labour which we exchange for what is supposed at the time to contain the value of an equal quantity." In the division of labor, therefore, in trade or other economic behavior, labor is expended. Value is the embodiment of human labor in the product.

This led Adam Smith to the view that "labour was the first price, the original purchase money that was paid for all things. It was not by gold or by silver, but by labour that all the wealth of the world was originally purchased; and its value, to those who possess it, and who want to exchange it for some new productions, is precisely equal to the quantity of labor which it can enable them to purchase or command."[255] Smith's reasoning of the hidden value of labor embodied in the product produced in the division of labor—not easily understood—changed, nevertheless, the character of economic behavior. It enhanced the dignity of human beings in carrying out all forms of labor and their contributions to the communal welfare.

Smith provided an analysis to substantiate his labor theory of value, going back to the hunting and foraging stages of human development. In these early societies, he reasoned, had "it usually [cost] twice the labour to kill a beaver" than "it does to kill a deer, one beaver should naturally exchange for or be worth two deer. It is natural that what is usually the produce of two days' or two hours' labour, should be worth double of what is usually the produce of one day's or one hour's labour."[256] In societies with a division of labor, different "species of labour" allowances are made for superior hardship and for uncommon dexterity and ingenuity. Based on this premise, Smith went on to define more complex systems of production requiring capital and the labor of others. Ultimately, he supported his labor theory of value by assenting to Locke's theory of private property.

Philosopher and political theorist John Locke (1632–1704) similarly alluded to labor in nascent societies. Locke's idea of private property distinguished what's mine from what's thine. "God hath given the world to men in common. . . . Yet every man has a property in his own person. The labour of his body and the work of his hands we may say are properly his. Whatsoever, then, he removes out of the state that nature hath provided and left it in, he hath mixed his labour with, and joined to it something that is his own, and thereby makes it his property."[257]

Adam Smith assumed that the labor theory of value would inspire all individuals to participate in the division of labor in their own self-interest. Wealth was wealth in so far as it promotes human welfare and increases life fulfillment. Wealth therefore was to a great extent dependent on the individual incentives of ordinary people not only participating as laborers in a free-enterprise system but also using their labor to create their own firms to compete in the marketplace. Smith imagined an explosion in the production of wealth not as an end in itself nor for the expansion of national power. Incentivizing ordinary citizens to participate in the creative endeavor of production as workers or as entrepreneurs would expedite the path to greater abundance for all, which Smith saw as a solution to the problem of poverty and indigence. Individuals free to pursue creative endeavors would remove the leash of serfdom in the free-market system. He embraced John Locke's idea of private property.

VIII

In the complex division of labor in social life, however, there are two disparate functions that are poorly understood and woefully confused—the need to participate in the complex division of labor, on the one hand, and the value embodied in one's contribution to the division of labor, on the other. Transferring the idea of the distinction of what's mine from what's thine in early societies to the complex order of the modern world is a fundamentally different matter. One may do little or no work in a complex capitalist system of monopoly advantage and yet come to possess enormous wealth (e.g., an absentee owner who has no work function in the firm or one who gains a fortune through the inheritance of an estate). Others may contribute considerably and gain a pittance. There may also be various economic functions that represent greater or lesser degrees of intellectual or manual work. Well versed in Hebraic, Greek, and Roman thought, John Locke gave the idea of private property a special designation that embedded itself in modern consciousness as a moral institution. Locke sought to safeguard the onset of individual freedom and minimize the oppression established historically in slavery and serfdom by establishing property rights as a social institution, despite the fact that history teaches that the distribution of property rights is conditional and derivative based on political power.

For John Locke and Adam Smith, the dogma of property rights became sanctified as an absolute right to property, enshrined in consciousness as both a legal and a moral right. In the waning years of serfdom and the onset of the market system through to the early nineteenth century, property rights as Locke defined them could be understood as ownership, an outcome of an individual's effective occupation, say working on a piece of land with one's tools or working in a workshop. Property rights, therefore, could be understood as an aid to a person's creative endeavors. For this reason, the United States Constitution and the French Declaration of the Rights of Man of the eighteenth century both treated property rights as one of the fundamental rights governments were duty bound to protect. With the expansion of an enormously complex industrial system of production and mounting monopoly power of business firms by the end of the nineteenth century, property rights from Locke's perspective became ever more illusory, unjust, and corruptive of the common good.

Smith's labor theory of value was sustained through the classical phase of capitalism: the early period of formalizing his theory into an economic model in the nineteenth century that includes notably the theories of David Ricardo, 1772–1823 (the theory of economic growth), Thomas Malthus, 1766–1834 (the theory of population), Jean Baptiste Say, 1767–1832 (Say's law of markets), and Jeremy Bentham, 1748–1832 (interventionist liberalism, the theory of utility—the greatest good for the greatest number).

IX

Technological evolution opens the portals of religious, philosophical, scientific, and moral analyses to help us make sense of what is eternal concerning the economic reality. Either we strive to elevate mass consciousness to grasp the plight of laissez-faire economics and its collapse after the Great Depression, or we remain in a state of idolatry to our present plight in which Adam Smith's philosophy has been turned upside down. The "free-market" system today is in reality a corporate warfare-welfare-managerial economic system. Such an ersatz free-market viewpoint has become a nefarious ideology at a time of deepening inequality, social injustice, intemperance, and waning wisdom. Without understanding and deciphering the eternal reality in which human life and the economic reality are embedded, the nation-state system in the hands of an oligarchy is destined to repeat the past. Laissez-faire economics has become a formula for continual warfare, the squandering of the earth's resources and wealth, and ultimately risking the survival of planetary life. Of utmost importance to bear in mind is that, despite the ideology of free-enterprise capitalism, the fact remains that human beings must eat, and to eat means participating in a division of labor and sharing in the benefits therefrom.

The free-enterprise system—rooted in the freedoms of the modern world and the cardinal virtues of the ancient and medieval worlds—has morphed in practice into a reversal of its economic philosophy. The corporate warfare-welfare-managerial economy has moreover gained dominance over the governing center of nations in both hemispheres of the world. As the British economist, academic, and author Noreena Hertz warned in her book, *The Silent Takeover,* we are at a critical juncture which requires a response to corporations having furtively taken over many of the roles belonging to government in a democratic society, leaving citizens without political recourse to many economic problems.[258]

Confusion reigns. Some remedy must be found to assuage the global inequality among nations, injustice within nations, and vanishing wisdom afflicting human life in a world in which nations are becoming ever more interdependent and interconnected. Yet, the oligarchy that many nations spawn—justified in the name of freedom—gives rise to an international system of predator nations, many enmeshed in war destructive to the world's ecosystems and planetary life. Many contemporary economic treatises, some bearing mocking titles, remind us of the outcome of international capitalism: *The Death of Economics*; *The Politics of the Rich and Poor*; *Bad Money*; *Zombie Economics*; *Econned*; *Griftopia*; and *The Myth of the Rational Market*; among others.

Humanity must confront the global crisis in humanity, an important aspect of which is establishing a world community, the sharing of the world's resources, and an awakening to the truth that the human race is one family sharing the resources of planet earth. Consciousness graced by literacy has access to the noosphere, to the sphere and repository of human knowledge made known by Teilhard de Chardin. Humanity must awaken to the revelations of spirit and energy embodied in the temporal-spatial world. Berdyaev maintained that the human personality and its efforts in understanding reality do not take place with reference to the future, "but to the eternal present of which future and past are one."[259] From the perspective of the temporal-spatial reality, creativity appears as nothing; a past spiritual event buried within our cultural heritage.

CHAPTER 8

Marx's Appraisal of Laissez-Faire Capitalism

I

As early as the beginning of the nineteenth century, a movement arose in opposition to capitalism, which had become marked by rising poverty, social injustice, and moral ineptitude. The Welsh social reformer, and one of the founders of socialism, Robert Owen (1771–1858) and his followers spearheaded a moral reform movement. By mid-nineteenth century, the philosopher, economist, revolutionary, and precursor of the depth psychologists Karl Marx (1818–1883) and his lifelong friend and collaborator Friedrich Engels (1820–1895) rose to prominence and assessed both the validity of Adam Smith's philosophy of private property capitalism and the claims of Robert Owen and his socialist followers. Marx rejected out of hand the perspective of the utopian socialists. He embraced Adam Smith's labor theory of value and regarded private-market capitalism as the initial stage in resolving the historical problem of poverty and economic injustice. Marx and Engels's critique of capitalism addressed its fundamental, systemic shortcomings, which had become apparent by the first half of the nineteenth century, including its moral problem (the exploitation of labor); psychological problem (various forms of alienation on the part of the working masses); economic problem (the concentration of wealth in the hands of the owners of capital); and sociological problem (a class struggle accompanied by revolutionary social forces).

In contrast to the socialist reformers, Marx maintained that economic relationships are the primary driving force in any society. "In the social production of their means of existence men enter into definite, necessary relations which are independent of their will, productive relationships which correspond to a definite stage of development of their material forces." It is not "the consciousness of men that determines their existence, but, on the contrary, it is their social existence that determines their consciousness." Consciousness is susceptible to social conditioning by a juridical and political superstructure that arises from the mode of production of the material means of existence. According to Marx, history teaches that a "social system never perishes before all the productive forces have developed for which it is wide enough; and new, higher productive relationships never come into being before the material conditions for their existence have been brought to maturity within the womb of the old society itself."[260] Marx claimed capitalism was in the process of nurturing in its womb social forces capable of bringing about its demise. Marx's scientific, philosophical, and political adeptness sought to hasten a revolutionary transformation.

Adam Smith's free-enterprise system presumably prevented the concentration of wealth that had historically afflicted humanity. "Perfect liberty" in a market system would hinder the possible growth of private profits and the concentration of wealth in the hands of the few. In theory, competition in the free-enterprise system would ensure that the profits of business firms could not increase or decrease in the long run above or below zero. When profits rise above zero, beyond paying for the factors of production—land, labor, and the return to capital (including depreciation allowance needed to replace capital)—entrepreneurs in their self-interest would be encouraged to enter the market. When profits go below paying for the three factors of production, some firms would be driven out of the market.

According to Marx, this presupposition was false to the actual reality of the market system, based on the labor theory of value. Capitalists employed men, women, and children, and worked them for as many hours as possible each day. This increased the worker's output (the labor value embodied in the product) to a level beyond the wage received. The moral question concerned the difference between the workers' wage per day and the value of the product according to its supply and demand in the product market in which the product is sold. Labor received only a portion of its value set by the labor market, amounting to a wage necessary to sustain the survival of workers and their families. The remainder, the surplus value—the profits made on the product in its market—the capitalist appropriated as profit, based on John Locke's conception of private property in a developing society. The drive to increase profits thereby enticed business firms to hire more and more women and children, when possible, for cheaper wages and work them for longer hours. The injustice started with, but was not exclusive to, the exploitation of labor.

II

According to Marx, an economic phenomenon took place in the market system, a dynamic cycle of booms and busts in economic activity. These business cycles began with the exploitation of labor. The busts, or downward slide of economic activity, were due to insufficient consumer demand. Workers en masse were unable to purchase the goods they produced in ever-greater quantity. This inevitably gave rise to a downward spiral in economic activity despite enormous unfulfilled needs on the part of the mass of workers and their families. The upturn of this recurring phenomenon brought about high levels of unemployment amidst a glut of goods and a life of poverty for the unemployed masses.

The exploitation of labor in every downward swing in the economic cycle resulted in an increase in the economic efficiency of labor. The stronger, more successful firms were able to buy out the weaker, debt-ridden firms, well below their market value. This gave rise to the ability of the larger firms to lower their prices for the commodities produced, providing them with a competitive edge in the market. A trend toward economies of scale took place on the part of larger firms, undermining any presumption of perfect competition or perfect liberty.

Smith's labor theory of value, moreover, presumed the labor embodied in goods and services was the essential source of value. Capital—including technology and all forms of wealth—turned out to be accumulated labor energy. What was referred to as "private property" was in reality the embodiment of labor energy inherent in the product. Marx maintained that over a series of cycles of booms and busts, a day of reckoning would lead to a collapse of the economic system. Yet capitalism, Marx alleged, was on the path to resolve a previously intractable historical problem: the production of wealth at an increasing pace that promised to stem the heretofore historical affliction of poverty for the mass of humanity. Despite forecasting the ultimate collapse of capitalism, Marx was optimistic that the phenomenal growth in capital and wealth was not temporary but a lasting characteristic of the industrial revolution and a modern era of increasing economic efficiency.

In addition to the exploitation of labor (owners usurping the surplus value) and the growing concentration of wealth (efficiency of labor through technological advancement), Marx recognized the growing alienation of labor. He identified and distinguished *four forms of alienation* afflicting the working masses that would ultimately generate a revolutionary fervor. Workers become alienated from the product of their work. What they produce does not belong to them. In lieu of their labor, they receive a return in value (wage) that condemns them to a life of subsistence. They lose any meaningful relationship to the product except as a means of survival. "For it is clear the more the worker expends himself in work the more powerful becomes the world of objects which he creates in face of himself, the poorer he becomes in his inner life, and the less he belongs to himself."[261]

Labor alienated from its product brings about another loss to the worker: access to the resources of nature itself, which are privately owned. If unemployed, workers lose their means of existence. "Thus, the more the worker *appropriates* the external world of sensuous nature by his labor the more he deprives himself of *means of existence*, in two respects: first, the sensuous external world becomes progressively less an object belonging to his labor or a means of existence of his labor. The natural world becomes owned privately or by the state. For the unemployed, there is nowhere to turn to gain access to the fruits of nature in order to survive. The natural world becomes progressively less a means of existence in the direct sense, a means for the physical subsistence of the worker."[262] Workers thereby become slaves of the objects they create while being cut off and separated from their means of existence—their access to the fruits of nature.

Marx identified a *second form of alienation*, the alienation of the worker during the process of production—that is, in the actual activity of work itself. Productive activity becomes one of drudgery, an activity of alienation and an alienation of activity. Workers become detached, disengaged, and distraught. Fear of survival and the likelihood of unemployment and destitution compel them to carry on. "Consequently, if the product of labor is alienation, production itself must be active alienation—the alienation of activity and the activity of alienation. The alienation of the object of labor merely summarizes the alienation of the work activity itself."[263] The worker "feels himself to be freely active only in his animal functions—eating, drinking and procreating, or at most also in his dwelling and in personal adornment—while in his human functions he is reduced to an animal. The animal becomes human and the human becomes animal."[264]

The *third form of alienation* has to do with the essential nature of human beings. Freedom and the self's creative vocation distinguishes the human being from all other creatures. According to Marx, the alienation of workers from their species-essence (their freedom and creative vocation) suppresses their essential human character. The work they do fails to fulfill their personal, social, and communal life. Thus, in addition to their alienation from the product and the activity of production, they become alienated from the exercise of their intuitive intelligence and their development as a whole human being. Workers become commoditized; the community of production within the firm becomes no more than human beings bought as a product of production, shorn of their human attributes. Indeed, the whole world of natural resources becomes commoditized—plants, animals, and humans alike—greedily for the ends of private profits and the accumulation of wealth. Adam Smith's presumption of self-enlightenment, justice, and wisdom as an outcome of "perfect liberty" of the free-market system turned out to be in actuality its opposite—workers commoditized, alienated, and submissive. They fall into the historical trap of mental and emotional enslavement to the owners of capital.

Workers in a laissez-faire system were nurtured psychologically on the notion that they were free workers in self-regulating markets. The problem of alienation and exploitation in a capitalist society—unlike the previous systems of slavery and serfdom—was thereby projected onto workers themselves; they became inured mentally and emotionally to the illusion that they participated in a system of "perfect liberty" as "free workers." Having lost control over the means of production, they found themselves having lost their link to nature's bounty of resources. Their subsistence was threatened as the resources of the earth fell into the hands of private owners. Treated as a commodity of production, "free workers" became replaceable by technology whenever possible to increase the profits of the business firm. Fear of personal survival, conscious or not, diminished and denigrated the workers' human dignity. The cardinal virtues underlying Adam Smith's philosophy—wisdom, courage, temperance, and justice—were lost to the workers as well as to the capitalists who preyed upon them for profit.

Any personal rebellion on the part of workers risked their expulsion from work; if unemployed, they were shorn of their subsistence as well as possibly a place to live. The whims of the owners of capital and of market conditions induced a mental and emotional enslavement that sapped the benevolence from both workers and the owners of wealth. "Productive life is however species life. It is life creating life. In this type of life activity resides the whole character of a species, its species-character; and free conscious activity is the species-character of human beings." In this *third form of alienation*, the person's life "itself appears only as a *means of life.*"[265] Thus human beings were more and more subject to the third form of alienation—*alienation from their species-essence*—their freedom, creativity, and creative vocation. They became a commodity of the owners of the means of production.

Marx disclosed a *fourth form of alienation*: the alienation of workers from each other. In the division of labor which is communal, workers, while suppressing or repressing their own species-essence—their own creative and spiritual natures—failed to honor the dignity and humanity of their fellow workers. The crude treatment they experienced in the work environment (workers employed as a purchasable object for the profits of the owners of capital) became a means of survival. This had detrimental effects on the relations between and among workers themselves. Workers tended to treat one another as commodities. In the presumed name of freedom, the working masses became commoditized, treating themselves and each other as commodities, in the name of "perfect liberty."

III

Marx summarized the outcome of private property of the means of production: *private property* is thus derived from the concept of *alienated labor*; that is, alienated man, alienated labor, and alienated life. Marx also clarified an underlying dynamic of private property and alienation in a democratic society: "the analysis of this concept [alienation] shows that although private property appears to be the basis and cause of alienated labor, it is rather a consequence of the latter [alienated labor]."[266] Marx made transparent a profound psychological paradox underlying capitalism: workers making up the overwhelming majority of the population must be alienated from themselves in a democratic political system in order to allow the embodiment of their labor to be confiscated from them as private property. Under the illusion that they lived in a free-market system and were free operatives (neither a slave of the ancient world nor a serf of feudalism), workers were caught mentally, emotionally, practically, and spiritually in a state of alienation—a state of being that allows, reinforces, and perpetuates private property of the means of production, as well as the workers' state of alienation, in a society in which they possess a voice in governing. Furthermore, Marx recognized that in so far as private property is the consequence of self-alienation, it is self-perpetuating. "Only in the final stage of the development of private property is its secret revealed, namely, that it is on the one hand the *product* of alienated labor, and on the other hand the *means* by which labor is alienated, the *realization* of *this alienation*."[267] Ultimately, only a transfiguration of consciousness—a change in the mentality of citizens en masse—could bring about personal self-enlightenment that would rectify the self-submission of labor to the owners of the means of production.

Given the dynamic nature of capitalism, its exploitation and alienation of labor, and its concentration of wealth, Marx envisioned an inevitable revolutionary reaction—a spiritual regeneration of humankind. He presumed it would furtively ferment in the womb of the capitalist system itself, giving birth to rebellious forces. By the 1840s, labor movements were coalescing, as workers united to challenge the authority and supremacy of business firms. Marx's revolutionary endeavor sought to bring to light the mental, emotional, and physical plight of the working masses in his *Manifesto to the Communist Party*, 1848. He envisioned either a peaceful or violent revolution that would inevitably give rise to the transfiguration of consciousness. In contrast to his earlier *Economic and Philosophical Manuscripts*, 1844, Marx presented an outline of the protracted stages that would result presumably in self-enlightenment.

By the Great Depression of 1929, the concentration of wealth and inequality in income had become so extreme that the Western World experienced an economic collapse. Three forms of merging—forms in the concentration of wealth pointed out in the previous chapter—brought about the Gilded Age of the late nineteenth century: horizontal mergers (buying firms producing the same product), vertical mergers (buying firms of suppliers), and conglomerate mergers (buying firms of products in other industries). Business firms sought to defy, avoid, or overcome competition in the pursuit of greater profits. Growth in the size of the firm and growth of profits made a mockery of free-market economics conceived by Adam Smith. By mid-twentieth century, multinational mergers heightened the concentration of wealth as conglomerate corporations expanded their production and distribution of goods in international markets. The name "free-enterprise" had become a misnomer for "private-enterprise" capitalism that survived after the Great Depression. It gave birth to nonviolent revolutionary change in the United States, Great Britain, and France. Other Western countries collapsed economically and politically. Italy, Germany, and Spain ended in violent fascist revolutions.

IV

Marx recognized Adam Smith's metaphysical shortcomings but sustained an optimism that capitalism's system of exploitation of labor would expedite capital formation and provide a solution to the intractable problem of poverty. Marx therefore accepted private-market capitalism in the budding democratic nations and viewed it as a necessary stage in social and economic evolution. He envisioned democratic nations advancing toward the final stage in human evolution. Unlike Adam Smith, Marx was living through and had an awareness of the rapid pace of change wrought by the industrial revolution in the nineteenth century. He sought to awaken the working masses to the universality of their communal character and their vital connection to nature.

Contrary to the disapproval of Marx's philosophical perspective by many today, psychologist Erich Fromm recognized Marx's messianic mission: "to liberate man from the pressure of economic needs, so that he can be fully human."[268] Erich Fromm maintained that "Marx's philosophy constitutes a spiritual existentialism." Marx's emphasis on the self's spiritual quality put him in opposition to the materialistic and mechanistic view of modern science. Marx sought to highlight not only the quantitative (factual, empirical data) but the inner qualitative aspect of human beings. His existential position presumed that existence precedes essence. In his *Economic and Philosophical Manuscripts*, Marx explained his existential perspective. "Even when I carry out scientific work, etc. an activity which I can seldom conduct in direct association with other men, I perform a social, because *human, act*. It is not only the material of my activity—such as the language itself which the thinker uses—which is given to me as a social product. My own existence is a social activity. For this reason, what I myself produce I produce for society, and with the consciousness of acting as a social being."[269]

Spiritual enlightenment—or as Marx called it, the supersession of private property—is the self's sensuous appropriation of the human essence and of human life. It is not in the sense of immediate, exclusive enjoyment, nor is it in the sense of possession or having. Awakening to the moral reality and to self-realization is not based on self-interest and self-love that inspires one to amassing property and wealth. Self-awakening is the outcome of the transfiguration of consciousness. "Man appropriates his manifold being in an all-inclusive way, and thus as a whole man. All his *human* relations to the world—seeing, hearing, smelling, tasting, touching, thinking, observing, feeling, desiring, acting, loving—in short all the organs of his individuality, like the organs which are directly communal in form are in their objective action (*their action in relation to the object*) the appropriation of this object, the appropriation of human reality."[270] Marx based self-enlightenment on a transfiguration of consciousness in which the self awakens to the meaning of personal, social, and communal life. Nature is no longer merely an external material reality; it is a vital extension of the self's life and being and its means of sustenance.

For Marx, the acquisitive mentality based on self-love and self-interest is not the beneficial means to freedom and creativity which inspire personal and moral virtues. The answer lies in the self's concrete way of life: in the actual way human beings live their lives as moral beings, rising above selfishness, avarice, and envy. The self's relationship to the world undergoes a radical transformation. The "spiritual senses" become transformed into the humanized organs of the self's individuality as a species-being, having the capacity to overcome alienation and to self-validate the meaning of the self's relationship to nature, to the community, and to the cosmos. The self awakens, recognizes, and validates qualitatively that the objective world is, as Marx deemed, "the confirmation of *human reality*. It is human effectiveness and human *suffering*, for suffering humanly considered is an enjoyment of the self for man."[271] The self, Marx maintained, thereby comes into possession within itself of the mental equivalent of the true human reality it is participating in. It awakens to the crystallized spirit, the embodiment of human freedom and creativity. The human world is in reality the manifestation of the life and world of the spirit. The awakened self—the transfigured and transformed self—recognizes that the objective world is the embodiment of spirit and energy.

In examining the material basis of history and being, Marx became critical of idealistic theories and sought to become conversant with factual, logical, and philosophical knowledge. His approach included not only the objective reality, but the interplay between the two worlds the self occupies simultaneously: the inner subjective and the outer objective domains. Marx's goal was to discern universals underlying the stages in human evolution. Through this assessment of historical reality, he sought to disclose and make conscious its underlying spiritual embodiments. Exposing the material and ideological evolution of social existence, he endeavored to highlight the underlying character of the self's essential nature: the human being's "own self-realization" which "exists as an inner necessity, a *need*."[272]

V

Marx envisioned the post-capitalist world as the beginning of *human history*. He characterized human history as the struggle for true human realization, a struggle between two opposing doctrines: one underlying the capitalist democratic society (which gave rise to crude individualism based on private property rights) and the other, the doctrine of communism (which advanced the communal nature of human life and the social nature of property). This revolutionary struggle on the personal, social, and political levels in democratic societies, he maintained, would put humanity on the path to resolving the injustices of private-market capitalism; that is, the exploitation of labor (surplus value and property rights), the concentration of wealth (inadequate purchasing power and business cycles), and self-alienation (the growing reserves of the unemployed and their increasing suffering). The struggles he believed—one on the mental and emotional level; the other on the social, political, and economic level—were already taking place in the womb of capitalism, challenged by the doctrines of communism and socialism.

The revolutionary goal in his doctrine of communism was to introduce the complementary relationship between individualism (a mechanistic view of social reality) and communism (a communal view of social reality). Marx sought to dispose of and supersede the ideological and moral insensitivities spawned by the ideology of capitalism that justified itself in Adam Smith's flawed metaphysics. The mental and political struggles between two doctrines, individualism and communism, involved the nature of society: the struggle between private ownership and communal ownership of property—the means of production. According to Marx, this twofold struggle would pass through three phases in the postmodern world, what he called the advent of human history. His communist doctrine sought to identify the nature of society and the community; it was a metaphysical perspective of the social, communal, and moral nature of human reality. It was revolutionary in so far as it intended to dislodge the mental and emotional conditioning of the working masses from their blind acceptance of private-enterprise capitalism. The doctrine of communism was an ideological assault on crude individualism—the enslavement of the self to false consciousness. This would entail a social and political revolution to change the concrete interaction of human beings in the world of work.

Marx presented his philosophical perspective in its simplest form in his *Manifesto of the Communist Party*, written for the working masses four years after his *Economic and Philosophical Manuscripts of 1844*. He sought to provide a three-pronged assault: to educate the masses, to sketch out the metaphysics of the three stages of communism in the post-capitalist world, and to encourage revolutionary action to quicken the pace in superseding private property. His goal to bring about a transfiguration of consciousness was to go beyond the mechanistic thinking of the social sciences and Adam

Smith's ideal perspective of the wise and just person who seeks the welfare of the community.

According to Marx, Adam Smith's labor theory of value and his appeal to self-interest and self-love were a preliminary means of inspiring humanity beyond the cauldron of centuries of self-submission fettered to the social forces of feudalism. Unfortunately, Smith's ideal system did not ultimately avert the historical tragedy of freedom and human suffering. Instead, Smith's ideal bred an opposite social condition to that of the ascetic, self-submission of humanity during the period of feudalism: it bred self-indulgence, greed, and envy. Marx maintained that historically the division of labor gave rise to a division of society into two classes, an intellectual class made up of two factions: the ruling, governing faction supported by an active intellectual faction which promoted the ideological justification for the reigning elites. The governing class gained control over the means of production as happened historically and, with the backing of its intellectual faction—using moral justification and persuasion—gained the acceptance of the working masses.

Marx envisioned a class struggle inevitably taking place over time between the administering and adjudicating functions of the ruling class and the working masses, which gave rise to the need for the creation of the state. Marx distinguished the state from the governing and intellectual class: the state as the coercive arm of the ruling echelon in society. The state ensured internal social cohesion in the class struggle within society and also functioned in the international arena, in the affairs of inter-societal relations— between and among societies whether nation-state or empire. "This crystallization of social activity, this consolidation of what we produce into an objective power above us, growing out of our control, thwarting our expectations, bringing to naught our calculations, is one of the chief facts in historical development up till now."[273] Given these contradictions, the community, Marx claimed, "takes an independent form as the State, divorced from any real interests of individual and community, and at the same time as an illusory communal life."[274] In history "all struggles within the State, the struggle between democracy, aristocracy, and monarchy, the struggle for the franchise, etc., etc., are merely the illusory forms in which the real struggles of the different classes are fought out among one another."[275]

Philosophically, morally, and humanly, Marx held that in the capitalist society the "worker becomes poorer the more wealth he produces and the more his production increases in power and extent." With the quickening pace of technological innovation and concentration of wealth, "the worker becomes an ever cheaper commodity the more goods he creates. The *devaluation* of the human world increases in direct relations with the *increase in value* of the world of things. Labor does not only create goods; it also produces itself and the worker as a *commodity*, and indeed in the same proportion as it produces goods."[276] With the expansion of capitalism, workers become commoditized and are taken as a mere factor of production. Empathy and compassion in human and social interaction are removed from consideration in the profit-making of the business enterprise. Private capitalism involved itself primarily with profit-making.

The working masses and the governing class, justified morally by its intellectual faction, appropriate the existing mode of production mentally and become mired in a state of self-alienation. At some stage in the mode of production and social relations, monstrous injustices develop that require a change in human relationships. The suffering of injustice, deprivation, and impoverishment for many among the working masses arouses and unleashes revolutionary social forces. Merely endeavoring to bring about superficial social change no longer serves to avert the terrible destructive power percolating and poisoning human interaction in the womb of society.

VI

Communism, according to Marx, is the doctrine that sets forth an antithesis to individualism. It seeks to provoke within capitalism a revolutionary struggle for the minds and hearts of the working masses. Capitalism, he maintained, had already entered the beginning of its final stage by mid-nineteenth century. By encountering and sustaining social forces, capitalism would expedite its ultimate demise and its transition to human history—to the progression beyond the ideology of both capitalism and communism. Marx outlined the protracted struggle necessary to transfigure consciousness that would usher in the spiritual awakening of humanity: to depose and supplant the myth of private property deeply embedded in human consciousness. The doctrine of communism, he presumed, would be necessary to counter, intellectually and morally, the fallacy of individualism and its absolute right to private property.

Marx envisaged three stages in the supersession of self-estrangement apropos individualism and communism. The first crude stage to supersede private property risked the possibility of widespread violence. Self-alienated workers reacting to their former enslavement full of resentment, vengeance, and rage could establish a revolutionary force against the reigning class. Gaining control over the means of production would loom so large in their minds that they would seek "to destroy everything which is incapable of being possessed by everyone as private property," even to the extent of eliminating talent by force. It could result in immediate physical possession as the unique goal of life and existence. Under such conditions, the "role of worker is not abolished but is extended to all men."[277]

Marx also envisioned the possibility of a nonviolent path. It would be carried out as he thought likely to occur (and did occur) in the United States and Great Britain through the establishment of a diversified economic system. In contrast to a violent revolution, this would be the first stage in the transition to social welfare procedures that would ease the plight of the working masses suffering from lack of employment. Marx envisioned this struggle of the working masses with the liberation of women: the relation between man and woman becomes the barometer that confirms the degree to which the species-essence of human beings is fulfilled. "From this relationship man's whole level of development can be assessed. It follows from the character of this relationship of man to woman how far *man* has become, and has understood himself as, a *species-being*, a *human being*. The relation of man to woman is the most natural relation of human being to human being. It indicates, therefore, how far man's natural behavior has become human, and how far his human essence has become a natural essence for him."[278] It also disclosed the extent to which freedom supplanted the domination of the state in the life of human beings.

In the first stage, crude communism, the punitive arm of government would remain under the dominance of private property. The shackles of alienation are not yet fully understood or self-transcended. In the first and second stages, the communal doctrine in the struggle carried out against the ideology of private property rights (communal wealth concentrated in the hands of the few), human beings become ever more aware of the possibility of the supersession of private property, as well as the supersession of alienation; they gain an increasing awareness of the significance of superseding private property exemplified through welfare measures—the state intervention in the distribution of material wealth. The struggle in the second stage, "politically-contaminated communism," continues to a greater or lesser extent by the residual effects of the long-held beliefs in the ideology of private property. The communal nature of human beings begins to be understood, but not its essence.

Marx regarded the transfiguration of consciousness and the transformation of social life as a protracted affair with no timeline in the transition from this first revolutionary stage to the second stage in postmodern society (that is, the onset of human history). He characterized the second stage as political in nature. This would entail a precarious outcome and would be dependent on the degree to which the first stage had been despotic or had inclined toward the beginning of a democratic transformation of the social forces of production.

Marx conceived the outcome of the struggle between communism and capitalism in the third stage, "positive communism," a protracted endeavor in the positive supersession of human alienation and the real movement to a democratic society, especially to a democratic means of making the property (the means of production) available to all citizens. How this was to be accomplished he left to future democratic societies. But its maxim was "from each according to his ability, to each according to his need." He envisioned this as a globalizing process preceding a democratic world federation of democratic nation-states in which two great struggles would be resolved—the end of human beings struggling against nature and human beings struggling against one another. The eventual form that socialism—collective ownership of the means of production—would take and the political and social institutions that would evolve he left to the freedom of human beings in what he referred to as an advancing "civil society." Marx presumed this outcome depended on the gradual increase in self-enlightenment in which humanity would begin to awaken to its social and communal nature, its rightful relationship to nature, and its global interdependence.

Marx acknowledged that this third stage in human and spiritual evolution was not reducible to the doctrine of communism, nor to any other doctrine, including that of socialism. "In order to supersede the idea of private property communist ideas are sufficient but genuine communist activity is necessary in order to supersede real private property." Marx foresaw this period of human history, no matter how long it would take, as inevitable. "History will produce it, and the development which we already recognize in thought as self-transcending will in reality involve a severe and protracted process."[279] This stage, Marx conceded, would be the real appropriation of human nature through and for man. Humans would return to themselves, as social (i.e., authentic) human beings and assimilate all the wealth of previous development.

Marx characterized this third, final stage in human history as follows: It is "the definitive resolution of the antagonism between man and nature, and between man and man. It is the true solution of the conflict between existence and essence, between objectification and self-affirmation, between freedom and necessity, between individual and species. It is the solution of the riddle of history and knows itself to be this solution."[280] He thus envisioned the self awakening to the eternal reality, to the tragedy of freedom, and to the struggle for self-realization. This awakening would entail the birth of a democratic government based on the brotherhood of man and the withering away of the state—the coercive arm of government. It would give rise to a global federation of interdependent democratic societies.

Although Marx regarded this spiritual evolution to be inevitable, he provided a caveat. He regarded communism in its various stages to be the negation of that which has negated (i.e., alienated) humans historically. Communism constituted the historical development through stages in which humans would be freed from the shackles of private property and be transformed mentally, emotionally, and morally. Yet for Marx, communism was only the form, not the essence, of the future. "Communism is the phase of negation of the negation and is, consequently, for the next stage of historical development, a real and necessary factor in the emancipation and rehabilitation of man. Communism is the necessary form and the dynamic principle of the immediate future, but communism is not itself the goal of human development—the form of human society."[281] Marx was not naïve about the potential for "communism" in transition to give rise to new forms of enslavement, in spite of the fact that he saw it as an inevitable stage in human evolution. This caveat had to do with the truth that communism as a communal form of social interaction depended not on its theoretical or ideological formulation but on the concrete transfiguration of human consciousness, the awakening to truth about human life and human realization. It would entail the actuality of the brotherhood of human beings globally.

Marx held that the transfiguration of consciousness and the transformation of the self to its creative vocation require something beyond the doctrine of communism and humanity suffering through stages in the postmodern world. They require the awakening of humans to their responsibility, to one another, and to the community. Marx's third stage of communism in human history therefore presumes an awakening of the self to the eternal and the life and world of the spirit. The self's awakening to its species-essence would constitute spiritual enlightenment. Humanity's awakening necessitates that communism as an ideological doctrine in the struggle be transcended. This would entail the birth of the self beyond the economic, political, communal, and ideological forces in the protracted struggle.

Marx's shortcoming, however, was his failure to grasp the full significance of human freedom: the prospect to do good or evil that puts in question the inevitability of arriving at the third stage of communism— the transfiguration of consciousness worldwide that would give birth to a democratic federation of world cultures and civilizations. Democracies in the West have made some inroads in the "first crude stage of communism" since the Great Depression of 1929 by initiating social welfare programs. But countervailing trends to safeguard private property capitalism not only sustained communism's ideological clout in the West, its social welfare programs continue to be attacked and derogated by reactionary forces as capitalism spreads worldwide. Marx's thought was made anathema by transplanting the edifice of private property capitalism—the labor theory of value—onto a new foundation, the theory of utility, to be discussed in the next chapter.

VII

Marx was a forerunner of the twentieth-century depth psychologists Sigmund Freud, Alfred Adler, and C. G. Jung, who grasped that the human psyche is divided, conflicted, and in a state of neurosis, overwhelmed by unconscious forces, a false and confused ego-consciousness, and a superego ("conscience") shaped by social forces. Jung claimed that the unconscious was collective and, thereby, postulated certain archetypes characteristic of all human beings. Yet these psychologists, well-grounded in the concepts of the alienated self, failed to envision an awakening of the self to the superconscious—the spiritual reality. Marx envisaged the possibility of a solution to the riddle of history that presumed the self's awakening beyond the socially conditioned state of being.

The depth psychologists, in contrast to Marx, were concerned more with the unconscious mind and repression. Psychologist Erich Fromm grasped the fundamental differences between Marx and Freud. Marx was the first to envision "that realization of the universal and fully awakened man can occur only together with social changes which lead to a new and truly human economic and social organization of mankind." For Freud, on the other hand, society only influences the human being "by greater or lesser repression of his physiological and biological equipment." For Marx, "repression is essentially the result of contradictions between the need for the full development of man and the given social structure—hence the fully developed society in which exploitation and class conflict have disappeared does not need ideologies and can dispense with repression."[282] The wealthy man, Marx affirmed, is "one who needs a complex of human manifestations of life, and whose own self-realization exists as an inner necessity, a need. Poverty is the passive bond which leads man to experience a need for the greatest wealth, the other person."[283]

Psychiatrist Viktor Frankl and the existential psychologists went beyond the depth psychologists. Though Frankl clamed to having learned much about the human soul from the three prominent depth psychologists (Freud, Adler, and Jung), he recognized their limitations and their aversion to the term *soul* which, Frankl understood, is embedded in the eternal. Frankl broke from the ranks of the depth psychologists and established the school of logotherapy. Going beyond ego-consciousness rooted in time and its neurotic struggle with the unconscious, Frankl stressed the human capacity for self-transcendence and gave voice to the superconscious mind: the self-awakening to the realm of meaning and the possibility of self-transcendence, and the self's capacity to come in possession of truth, beauty, and goodness beyond the phenomenal, temporal-spatial reality.

Marx, as did Dostoevsky and Nietzsche, sought to unveil the self-deception of ego-consciousness. All three sought to find a way to overcome the wounded personality of modern man. Nietzsche denounced the "good" and searched for good beyond the pale of "good" and "evil" of the herd mentality and slave morality. Nevertheless, Nietzsche failed to grasp the truth of the mystical revelations of Christianity, basing his understanding on historical Christianity, its authoritarian, materialist corruption. Nietzsche's reversion to Dionysian pre-Socratic thought and his genius in creating his artistic image of the superman, Zarathustra, are nevertheless a far cry from the truth embodied in the life of Christ and the Resurrection, which Nietzsche excoriated as weakness. Christianity portrays the cosmic revelation of humankind's twofold nature: a natural being with a divine-spiritual potential, born in the likeness and image of the Creative Source of Life and Being.

Tolstoy underwent a spiritual awakening but did not advance beyond the phase of redemption. His teachings are rooted in religious law. As Nicolas Berdyaev pointed out, Tolstoy's resurrection was genuine but limited, and there was something moralistic in his teaching. Tolstoy fell short of recognizing the possibility of a new epoch of creativity, prefigured by Kierkegaard, Solovyev, Dostoevsky, and Berdyaev, among others. Marx, who shied away from religion and took a predominantly humanistic perspective, nevertheless posited the need for a transfiguration of consciousness and moral transformation. This was not the case, ultimately, for the depth psychologists—neither of Freud nor his followers.

From our perspective in the twenty-first century, we may, and hopefully should, become aware that the essential path to resolving the global crisis in humanity is not derived primarily, as implied by Marx, from and through the evolution of social reality and its stages per se. Nevertheless, Marx affirmed the realization of an essential reality beyond capitalism and communism and beyond individualism and socialism. Awakening to the eternal must be seen as the creative activity and the activation of the spiritual power intrinsic in the human personality. Conscience—superconsciousness apart from the conscious and unconscious mind—is not awakened by society and social institutions per se, though it can be and generally is conditioned by customs and social values. The self is burdened with the creative task of awakening to the superconscious through spiritual literacy that has the capacity to bring about a transfiguration of consciousness and a transformation of one's personal life. Conscience aligned with the eternal presupposes, therefore, the self's resurrection—death and rebirth—on this side of the grave.

Our creative vocation is tasked with transcending the natural reality of time and space. This includes opinions of good and evil passed down to us. It means that, in contradistinction to what Marx advocated, there may not be a final revolution in so far as freedom is intrinsic in the cosmos and universe. Freedom points to an open-ended prospect inherent in the path and choices humans make. Marx valued an achievable struggle as a means of rising beyond individualism and communism and beyond capitalism and socialism, necessary to fulfill the prospect of moral transcendence and the spiritual transfiguration of consciousness. Yet, should today's nations manage to avert a nuclear catastrophe or space warfare, the Era of the Spirit, beyond the Era of the Law and the Era of Redemption, may help humanity find a means of rising above our patriarchal fixation on power, violence, and warfare that could destroy planetary life. An Era of the Spirit may help nurture revelations embodied in the cardinal virtues, the theological virtues, and the transcultural awakening of humanity to spiritual literacy. Failing to educate our children in spiritual literacy will result in each generation being born into a natural reality ignorant of a hidden, undetectable world of spirt and energy. Our hope, emphasized throughout this book, is to make spiritual literacy an intricate, meaningful, and necessary part of formal education globally.

Humanity must release the spiritual reality from its exclusive expression in religious institutions, their revelations, and their sectarian divisions. Still, we must hew a spiritual path beyond atheism, agnosticism, and humanism, as well as authoritarian forms of religion. World religions today are in crisis, and the spiritual freedom and understanding of many worshippers are being woefully disfigured. There must be a judgment on Christianity itself, with its asceticism often viewed as an end rather than a means. We must also be mindful of the false moral conclusions that can be drawn from the doctrine of original sin— the Christian doctrine of humanity's state of sin resulting from the fall of man, stemming from Adam's rebellion in Eden— and its misrepresentation of man's creative vocation. There still remains the frightening and misunderstood dogma of hellfire and damnation. We must also admit that Christianity as a religion is not God (the eternal), although as Berdyaev maintained, the "ideal relation between the human and the divine is shown in the life of Jesus Christ." This should be taken, Berdyaev made clear, "not dogmatically but existentially, that is to say in a way which was free from all idolatry. But that will be to receive it in Spirit and in Truth."[284]

Reinhold Niebuhr acknowledged that revelations are embodied in all cultural disciplines, not in religious revelations alone. He would embrace the goal of spiritual literacy set forth in this book—spiritual literacy grounded in religion, philosophy, the sciences, and the liberal arts; that is, within the branches of learning embodied in culture which are, in reality, spirit and energy, embedded in the cosmos and universe. Niebuhr foresaw the need to limit the power of the state as "one of the chief marks of distinctions between an open society and a totalitarian one." He recognized that the conscience of the individual is not infallible even "when it is ostensibly informed by a genuine desire to submit to a higher divine judgement. Therefore, even the most democratic states have learned to insist on certain standards of common decency and public order even against the dictates of religiously inspired conscience."[285] As in his earlier works, Niebuhr returned to the mystery in biblical faith which furnishes the key that makes meaningful the promise of personal fulfillment. "Sin and guilt are intolerable burdens without forgiveness which is available to those who acknowledge rather than hide the ultimate predicament of man." Biblical faith provides us with "glimpses of meaning in the ultimate mystery ('the light that shineth in darkness') which furnish the keys to the understanding of directly experienced realities." This is our "hope that both the individual and the total drama of life will end in 'the forgiveness of sins; the resurrection of body; and the life everlasting.'"[286]

CHAPTER 9

The Utilitarians and the Keynesian Revolution

I

In his controversial, impassioned critique of capitalism, the British economist Paul Ormerod maintained that there is no such thing as free self-adjusting markets. "The need to make the intellectual leap which grasps that behaviour at the macro-level of any system with any degree of complexity cannot be deduced by simply adding together the actions of its component parts."[287] Economics as a field of study is unique in the sciences. In contrast to physics, economic theory presumes to describe how the world actually operates. Orthodox economics became isolated from its roots in the late eighteenth and early nineteenth centuries, despite the pretensions of many economic practitioners who, isolated from the physical sciences, aspired nonetheless to knowledge of free-market economics. Economists took pure theory—the notion of the sacred mechanism of the free market—to describe how the world actually operated. The concept of a free market became an ideological prop in economic theory to rally the masses, even though the free market no longer applied. By invoking Adam Smith, Ormerod claimed that Smith was a philosopher who well understood that "society is more than the sum of its individual parts."[288]

There are many factors unaccounted for in Adam Smith's free-market system. The social and material infrastructures of society were left out of the picture. To start with, women at home raising children, maintaining the well-being of the family and endeavoring to keep the primary breadwinner fit to work, were given zero value in his economic equation. And so were a whole host of underlying services supporting and sustaining any well-functioning market system. Also totally overlooked were the costs of education, policing, administering of justice, firefighting, maintenance of the infrastructure, and so forth.

After Marx embraced the labor theory of value as the foundation of Adam Smith's laissez-faire economics, three economists independent of one another proclaimed an opposing principle underlying value, the principle of utility: an Englishman, W. Stanley Jevons; an Austrian, Karl Menger; and a Frenchman, Léon Walras. According to economic historian Daniel Fusfeld, utility theory "had been ignored until Marx attacked the private-enterprise system.... To compound the coincidence, the discovery came only a few years after Marx had published his attack on capitalism, using the labor theory of value as a base for his exploitation theory.... When that happened the labor theory of value had to go, and economists had to give serious attention to problems of income distribution and business cycles. A new approach to economics was born."[289] The utility theory of value explains the degree to which the commodity valued is presumed to be the satisfaction the self obtains from consumption of a good or service. The utility theory of value not only rendered the cardinal virtues (justice, temperance, wisdom, and fortitude) extraneous with respect to the economic reality particularly, but to social existence generally. Earlier economists had ignored the principle of utility and its absence of any logical relationship between the usefulness of commodities and their prices. This chapter endeavors to sort out the response of the utilitarian economists to Marx's critique, as well as the outcome of capitalism and the Keynesian revolution.

In removing the cardinal virtues from the foundation of capitalism as envisioned by Adam Smith and replacing them with the theory of utility, the utilitarians assumed that they had circumvented Marx's acceptance of Smith's labor theory of value. Marx maintained that evolving democratic societies worldwide would awaken the working masses to an economic reality beyond both individualism and communism. The utility theory of value rooted economic value in the self's irrational appetites, desires, wants, and needs. Shared responsibility for the collective well-being of humanity and the well-being of planetary life were no longer part of the prevailing thinking in private-enterprise economics.

II

By the end of the nineteenth century, the British economist Alfred Marshall conceived that market price (economic value) was determined by both supply (the productive function) and demand (the consumption function), in addition to government expenditures. Prices (value) of goods and services, as well as the costs (value) of the factors of production (land, labor, and capital), were no longer based on labor energy embodied in them. They were based presumably on the satisfaction—the fulfillment of desires, wants, and needs—of consumers. Marshall and the utilitarians thereby were able to maintain Adam Smith's philosophy of free-enterprise and self-adjusting markets by gutting his theory of the primary source of value—labor energy.

Marshall replaced the freedom, dignity, and creativity in the division of labor by something much more elusive, pernicious, and destructive to freedom. He was oblivious to the cardinal virtues. Smith's theory was not without shortcomings philosophically, morally, and economically. Nevertheless, Smith intended to bring about an economic system that would constrain profits through competition and thereby constrain the growth of a wealthy class that could affect the functioning of government. Marshall's utility theory of value, conversely, increased profits of business firms while leaving the irrational appetites to the flux of time and the cardinal virtues sacrificed to the vagaries of utility. The concentration of wealth was taken thereby to be the reflection of "free" human beings expressing their freedom in economic affairs by their satisfaction, contentment, and happiness (i.e., their utility). Their pattern of consumption was presumed to reflect an economic system of free markets in a free society with self-adjusting markets. Government regulations in the economic arena were considered not only unnecessary but detrimental to freedom and economic growth.

Consciously or not, the utilitarian economists from 1870 to 1900 fashioned, as the economic historian Daniel Fusfeld claimed, "new theoretical formulations that served to refute the Marxist proposition about capitalism."[290] The utilitarians thereby sought to evade and dodge Marx's critique of capitalism, transferring value from labor energy generally to utility theory specifically. They were successful, ideologically. Marx's ideas of a final revolution beyond communism and individualism and beyond socialism and capitalism, which would give birth presumably to a positive supersession of private property and the supersession of alienation, were ignored. Marx envisioned human progress as the outcome of a protracted global struggle that would resolve the antagonism between man and nature, existence and essence, objectification and self-affirmation, freedom and necessity, and individual and species. Even before the collapse of state capitalism in the Soviet Union in 1991, claimed (mistakenly or intentionally) by the West to be a concrete realization of Marx's philosophy, Marx's significant and profound contributions to economic, social, and political thought had been cast aside. His ideas were regarded as irrelevant in economic and political discourse despite the fact that Marx outlined in the nineteenth century numerous welfare programs necessary to sustain capitalism and keep it from collapsing. Adam Smith's important contributions to private-enterprise economics rooted in the cardinal virtues were also deemed irrelevant. Ideologically, private-market enterprise came to justify and embrace monopolistic and oligopolistic economic markets. This sleight of hand turned Adam Smith's philosophy on its head and made Karl Marx's philosophy irrelevant.

John Maynard Keynes, the chief proponent of utilitarianism, realized and proved correct that the utility theory of value would bring about a useful, though unscrupulous and ruthless, means of wealth formation. Like Marx, he accepted private-market capitalism primarily as a stage in the evolution of economic reality. In effect, the utilitarians (Keynes joined them), in unseating the labor theory of value, severed economics from its proper linkage to the natural, human, and eternal reality. This approach constituted a break in the chain of spiritual evolution and human striving toward the eternal, presumed to be the foundation of economic and social life. The communal nature of human beings and the well-being of planetary life and its resources were set apart and put under siege.

Instead of appealing to the cardinal virtues, advocates of the utility theory of value encouraged selfishness, avarice, and wantonness—crude individualism. Keynes held this behavior to be shameful, wanton, and vulgar ("foul," as he famously put it). He embraced it nevertheless until humanity could regain its sanity; that is, until humanity awakened to traditional knowledge and virtue. "I see us set free, therefore, to return to some of the most sure and certain principles of religion and traditional virtue—that avarice is a vice, that the exaction of usury is a misdemeanor, and the love of money is detestable, that those walk most truly in the paths of virtue and sane wisdom who take least thought for the morrow . . . . But beware! The time for all this is not yet. For at least another hundred years we must pretend to ourselves and to everyone that fair is foul and foul is fair, for foul is useful and fair is not. Avarice and usury and precaution must be our gods for a little longer still. For only they can lead us out of the tunnel of economic necessity into daylight."[291]

Keynes well understood the risk and hazard of the utility theory of value to the socio-economic reality, as he well understood the necessity and beneficence of the cardinal virtues. His intentions to preserve the democratic society and private-enterprise capitalism, principled as they may have appeared, nevertheless encouraged injustice as a means to future justice. "Usefulness" in place of virtue—regarded as vulgar and despicable—he deemed crucial to human welfare. Virtue could be forsaken for another century in the name of future abundance for all. Indeed, Keynes sought an economic approach that—mindful of the revolutionary fervor and possible violence of Marx's more radical approach—would more likely avert greater suffering in humanity's transition to virtue.

III

The utilitarian economists created a technical calculus so complex it confounded the minds of the intelligentsia, barring the few—let alone the consciousness of citizens generally. For the utilitarians, the value of the three factors of production—land (rent), labor (wages), and capital (technology, profits)—was based on *marginal productivity*. This purports to estimate the desirability of business firms to employ land, labor, and capital to the limit of declining profits. The measure of marginal productivity represents, in the union of the three factors of production (land, labor, and capital), the ability of one additional increment of any one of the three factors to increase the total product cost. Increasing corporate profits becomes the primary goal of economic activity, regarded as the prime mover of the economic order.

The value of goods and services was based on *marginal utility*, which purports to measure the relationship between desirability and price, a measure of the degree of satisfaction each individual presumably derives from buying and consuming goods—to the limit of declining desirability and satisfaction. Such a measure becomes an aggregate of all consumers for a given product and its price in competition with other products. Value (price of goods and the cost of the factors of production) presumably reflects the intersection of these two measures: marginal productivity (the ability of one additional increment of a variable factor of production to increase the total product) and marginal utility (the least utility attributed to any one item of a supply of goods) for each product market. This presupposed that rational consumers, confronted with a vast array of choices on which to spend income, seek to maximize satisfaction (utility). When consumers allocate spending so that the last (marginal) dollar spent on one commodity gives no more and no less satisfaction than the last dollar spent on anything else, utility at the margin sets the value of consumer goods. It is assumed that all rational consumers do this so that utility at "the margin" is equalized. Marshall assumed "that in the long run prices in competitive markets would tend toward the lowest possible costs of production at which the amounts desired by consumers would be provided."[292]

The utility theory of value explains value according to the degree to which the thing valued contributes to man's most urgent necessities. The obvious objection that some commodities, like diamonds which contribute nothing to the actual physical needs of existence, may stand high in value, and other commodities like water, which do contribute to basic physical needs, may stand low in the scale of values, led to the modification of the utility theory of value and the development of the final utility theory of value. The values of the forces of production (the cost of land, labor, and capital) presumably establish the increasing of capital on the part of owners to the limit of declining profits. Thus all goods and services reflect utility, which expresses the satisfaction of appetites, wants, and needs of consumers en masse; all investments of productive forces in the firm reflect the most profitable ventures of capitalists, en masse.

IV

Keynes created a mathematical system of analysis based on the entire macroeconomic order. It was a work of genius, though couched in mind-boggling, obscure terms disclosing how utility channels economic behavior in society as a whole. Keynes was under no illusion that the utility theory of value was anything but a stopgap measure—a sort of subterfuge to escape economic planning on the way to producing enough for all. Besides, he sought to mitigate any radical attempt to disrupt the system of the goose that laid the golden egg—growing capital formation expedited by usury. Capitalism had become so complex and interdependent within the cadre of Western nations and their overseas colonies that he understood that there was no way it could be changed in the short run. In effect, Keynes maintained that the immorality of avarice and usury (gaining greater profits in financial markets beyond moral limits) should be tolerated as the means (a temporary economic necessity) to forestall a revolution that could incur greater violence and suffering. The daylight of virtue, he presumed, must trail capital formation: the longed-for abundance for all accompanied by human dignity befitting the laboring masses. The future would then be heir to the light of self-enlightenment transmitted in traditional knowledge. He envisaged the lives of citizens in a democratic society being suffused once more by the ancient verities of the cardinal virtues.

Keynes's economic approach was revolutionary in so far as it called on government to play a limited though influential role in economic affairs. He limited government's role to moderating economic crises (business cycles) in order to minimize economic and human suffering on the bust, or downward, phase of the business cycle while seeking to balance government expenditures on its boom, or upward, phase. His focus on macroeconomics gave him a wide perspective of how utility theory rooted in greed, envy, and acquisitiveness affects the cyclical momentum of the business cycle. He sought to identify the major social, psychological, and economic forces operating, and what government measures could be introduced to stabilize them without bringing into being a planned economic system.

Ultimately, Keynes discovered mathematically that the level of employment depends on both the total amount consumers spend for goods and services and on the total amount businesses spend for new capital (investments). Total spending is also affected by government spending and revenues. His mathematical analysis disclosed that in the short run consumer spending rises and falls according to the level of employment. Consumer spending stimulates investments owing to two factors: the rate of return on investments (profits) and the interest rate on new capital investments (business purchases). Both of these measures influence employment rates. Keynes found that government should and could play an active role to stabilize the economic system by slowing down the rate of unemployment on the bust side of the business cycle (at a time when the anticipated rate of return on new investment by business firms decline). Government could act to slow down (or reverse) the momentum of decline brought about by unemployment by bumping up its purchases, thereby helping to increase employment. Keynes recommended and outlined two government programs, fiscal and monetary policies that would stimulate the economic order in poor times and slow down economic activity when inflation threatened economic stability.

Economic historian Daniel Fusfeld characterized the problem underlying private-enterprise capitalism during the aftermath of the Great Depression: "The growth of big business, big government, and big labor makes it clear that the impersonal operation of market forces has now been at least partially supplanted by the ability of important groups in labor, management, and government to influence significantly the way the economy functions. The organization and locus of political and economic power influence economic decisions as never before."[293] The Keynesian revolution was, in reality, the legitimation of the role of government in a private-market economic system. In 1946, the United States passed an Employment Act influenced by Keynes's macroeconomic analysis: Congress declared that "it is the continuing policy and responsibility of the Federal Government to use all practicable means . . . for the purpose of creating and maintaining . . . conditions under which there will be afforded useful employment opportunities . . . for those able, willing and seeking to work, and to promote maximum employment, production, and purchasing power."[294]

Beyond lessening inflation during the boom phases and suffering during the bust phases of the business cycle, Keynes's venture into macroeconomics brought him face to face with a future, if not present, specter that would haunt, if not ultimately do away with, private-enterprise corporate capitalism. He discerned mathematically that the economic order could arrive at equilibrium at less than full employment, such that structural (technological) unemployment could not be remedied merely by the combination of monetary and fiscal policies. He decided that monetary measures (manipulating the money supply) and fiscal policies (manipulating revenues and taxes) to be countercyclical to booms and busts; they were temporary stopgap measures and not permanent solutions to the problem of private-enterprise corporate capitalism and the democratic society. The increasing pace of economic efficiency through uncontrolled technological innovation in combination with the concentration of wealth in fewer and fewer hands foreboded a possible future economic collapse of capitalism. Keynes feared that the stability of the economic system in the future could occur at employment rates similar to depression levels.

Economists discovered a heretofore hidden, alarming outcome of corporate welfare capitalism. Unless savings are channeled back into the stream of investments, total spending falls, bringing about in turn ever-increasing levels of unemployment. The economic order turned out to be something akin to a treadmill: ever-increasing levels of technology and efficiency of labor give rise to ever-increasing levels of unemployment requiring, in turn, an ever-increasing pace of investment. Business investments, on the other hand, would give rise to upgrading and implementing new technology that replaces labor and increases labor efficiency, thereby increasing the number of workers falling into the ranks of the unemployed.

Worse yet, economists found themselves in a quandary: stagnant economic conditions were accompanied by inflation (stagflation). High levels of unemployment and falling consumption accompanied a general increase in price levels. This tragic outcome meant that inflation would remain high in spite of a slowdown in economic growth, thereby giving rise to decreasing levels of employment and total consumption. This was counterintuitive to Keynesian thought, which presumed inflation (general rise in prices) could take place on the boom side of the business cycle and a general fall in prices on the bust phase of the business cycle. Keynes realized that economic equilibrium could occur at less than full employment, even when fiscal and monetary policies made welfare programs available. Though he believed that his policies would tide humanity over for a hundred years to produce a society of abundance. The truth is his government-management-of-the-utilitarian approach is still seeking to this day the cherished cornucopia of an abundance of wealth for all—to no avail.

V

The Keynesian revolution (government-managed economics through fiscal and monetary policy and welfare programs) challenged the philosophy of rugged individualism entrenched in the consciousness of many citizens. Rugged individualism was not born of the cardinal virtues. It arose from another strain of thought—social Darwinism. The theory arose in the late nineteenth century and claimed that the laws of evolution, which Charles Darwin observed in nature, applied also to society. Social Darwinism put forth the view that social progress resulted from conflicts in which the fittest or best-adapted individuals tend to prevail. It gave rise to the slogan "survival of the fittest." It was quite at odds with the optimism arising from Adam Smith's philosophy and the economic view of the utilitarian economists. Social Darwinism sprang from Herbert Spencer (1820–1903), William Graham Sumner (1840–1910), and their followers—all staunch proponents of laissez-faire economics. They were, in part, the precursors of today's economic and political libertarians. Spencer taught that there should be unfettered individualism to allow the forces of natural selection to ensure the survival of the fittest. He and his fellow Social Darwinists regarded government as a necessary evil and regulation of industry as pernicious, purging the strength and viability of the human character.

William Graham Sumner presumed that the social system as a whole is both conservative and progressive, both resisting and effecting change. Progressive measures in social institutions, Sumner contended, whether economic or political, ought to be surrendered only reluctantly to change. Acceptance of the new without due diligence threatened the citizens of society. Any changes weakening the ability, drive, intelligence, and, thereby, the competitiveness of the individual in society should be resisted. Such measures, he maintained, would compromise rugged individualism. Any new demands must be scoured for evidence of potential personal improvement. Competition, for Sumner, assured that those afflicted by sloth, ignorance, and feebleness, making them helpless and hapless members of society, would be better left to wither, thereby improving the vigor of the stock of humanity. For both Spencer and Sumner, success and failure correlated, respectively, with right and wrong, with wealth and poverty, and with righteousness and uselessness. They advocated rugged individualism as a means to ensure and sustain a healthy society and economy.

Thus, they held to social Darwinism as the true foundation of laissez-faire capitalism.

In the years following the Great Depression of 1929, Keynes's monetary and fiscal policies were supplemented by social welfare programs established by government to help redistribute wealth to the dispossessed and unemployed. This buoyed total spending. Several welfare programs were recommended to avoid a violent revolution. Corporate capitalism soon embraced, in addition to Keynes's fiscal and monetary policies, social welfare measures introduced during the Franklin Delano Roosevelt administration in the 1930s. Among them were Social Security, workman's compensation, unemployment insurance, centralized banking, and public education. Before the Great Depression of 1929, President Herbert Hoover was sensitive to the need for welfare measures. However, he considered such measures not a matter to be foisted by government mandate but rather as a choice made by the perceived political needs in governing a democratic society.

All these measures are contrary to the idea of self-adjusting free markets. Keynesian economic policies, and the social welfare programs that followed, gave birth to corporate welfare economics (or what is called a mixed economy) in Western democracies. It served to compensate for what Marx called the surplus value of labor appropriated by capitalists, a major factor expanding the concentration of wealth and the breakdown of capitalism. Marx claimed that the worker received only that portion of the value he created necessary for his upkeep, the remainder passed to capitalists as profit or surplus value. Corporate welfare economics still remains a thorn in the side of the proponents of rugged individualism and those who hold to the belief that the ideal of free-enterprise economics is being compromised by government economic policies that seek to improve social conditions.

Unlike Keynes, many contemporary advocates of free-enterprise economics do not see, nor wish to see, that Adam Smith's ideal had been compromised in practice from the beginning. They fail to see and prefer not to see what Keynes referred to as foul: social injustice and the failure to render to labor and to the infrastructure of the community their due in a system of markets that became structurally dysfunctional. Nonetheless, after the Great Depression, welfare measures became a necessary collective, government-sponsored sharing of the wealth to help reduce the level of unemployment and to help stabilize the business cycles of booms and busts. These welfare measures made available goods and services necessary to sustain the lives of countless workers who had been displaced and needed a helping hand to survive. Rightwing economic and political thinkers, who arrogated to themselves the title of conservative concerning these welfare measures, identified them as entitlements; in other words, economic means viewed as undeserved. Ironically, these welfare measures enabled corporate capitalism to survive.

VI

Keynes's macroeconomics speeded up the implementation of technological innovation, thereby increasing the pace in the efficiency of labor even though it escalated the trend toward structural unemployment. Keynes foresaw this complex issue happening well into the future. On the macroeconomic level, savings must be constantly translated into investments to keep the economic system near full employment. Corporate welfare capitalism was caught in an irresolvable paradox: less and less labor was needed to produce more and more goods and services as new, increasingly automated, robotized means of production were implemented in the workplace. These measures gave rise to an economic order akin to a person walking on a treadmill with the speed continually ramped up. Investments foster technological advancements that reduce the need for labor, providing greater efficiency of labor that brings about greater savings (concentration of wealth); these savings must be converted into investment (new technology), creating greater savings while further reducing employment.

Compared with what transpired in other Western democracies, Keynes's recommendations implemented in the FDR administration and expanded in succeeding administrations not only skirted a planned economic system but extended the life of corporate welfare capitalism. Examples of Western counterparts include the planned economies (state capitalism) brought into being in the Russian Revolution of 1917, and the fascist revolutions in Italy (1922), Germany (1933), and Spain (1936). Capitalism from the beginning has required government as a vital partner, which the conservative dissent of the 1980s actively glossed over. Government ensures public capital—revenues from taxation—to build the needed infrastructure of society, to subsidize private enterprises in various ways to pay for research, to protect the rights of private property, to sustain public education, to provide for an educated workforce, to protect citizens from internal and external enemies, to protect copyrights, and so forth.

All of these measures were left out of the conservative dissent's agenda, both in the United States and Great Britain. Those opposing the Keynesian revolution failed to take into account that social welfare programs constituted a safety net that gave welfare capitalism an extension of time, delaying its collapse. Touting greater reliance on self-adjusting market forces without tampering with the utility theory of value, the post-Keynesian dissent on the political right dismissed fiscal policies and sought to reduce the role of government by deregulating business firms, promoting increased production of war goods, and reducing corporate taxes to incentivize entrepreneurs. More and more growth was considered the most effective solution to the problem of structural unemployment. American neoconservatives favored expensive foreign intervention, including the invasion of Iraq in 2003 to replace a dictator and to institute a new system of government, and the war in Afghanistan from 2001 to the present, both involving massive federal spending on the military. Moreover, neoconservatives sought to privatize schools, prisons, hospitals, and government functions with the promise that huge profits would benefit big corporations while ignoring interest in the common good.

As a result, economics has come full circle as neoconservatives seek to drink once again from the wellspring of Adam Smith's conceptual framework, claiming to restore self-adjusting markets. As economic historian Daniel Fusfeld put it, to create "new bottles for old wine." But turning back to an economic reality of global conglomerates—multinational firms spreading their tentacles worldwide into emerging third-world countries in search of cheaper labor and higher profits—is as futile as returning to feudalism. The world today is globally interconnected and financially codependent, despite the form of capitalism practiced—whether state capitalism in planned economies (the Chinese model) or corporate welfare-warfare capitalism in Western democratic societies. The political system is under the sway of financial institutions too big to fail and economic global forces intertwined in a financial world of international codependency.

VII

As early as the second decade of the twentieth century, the British economic historian R. H. Tawney fully assessed the error at the root of the philosophy of capitalism and the theory of utility. "It is obvious, indeed," Tawney contended in his book, *The Acquisitive Society*, "that no change of system or machinery can avert those causes of social malaise which consist in egotism, greed, or quarrelsomeness of human nature." Nevertheless, human beings do possess the capacity "to create an environment in which those are not the qualities which are encouraged." Hence, no change of system, Tawney claimed, "can secure that men live up to their principles. What it can do is to establish their social order upon principles to which, if they please, they can live up and not live down. It cannot control their actions. It can offer them an end on which to fix their minds. And, as their minds are, so, in the long run and with exceptions, their practical activity will be."[295] Tawney addressed freedom and human dignity: our fundamental character, possessing the capacity of self-transcendence and spiritual literacy.

The creative inspiration of Adam Smith's ideal model may have offered a virtuous end on which to fix our minds. But it was flawed philosophically and readily gave rise by the end of the nineteenth century to its opposite. In shifting economic value from virtue in Smith's economic model to utilitarianism, the irrational appetites ramrodded the rational faculty and took possession of the will in the name of economic freedom. Tawney described the world humanity brought into being. We failed to have something to live up to, something that would bolster human resistance to self-alienation, except in acquiring more and more satisfaction from satiating irrational appetites. He spelled out the consequence of the abdication of the self's communal purpose in the division of labor within any social organization. Prior to the private-enterprise system of economics, the communal principle underlying social and economic life was generally affirmed, no matter how imperfectly it may have been realized. With the onset of private ownership as the foundation of private-enterprise economics, Tawney maintained, there "was the gradual disappearance from social thought of the idea of purpose itself. Its place in the eighteenth century was taken by the idea of mechanism."[296] The social order was conceived as nothing more than a mechanical linking of individuals interacting for the ends of self-gain. Egotism and greed replaced "the conception of men as united to each other, and of all mankind as united to God, by mutual obligations arising from their relation to a common end," no matter "how vaguely and imperfectly realized."[297]

Tawney brought to mind the significance of the link between the natural reality of time-space and the eternal. Forsaking the eternal turned out to be a spiritual (that is, a metaphysical) regression of consciousness: "The keystone holding together the social fabric, ceased to be impressed upon men's minds when Church and State withdrew from the center of social life to its circumference. What remained when the keystone of the arch was removed, was private rights and private interests, the materials of a society rather than a society itself."[298] The natural order, the reality of time-space, came to replace the spiritual underpinning of reality. Humanity was lost in the finite, in history, in the mayhem of the flux and vagary of time.

Private property rights were absolutized. "Thus conceived society assumed something of the appearance of a great joint-stock company, in which political power and the receipt of dividends were justly assigned to those who held the most numerous shares."[299] The communal nature of human reality with its roots in the transcendent was sloughed off. It was replaced by a mechanical system of competition in which markets were more and more severed from their complement—cooperation. Tawney provided us with a vivid description of the outcome of the modern era. It is not as one is led to believe, a cacophony of economic exchanges in self-adjusting markets that justified the value of what was produced, distributed, and morally shared with the laboring class, and of the maintenance of the infrastructure of society. It more readily represented a political economy of conflicting social and political forces within the corporate structure of an economic order in which all participants sought the maximum self-advantage goaded by greed, egoism, and envy.

Tawney did not make a case against private property rights per se. He understood that greed, envy, and acquisitiveness just as easily infect socialism; that is, any collective form of ownership of property, such as the nationalization of an industry or state-sponsored capitalism, among others. What troubled him was the outcome of private ownership divorced from work; that is, property that was an outcome of creative work as opposed to property that was an alternative to work. In the latter, absentee owners were fixated on finding a means of enhancing the receipt of dividends in their owning of shares in a company. They were passive owners without a creative function in the enterprise itself. Tawney contended that collective forms of ownership of property as well as private ownership of property should be judged according to their function in the creative process of production. He regarded as natural and healthy the activity/function of creative work, and as unnatural and unhealthy the passive property owners who did not create but were parasitic on the life and work of those who did create—the workers.

Tawney put in perspective the fact that private enterprises were compatible with small-scale, personal, and local firms in which creative work could be carried out in a natural, healthy manner. He was scornful of those participating in a division of labor who politically whine and wrangle to grab on to the most profit possible. He was tolerant nonetheless toward labor unions which campaign against the corporate power structure of business firms. Morally speaking, he equated the head of a business or financial firm with the captain of a ship. The tradition of the latter was one of service, and the captain was the last to leave the ship. What the leaders of business and financial firms have a right to demand, and what concerned their fellow men to see they get, was enough to enable them to perform their work. Apropos the cardinal virtues, what should CEOs see as "enough"? For Adam Smith, it had to do with the temperance of the appetites in the soul under the dictates of wisdom that spearheads justice in oneself as well as in the communal order. As Tawney claimed, "If a man has important work, and enough leisure and income to enable him to do it properly, he is in possession of as much happiness as is good for any of the children of Adam."[300]

Tawney called our attention to the fact that in our sinful state the self is alienated from itself. The tragedy of freedom is the sinfulness stored in the self of all of us. It is well-masked by ego-consciousness conditioned by literalized religions worldwide, as well as ideologies, myths, and the realm of common phantoms and illusions of the period we live in. The self falls into the righteousness of the Pharisees. Its intuitive intelligence becomes restrained. What often appeared as hypocrisy was spiritual illiteracy and the confusion of the ego (the conditioned, alienated self) assumed to be the true self rooted in the eternal. Long, arduous, and full of suffering is the road ahead for the ego in preparation for death that leads to self-conversion, and to the self's transfiguration of consciousness and self-transformation. Living in idolatry of the social-natural reality gives yields either to egoism and egotism (self-enslavement) or to the possible transfiguration of consciousness (self-liberation). This is what Tawney meant when he maintained, aptly, that what a person "has a right to demand, and what it concerns his fellow-men to see that he gets, is enough to perform his work."[301]

When understood spiritually, this "enough" turns out to be the ecstasy in working in community with others, which flows from and suffuses the self's creative endeavors regardless of the work done, whether it is that of a janitor, a captain of industry, or a chief executive of a nation. A realization of "enough" is in fact the realization of the true self contributing to the creative efforts of the community in gratitude to forebears, to the inheritance of the gifts bequeathed, and to the cosmic mystery of the self's divine stature. Undergoing a transfiguration of consciousness, the self undergoes self-transformation. But for many, suffering is unfortunately no guarantee that the soul will incline toward transcendence. Awakening spiritually is at the heart of the solution to the global crisis in humanity afflicting the world today.

Tawney appraised the legitimacy of absolute property rights. His principle of the creative function of work within the economic order stood in contradiction to "predatory property" and crony capitalism that gave rise to "residuary profits"; that is, to the confiscation of what Marx called the surplus value of labor. Tawney recommended a change in the character of property. He understood that under the name of property several different powers were vested—those of owners, workers, consumers, and the communal infrastructure. Political controversy continued to characterize property rights according to the early nineteenth-century dichotomy: the black-and-white issue of public and private ownership. This commonplace view still contrasted the two with one another: "as light with darkness or darkness with light," as Tawney claimed. "The shell of the traditional legal system the elements of a new body of relationship" had already been prepared." The true purpose is "the provision of service, not the provision of dividends;" service, function, or creative work frees human activity "from subordination to the pecuniary interests of the owner of property, because they are the magnetic pole which sets all the compasses wrong, and which causes industry, however swiftly it may progress, to progress in the wrong direction."[302] Tawney rendered a severe indictment of pecuniary interests of private ownership shorn of wisdom and justice.

It is not only the utilitarian view he was referring to as the compass set wrong, although this inclined human beings toward greater alienation. It concerned fundamentally the issue of the freedom and dignity of the human being: the simple and obvious system of natural liberty. The character of ownership—whether public, private, or managerial—should be based on obligation, responsibility, and the creative function of economic participants in the division of labor. A "combination of unity and diversity is possible only to a society which subordinates its activities to the principle of purpose. For what that principle offers is not merely a standard for determining the relations of different classes and groups of producers, but a scale of moral values."[303] Ultimately, Tawney envisioned the compass pointed toward industry holding "a position of exclusive predominance among human interests, which no single interest, and least of all the provision of the material means of existence, is fit to occupy."[304] The economic reality abetted by the utility theory leads to the enfeeblement of our social institutions: family, church, school, government, and, obviously, the economic order. Tawney's final recommendation should be taken to heart. Industry must be so organized "that the instrumental character of economic activity is emphasized by its subordination to the social purpose for which it is carried on."[305]

VIII

Adam Smith, Karl Marx, and John Maynard Keynes all sustained a vision of social purpose and the communal nature of economic activity. They embraced with amazing vagaries of optimism the wending of humanity toward a global human community beyond the nation-state. Greed and acquisitiveness still haunting contemporary societies belie such optimism. Looming on the horizon beyond the dark cloud of unknowing lurks the global crisis in humanity. Neither Keynes nor contemporary economists heeded, as Tawney did, Locke's outdated idea of absolute property rights, or Marx's cautioning of the outcome of the surplus value of labor that leads to the concentration of wealth. The truth is that corporate profits—especially beyond small-scale firms in which market forces are effective—must be shared for capitalism to stay afloat. Profits must be shared with and parceled out—apart from the capital needs of the firm—to the investment of owners, to the costs of the infrastructure of society, and to workers whose surplus value is rendered up to absentee owners.

On at least two issues, Marx and Keynes can be thought of as soulmates. They both accepted private-market capitalism as a stage through which human beings would suffer on the way to a more enlightened and just future. They accepted the fact that the survival of capitalism required a social safety net of welfare programs as a means of alleviating suffering amidst potential abundance. John Maynard Keynes, unlike Adam Smith and Karl Marx before him, presumed mistakenly—as is now clear and should have been clear then—that a world of economic abundance for all does not in itself necessarily guarantee a transfiguration of consciousness and spiritual liberation (i.e., a victory over self-enslavement).

All three fell under the illusion prevalent in the modern world that economic and social progress was the path to the fulfillment of human life. Their confusion was based on the presumption that economic growth provides the keystone to spiritual progress and self-enlightenment. The elevation of consciousness to the life and world of the spirit is a matter of personal freedom and human destiny, rooted in humanity's creative vocation. As a creature of flesh and blood and of the spirit, humanity is caught between time and eternity, suspended in a state of yearning and endowed with the tragic fate of freedom.

For all his philosophical and scientific astuteness, Marx assumed that revolutionary change through three stages of communism after the breakdown of capitalism would inevitably give rise to "human history" and spiritual enlightenment. Thus, he referred to communism as the final revolution that would precipitate the overcoming of self-alienation: the appropriation of human life and the supersession of alienation. This included the emancipation from and self-transcendence of the doctrine of communism itself. Self transcendence would be the return of humanity from religion, the family, and the state to the self's human and social life. It would bring about a state of being that would rise above the heretofore antagonism between humans and nature, and between fellow humans. It would be self-validated in the life experiences of human beings.

Marx envisioned human beings appropriating their "manifold being in an all-inclusive way, and thus as a whole being."[306] This state of self-enlightenment would impel human consciousness beyond the state of having—the acquisitive mentality of greed and self-submission. "The human being had to be reduced to this absolute poverty in order to be able to give birth to all his inner wealth." Ultimately, Marx envisioned the resurrection of human beings through the resurrection of the natural and social reality. "Need and enjoyment," Marx claimed, "have thus lost their egoistic character, and nature has lost its mere utility by the fact that its utilization has become human utilization."[307]

The confident optimism of Adam Smith, Karl Marx, and John Maynard Keynes in a future of virtuous and wise outcomes to economic and social affairs appears rather quaint given today's economic reality. A relentless pursuit of profits structured in a global system of interconnected, interdependent nations has now become a global problem—whether it's a product of corporate welfare capitalism or centralized, planned state capitalism. With exponential increases in the concentration of wealth in the hands of the few across all nations—the rise of billionaires globally—the world faces a matrix of economic, social, and political forces frightening to contemplate. Given the injustices spawned and the power wielded by the affluent class over the minds and hearts of the masses and its control over the mass media, a positive resolution of the global crisis in humanity is daunting.

Global capitalism is riddled with omens of a future worldwide financial collapse accompanied by unimaginable human suffering and starvation. The wanton assault on nature, the systemic poisoning of the ecosystem, and human influence on climate are foreboding signs. This is accompanied globally by social injustice, disparity in the distribution of wealth, terrorism born of sectarian religions, and nations stocked with weapons of mass destruction. Our hope in avoiding a world catastrophe lies in awakening to the major domains of reality that embody knowledge of the eternal intrinsic in the cosmos and universe.

CHAPTER 10

The Global Plight of Nation-States

I

Nation-states have become expansionary in their hankering after power since the establishment of the Treaty of Westphalia that ended the Thirty Years' War, which lasted from 1618 to 1648, considered at the time as one of the most destructive conflicts in European history. Compared to today, viewed from a transcultural perspective, political leaders continue to turn a blind eye to the eternal character of the cosmos and universe. A heedless relationship among sovereign nations exists in today's global crisis in humanity. Nearly a century ago, Reinhold Niebuhr acknowledged that in a world of interrelated and interdependent nations, the nation-state system would become problematic as it would prevent the necessary establishment of a world community. Lacking an adequate pursuit of freedom and justice, nations find themselves caught up in national pride, succumbing readily to the temptation of idolatry. The will-to-power of nation-states becomes demonic in so far as they seek to extend their sovereignty, whether their political system is monarchic, democratic, fascist, or communist.

The German sociologist Robert Michels coined the adage the "iron law of oligarchy": "who says organization says oligarchy." Michels' political theory addressed the oligarchic trend in organizations, including governments of nation-states. In democratic nations, the temptation of citizens is to idealize and venerate their nation. Ruling oligarchies use all means possible to safeguard their hegemony in the affairs of state.[308]

"No politically crystalized social group," Reinhold Niebuhr declared, "existed without entertaining or succumbing to the temptation of making idolatrous claims for itself. Frequently the organs of this group pride, the state and the ruling oligarchy which bears the authority of the state, seek to detach themselves from the group pride of which their majesty is a symbol and to become independent sources of majesty." Niebuhr condemned egotism prevalent in nations that "is not merely an expression of the natural impulse of survival," disclosing "the fact that its most typical expressions are the lust-for-power, pride (comprising considerations of prestige and 'honour'), contempt toward the other (the reverse side of pride and its necessary concomitant in a world in which self-esteem is constantly challenged by the achievements of others); hypocrisy (the inevitable pretension of conforming to a higher norm than self-interest); and finally the claim of moral autonomy by presentation of itself as the source and end of existence."[309]

During the twentieth century, nations were caught up in two world wars. The secretion of the toxin of power characteristic of the governing oligarchy within nations compelled them to sacrifice their citizens, arrogating to themselves righteousness and deeming the enemy to be the epitome of evil. This malady of nations continued well into the twenty-first century despite revelations concerning the eternal reality innate in the cosmos and universe.

During the twenty-first century, many nations have been mired in wars globally. The United States declared a "war on terrorism" in the aftermath of the 9/11 terrorist attacks on the World Trade Center Towers and the Pentagon, embroiling itself in the affairs of the Middle East by declaring war on Afghanistan and Iraq. The U. S. invasion triggered instability in the region, resulting in the establishment of multiple terrorist groups driven by religious sectarianism in Islamic states. Wars among and civil wars within Middle East nations expanded, drawing into the quagmire Iran, Saudi Arabia, Syria, Yemen, Somalia, and African nations, with no end in sight. The problem for European nations, and to a lesser extent for the U. S., is that millions of refugees sought to escape the rampant terrorism and warfare in their own countries. This brought about an ill-fated predicament in European nations faced with instability. Unfortunately, the predicament these nations found themselves in was not easily resolvable, as corruption, terrorism, and religious sectarianism continued to spread and seep into social and political affairs.

Nations engaged in warfare suffer damage to their ecosystems. Four decades ago, international economist E. F. Schumacher warned that the ever-advancing technology in industrial capitalism is giving rise to three crises globally. "First, human nature revolts against inhuman technological, organizational, and political patterns, which it experiences as suffocating and debilitating; second, the living environment which supports human life aches and groans and gives signs of partial breakdown; and, third . . . the inroads being made into the world's nonrenewable resources, particularly those of fossil fuels, are such that serious bottlenecks and virtual exhaustion loom ahead in the quite foreseeable future."[310]

The global crisis in humanity has unfortunately forsaken the hearts and minds of citizens in interdependent nation-states. We are approaching a world that is detrimental to the human personality, its creative vocation, and its spiritual freedom. Oligarchies spawned within nation-states have gained enormous power, afflicting the well-being of the human personality and devaluing its freedom. This book makes clear that the highest value of humanity is its creative vocation, which entails awakening to the eternal, and advancing spiritual literacy.

Global capitalism and the plight of sovereign nations during the modern era reversed and rescinded the rightful relationship of citizens to one another and to planetary resources. Citizens became confused when the term "free market" was used to identify a world of oligopolistic and monopolistic predatory firms navigating the globe for cheap labor to increase the income of their absentee owners. The idea of a free-market economy is an ideal presumably based on "perfect competition," which embraces an effective morality—a compensatory balance between egoism and altruism, and between self-interest and sympathy for others. Adam Smith presumed a "free-market" economy would prevent a social pathology, the concentration of wealth that has afflicted humankind historically. His free-market philosophy rooted in the ancient virtues was turned on its head by the end of the nineteenth century and replanted in the morally and psychologically tainted soil of utilitarianism.

II

American political theorist Sheldon S. Wolin examined the contemporary political reality in depth and provided an answer that condemns corporate welfare-warfare capitalism that is shaping the global economy caught in the painful struggle of chaos in a world of potential abundance. Wolin proclaims that nations give rise to wars in so far as their citizens remain heedless of the moral standards enlightened human beings understand. If the U. S. has lost its Republic—a form of government in which power resides in elected officials representing the citizen body according to the rule of law—citizens may find themselves facing the possible specter of "inverted totalitarianism." Wolin coined the term to identify a political system driven by abstract totalizing powers, which he contrasts with classic totalitarianism. The power of classic totalitarianism was the outcome of larger-than-life dictators—Mussolini, Stalin, and Hitler—who "literally built the organization of their respective dictatorships." They stood inseparable from their dictatorships, in contrast to inverted totalitarianism. Wolin envisions inverted totalitarianism following an entirely different course in which the leader is not the architect of the system but its product. As an example, he points to the leadership of George W. Bush who "no more created inverted totalitarianism than he piloted a plane onto the *USS Abraham Lincoln*. He is the pliant favored child of privilege, of corporate connections, a construct of public relations wizards and of party propagandists. . . . Inverted totalitarianism is largely independent of any particular leader and requires no personal charisma to survive; its model is the corporate 'head,' the corporation's public representative."[311]

"While Hitler, Mussolini, and Stalin were the principal authors of schemes that eventually led to disastrous overreaching, those who counsel the titular head of Superpower, the equivalents of the CEO, supply the hubris that confuses opportunity with capability and grossly underestimates the resources needed to accomplish the grandiose end of world hegemony."[312] Wolin alleges that the actual direction democracy is moving toward is "a political system, the very opposite of what the political leadership, the mass media, and think-tank oracles claim that it is, the world's foremost exemplar of democracy."[313] He envisions a politics of fear accompanying the struggle between "terrorism and imperialism" with the onset of the twenty-first century that is giving rise to the loss of basic liberties.

Exploitation of fear since 9/11 not only pervades the mental and emotional life of citizens; public officials have tragically learned to exploit fear. Public authorities savaging personal liberties by an astute management of fear tends to fashion a misguided patriotism.

Fear is spilling into the public arena, not only in the lives of workers by an ever-changing economic state of affairs, which has become the "constant companion of most workers, but by terrorism, natural disasters, illegal immigrants, and epidemics."[314] "The fact of terrorism, combined with the imaginary it has assumed in the national consciousness, will provide justification enough for retaining the security apparatus, subsidizing the defense industry, and nurturing 'the fear factor,' while accustoming the citizen to a legal regime that sanctions extraconstitutional powers, including the torture of prisoners and domestic spying."[315]

Wolin alleges moreover that the U. S. is witnessing something new in political affairs: a conservativism which is hostile toward social spending and which tends to intervene in the most personal affairs of citizens, including sexual relations, marriage, reproduction, and family decisions about life and death. He focused on the matrix of power and the direction of contemporary politics, entreating citizens to put aside timeworn assumptions they hold about democracy; namely, that even if they do not live in a fully realized democracy, an impressive number of its manifestations are actualized. Wolin turns to some of the fundamental changes occurring during the first decade of the present century that raises the question of what causes a democracy to change into some non- or anti-democratic system, and what kind of system is democracy likely to change into. What Wolin perceives evolving gradually and surreptitiously, he puts in the form of a philosophical and empirical analysis: "What if, in its popular culture a democracy were prone to license, ('anything goes')?" Yet in their politics, the demos "were to become fearful, ready to give the benefit of the doubt to leaders who, while promising to 'root out terrorists,' insist that endeavor is a 'war' with no end in sight? Might democracy then tend to become submissive, privatized rather than unruly, and would that alter the power relationships between citizens and their political deciders?"[316]

Wolin highlighted a coincidence of two forces in a popular democracy facing growing chaos: the utility theory of value in the economic realm— "anything goes" according to citizens' and leaders' irrational appetites and ever-expanding needs freed from the cardinal virtues—and an "imperial superpower" projecting its power inward to sustain order. This is the recipe, he admits, for the root causes of a potential revolutionary rise of a postmodern form of fascism: inverted totalitarianism. Wolin distinguishes the causes of this practice of inverted totalitarianism from the causes underlying "classic fascism" of the twentieth century. An inverted totalitarianism does not derive from "classic fascism" of the types embodied in Nazi Germany, Fascist Italy, Franco's Spain, or Stalinist Russia. Those regimes were powered by "revolutionary movements whose aim was to capture, reconstitute, and monopolize the power of the state."[317] Their main center of power provided the necessary leverage to mobilize and reconstruct society and its social institutions under government diktat.

The gradual transition to an inverted totalitarianism, consequently, is more a stealth gestation of social and political forces gradually coalescing during the last two decades of the twentieth century—forces conceived and evolving from ideological indoctrination of citizens with the illusion that laissez-faire capitalism and a republican form of democracy actually did exist; ideologies spun from complex philosophies little understood by a "distracted citizenry." The system of capitalism envisioned by Adam Smith's free-market philosophy from the perspective of the eighteenth century represented an intellectual construct of a decentralized government, with the market working best when left alone, operating freely, and guided by an unseen hand that brought self-interest into a complementary relationship with the common good. Wolin maintains that the "emergence of the corporation marked the presence of private power on a scale and in numbers thitherto unknown."[318] With the rise of huge corporations, a change in the balance of power occurred. This predatory nature of the economic system was envisioned, mistakenly, as befitting democracy. Indeed, it was taken as the mainstay of democracy.

With this economic-political sleight of hand—a welfare-warfare economic system henceforth embraced as the mainstay of democracy—the tragic terrorist act in the 9/11 destruction of the Twin Towers of the World Trade Center intruded into the lives of innocent Americans. The administration in power quickly responded to terrorism by harnessing its power onto "other forms of power, evangelical religions, and most notably by encouraging a symbiotic relationship between traditional government and the system of 'private' governance represented by the modern business corporation." This combination of institutional power "is not a system of codetermination by equal partners who retain distinctive identities but rather a system that represents the political coming-of-age of corporate power."[319]

Terrorism against the United States expedited, thereby, the protracted, covert gestation of industrial capitalism into an inverted fascism. By the end of the past century, there was in place the delusionary mindset foisted on the masses and abetted by the pundits and academics concerning economic decisions: a delusionary mindset conceived as the outcome of Adam Smith's free market, now morphed in reality into huge trusts, monopolies, holding companies, and cartels. These corporate structures (the negation of Smith's free market and perfect freedom) had gained the capacity "to set (or strongly influence) prices, wages, supplies of materials, and entry" into the market, determining the market forces themselves.[320] The crucial consequence of corporate business developing oligopolistic control over markets (i.e., where sellers are so few that the supply offered by anyone of them affects the market price and production decisions) had earlier given rise to the need for expanding government to safeguard democracy: to serve the common good and the interest of ordinary people by administering counterbalancing social welfare programs.

Progressives and populists of the late nineteenth and twentieth century, Wolin claims, "argued, perhaps naively, that in a democracy the people were sovereign and government was, by definition, on their side." They held the belief that the "sovereign people were fully entitled to use government power and resources to redress the inequalities created by the economy of capitalism."[321] The New Deal and the onset of regulatory agencies, the social safety net of the Social Security program, minimum wage law, the legitimation of unions to organize and bargain collectively, government programs for public works and conservation—all strengthened the conviction of progressives and citizens that democracy was functioning.

With the passage of time during the twentieth century and the onset of World War II and the Cold War, corporate economic power, Wolin claimed, became "the basis of power on which the state relied."[322] What was a gradual process became "an unprecedented combination of powers, distinguished by their totalizing tendencies, powers that not only challenge established boundaries—political, moral, intellectual, and economic—but whose very nature it is to challenge the limits of the earth itself."[323] The landscape of the economic, social, and political reality was recast. Such powers became instrumental in subtly and furtively "inventing and disseminating a culture that taught consumers to welcome change and private pleasures, while accepting political passivity."[324] This constituted for Wolin the seed bed that would nurture a new collective identity—imperial rather than a Republic, and far less democratic.

From this denouement of the twentieth century, Wolin set forth his tentative, hypothetical construct of inverted totalitarianism as a warning of social tendencies that point "in a direction away from self-government, the rule of law, egalitarianism, and thoughtful public discussion." In its place, the citizenry found itself confronting a slow but ongoing "managed democracy," what Wolin calls "the smiley face of inverted totalitarianism."[325] As a political philosopher assessing contemporary society, he asked readers to "question who we are as a people, what we stand for as well as what we are willing to stand, the extent to which we are committed to becoming involved in common affairs."[326] The risks in the way forward, as far as democratic principles are concerned, demand that citizens play an important role that cannot be abrogated. For example, how do citizens in a democratic society justify expending the energies and wealth of its "citizens and asking some of them to kill and sacrifice their lives while the destiny of their country is fast slipping from popular control?"[327]

III

The core of Wolin's contention consists of three major *interpenetrating social forces* that are an outgrowth of democracy itself and that, paradoxically, are ideologically cast as free-market capitalism and a republican form of democracy. The first is *growing apathy* among the electorate. In contrast to classical totalitarianism, "inverted totalitarianism thrives on a politically demobilized society, that is, a society in which the citizens, far from being whipped into a continuous frenzy by the regime's operatives, are politically lethargic, reminiscent of Alexis de Tocqueville's privatized citizenry."[328] The social forces cultivating political apathy on the part of the electorate are not simply due to the current TV culture. "Ordinary citizens have been the victims of a counterrevolution that has brought 'rollbacks' of numerous social services which were established only after hard-fought political struggles, and which the earlier Republican administrations of Eisenhower and Nixon had accepted as major elements in a national consensus."[329] For many among the citizenry, this counterrevolution based on complex economic issues has brought about skepticism if not cynicism and a sense of political futility. In contrast to classical totalitarianism, by fashioning the electorate as followers rather than citizens, "inverted totalitarianism can achieve the same end of furnishing substitutes such as 'consumer sovereignty' and 'shareholder democracy' that gives a 'sense of participation' without demands or responsibilities."[330]

After 9/11 and the experience of foreign terrorism wreaking damage on U.S. soil and taking innocent lives, the war against terror served to reinforce a sense of ineffectiveness or futility on the part of citizens. President G. W. Bush, for example, encouraged citizens to go out and shop. Herein resides a *second major social force*. The onset of terrorism tended to *reinforce the obedience of the citizenry* to the furtive expansion of the shareholder democracy—the citizen owning a share in what government does rather than being the government of, by, and for "the people." Shareholders are inactive recipients of what is being managed in their name. The threat of terrorism was, therefore, the second major force that generated a more complicit and pliable electorate willing to accept and endure a managed democracy. According to Wolin, the fear evoked was used in a subconscious, if not a calculated manner, by the Bush II administration to perpetuate fear and ensure obedience on demand. It also served to weaken the Vietnam syndrome, the general aversion of citizens to engage in foreign imperial ventures. In the declaration of war on terrorism, the Bush administration—having both a pliable public and a submissive Congress in waging a war against a new form of violence—took political advantage of the reins of power. Accompanied by lies and distortions, this violence projected its power outward toward an "axis of evil."

Wolin calls our attention to the seventeenth-century political theorist Thomas Hobbes who identified the means of securing a compliant and submissive public and legislature. A few words on Hobbes is necessary to understand Wolin's position. Hobbes can be described as both the complete utilitarian and the complete individualist, believing that humans, like all other organisms, have an instinctive drive for self-preservation. Hobbes characterized human nature in his famous quip that human life is "solitary, poor, brutish, and short," and that the human condition is a "war of every man against every man." Consequently, the power of the state and submission to the authority of law is justified only in so far as it contributes to the security of humans seeking their own self-interest. Society becomes merely an artificial body for humans in so far as they find it to their self-advantage.

Wolin quoted neoconservative intellectuals in the Bush II administration who claimed the "alternative to American leadership is a chaotic Hobbesian world," a world in which "there is no authority to thwart aggression, ensure peace and security or enforce international norms."[331] Wolin maintains that these Neo-Hobbesian thinkers without exception got it half right: they "suppressed that half of Hobbes's story which dealt with the domestic implications of his defense of the principle of absolute authority and of the sovereign's role as 'supreme pastor.'" Hobbes's position on the prominence of terror and fear "could be exploited to promote an awesome concentration of state power and authority, and, crucially, how that outcome could be represented as the product of popular consent."[332] Further, Wolin notes that "Hobbes's crucial assumption was that absolute power absolutely depended not just on fear, but on passivity. Civic indifference was thus elevated to a form of rational virtue.... Virtually unlimited power, on the one hand, and, on the other, an apolitical citizenry now assured of its security so that it [an apolitical citizenry] can single-mindedly pursue private concerns: a perfect complementarity between apolitical absolutism [a pliable, shareholder citizenry] and economic self-interest [on the part of the economic and political elite]."[333] The realities of both a democratic society and laissez-faire economics were, thereby, being turned on their heads.

Wolin assessed how Alexis de Tocqueville's nineteenth-century democracy would go wrong with Hobbesian thought. Tocqueville "imagines 'the new features' of a despotism evolving naturally and peacefully out of a democracy."[334] Wolin suggests that Tocqueville's idea of the new features of despotism and Hobbes's absolute sovereign may appear far-fetched concerning postmodern society in the twenty-first century in which global warfare was reignited by the neocons. Yet, Wolin was not amiss in reminding us that the "lesson of Hobbes and Tocqueville can be boiled down to a brief but chilling dictum: concentrated power, whether of a Leviathan, a benevolent despotism, or a superpower is impossible without the support of a complicit citizenry that willingly signs on to the covenant, or acquiesces, or clicks the 'mute button.'"[335]

The *third social force* is the attempt on the part of the neocons to reconstruct the nation's identity. Wolin submitted that their ideology set out in *The National Security Strategy (NSS) of the United States*, September 9, 2002, a year after 9/11, "represented the clearest formulation of the administration's understanding of the mission" of the U. S. "and of its totalizing reach. The document is also the best evidence of the ideology promoting inverted totalitarianism."[336] The NSS "begins by positing a conception of an expansive power that goes beyond previous understandings, and justifies it, not by an appeal to legal authority or political principle, but by a Manichean myth that depicts two formations locked in a death struggle"—the U. S. representing absolute justice (the innocent Utopia); the other, the absolutely unjust axis of evil (global terrorism, the evil Dystopia).[337]

Wolin contends that such a Manichean myth "crowds out all other distinctions, reducing politics to one focal point, a politics fixated upon a single foe, mobilized to combat an enemy unlike any encountered previously, 'a new condition of life.' Exhilarated by the prospect of a contest between good and evil, as confident of its own rectitude as it is of the unalloyed evil of its foe, *National Security Strategy* offers assurance that our society will emerge invigorated from the contest with terrorists."[338] The NSS notes further that, "For freedom to thrive, accountability must be expected and required. Thus, when the NSS document presents the 'free market' as one of the three constituent elements of the ideal political system, the market is a surrogate, a stand-in for globalization/empire."[339]

IV

Wolin envisions a surviving and flourishing democracy of citizens in society who are willing to shed their political passivity and acquire the character of a demos. "That means, creating themselves, coming-into-being by virtue of their actions."[340] It means the democratization of the self and the democratization of politics. Without fulfilling both these conditions, a democracy remains merely formal. Wolin realized the prospect of the self-transfiguration of consciousness: "to change one's self, to learn how to act collectively, as a demos. It requires that the individual go 'public' and thereby help to constitute a 'public' and an 'open politics,' in principle accessible for all to take part in."[341] Wolin claimed that social institutions and the moral state of citizens correlate with political responsibility and adeptness. He made clear that well-functioning social institutions depend on the self-transfiguration of the consciousness of the citizenry. "While it cannot be emphasized too strongly that democracy requires supporting conditions—social, economic, and educational—the democratization of politics remains *merely formal without the democratization of the self.*"[342] Citizens must rise above a strictly ego-centered, utilitarian relationship with respect to economic and political issues. "Becoming a self" means a citizen sees "the values of common involvements and endeavors and finds in them a source of self-fulfillment."[343] This becomes the precursor of self-awakening to the economic and political discourse going public: citizens taking part in discourse and decision-making. Citizens undergoing a wholesale shift in their state of consciousness that sets free their creative vocation and enhances their potential to think, speak, and behave "according to ethical and demanding mores."[344] Thus, democratic political consciousness requires nurturing "in local, small-scale settings, where both the negative consequences of political powerlessness and the positive possibilities of political involvement seem most evident."[345]

Wolin had no illusion that the demos will ever dominate politically. "In an age where identities are potentially plural and changing, a unified demos is no longer possible, or even desirable." Instead of a demos, what is needed are "democratic citizenries." For Wolin, any optimism comes from the prospect of encouraging and nurturing counter-elites of democratic public servants—"democratic citizenries." "What is at stake is a fundamental difference between, on the one hand, reason in the service of commonality [shared aims, cohesion, and the communal welfare] and, on the other, elite rationality of reason in the service of the economic polity [government in the service of the elites]."[346]

According to Wolin, "Public institutions are being savaged. A legislature, a court, a system of law, a civil service are the equivalent to a 'public ecology' and, like the natural world, an inheritance to be cared for and passed on."[347] The counter-elites (democratic citizenries) stand in opposition to elite rationalism. The latter "is encouraged by the ethos and ethic shared by political and corporate elites," whose outlook and approach are "expansionist, opportunistic, and, above all, exploitative." The whole public ecology, like the natural world and its ecology—inherited, cared for, and passed on to citizens— "can easily be 'used up' by, for example, corruption, partisanship in the wrong places, denigration of public servants, dismissal of scientific evidence and the reports of whistle blowers, systematic lying to the public, and the stretching of legal authority to the point where it sanctions torture."[348]

Overall, Wolin perceived a frightful scenario looming, given the decline of the democratic society: the private ownership of the airwaves, the lack of noncommercial broadcasting, a cowed and diminishing middle class, a public becoming ever more gerrymandered into political enclaves equally divided into contending political parties, and the forfeiture of virtue in a world dominated by crude individualism. These barriers to enfranchisement have been gradually expanding over the course of the twentieth century. The democratic society has become more and more fragmented by economic interests and cultural identities. "As the barriers to participation were gradually lowered and citizenship opened to all adults, what stood exposed, however, was not a compact body of citizens but the reality of a society fragmented—first, by economic interests, occupations, and social classes, each of which could be almost endlessly subdivided; and second, by cultural identities that resisted absorption."[349] Concern for the common good, the general interest of society, and the good of the whole were replaced by self-interest, the proliferating divisions of conflicting interests, and crude individualism—all detrimental to the dependable politics of a pluralistic democracy.

V

Wolin recognized the dangers of privatizing public functions—"notably education, welfare programs, administration of prisons, military operations, postal services, even space travel"—all of which would give rise to "the steady evolution of corporate power into a political form, into an integral, even dominant partner with the state."[350] He also understood and took a strong position against privatizing Social Security and public lands, and exploiting natural resources. What happened over the course of the past five decades was the cobbling together of artificial majorities: "the elites *temporarily* assemble or rally diverse interests without integrating them. Instead of seeking ways to block the coalescence of diverse interests, they employ the strategy of 'targeting' them with a 'message.'"[351] They whip up, as they did after the 9/11 terrorist attack, an appeal to patriotism and religious faith, or patriotism and millenarianism (i.e., the belief by a religious, social, or political group or movement in a coming major transformation of society, after which all things will be changed). What begins as rational calculations about voting ends up "in both an irrational citizenry and the compilation by 'the best and brightest' of an alarming record of irrational decisions, a Vietnam, a Lebanon (1982), or an Iraq."[352]

The real tragedy would be the loss of commonality, "the care and fate of the polity."[353] The politics of commonality can be seen in the long-standing attempt to privatize Social Security. Wolin grasped the underlying reality, whether conscious or subconscious on the part of the radical conservatives, to dismantle Social Security by transforming it into individual, privatized accounts. This was a perfect example of the difference between the politics of democratic commonality and corporate politics, represented by the contrast between the present Social Security system and the proposed alternative system based on private investment accounts. Under the existing system, one generation contributes to the support of another so that the program became a shared endeavor resulting in a common good. "Under the proposed replacement each person would be on his or her own, commonality would be lost and inequality promoted. That contrast, between self-interest and commonality of concerns, involves contrasting mentalities, each with its own form of rationality: one is exploitative, the other protective."[354]

Historically, revolutionary change managed to give rise to the "eternal return," as conceived by the ancient Greeks and Nietzsche, in which inequality and exploitation were reasserted. Citizens are in need of a creative solution to the global crisis in humanity, which is frightfully on a trajectory toward imperiling planetary life. The fate of the Westphalian nation-state in the postmodern era is a world that has become afflicted with the malady of an unjust distribution of property and wealth, and ultimately, a demise of the cardinal virtues.

Wolin recognized that the fundamental problem lies in the soul of human beings. The change must come from within and entails the awakening of the self to its human personality; an awakening beyond the historical that advances consciousness to the metahistorical (the meanings underlying historical facts) and to the metaphysical (the truth that underlies what is perceptible to the senses). Personal evolution is consciousness opening to conscience, to knowledge of the Good and the Eternal. This awakening would reverse the course of history and the path humanity now treads. As Wolin declared, the prospect of the survival and evolution of the democratic society resides in the people rising beyond self-tyranny—that is, in "becoming a self." A change in mentality—a change in the direction, structure, and content of consciousness—must reach a wider circle of the academic community and the intelligentsia in order to be broadcast to a broader mass of citizens. As a political philosopher, Wolin brought the self to the threshold of our evolving transcultural world.

VI

Utilitarian values have tended to deplete world resources and to disrupt, if not transform, the planet's ecological landscape and climactic conditions. Communal life, moreover, was disintegrating. An infirmity had infected the hearts and minds of human beings from the bottom to the top of the social hierarchy. Reinhold Niebuhr touched the core of freedom with respect to the future: "Mere development of what he now is cannot save man, for development will heighten all the contradictions in which he stands. Nor will emancipation from the law of development and the march of time through entrance into a timeless and motionless eternity save him."[355]

A dialogue between genuine conservatism and genuine progressivism holds out some hope. Such a dialogue however must be anchored in the collective wisdom of traditional knowledge rather than in the self-calculation of economic and political elites seeking to safeguard their wealth and privilege. Conservative and progressive forces grounded in an awareness of the eternal can recognize the potential in democratic societies to navigate a positive way forward in a world caught up in, and hindered by, an increasing transformation of the ecological landscape. The way forward calls for the awakening of both conservative and progressive forces to the truth established in our transcultural world that ensures a meaningful dialogue free from animosity, mendacity, and corruption (i.e., social entropy). To safeguard a democratic society from political paralysis and the movement toward a state of Wolin's inverted totalitarianism, two sociopolitical forces—conservatism and progressivism—must inevitably collaborate and cooperate, reigning in corruption. As adversaries, both are prone to injustice. Thoughtful optimism in avoiding an inverted totalitarianism in the global crisis in humanity resides in knowledge of the history of the twentieth and twenty-first centuries. The goal of these antagonistic forces is not compromise *per se*, but the compelling need for assuring truth rooted in the cardinal virtues.

A dialogue between conservatism and progressivism grounded in the eternal has the capacity to safeguard the pathway forward in a world no longer lacking in the knowledge and practice of the cardinal virtues. The dialogue can only be brought about by spiritual literacy, which makes intelligible the virtues of wisdom and justice as the bedrocks of commonality, solidarity, empathy, and personal well-being. As the social, economic, and political orders of reality within and among nation-states tend to become trapped and embroiled in injustice, inequality, and lack of wisdom owing to the decline of knowledge of the cardinal virtues, corruption is giving rise to the empty rhetoric of politics, each side seeking victory over the other. This will exacerbate social and political revolutions worldwide, increase social chaos and international warfare, and intensify the possibility of destroying the ecosystem and rupturing community life. Unless and until conservatives and progressives work hand in hand to find a life-enhancing way forward in the nuclear age, human and planetary life will continue to be imperiled.

Knowledge inherent in the domains of religion, philosophy, the sciences, and the liberal arts had revealed the eternal in the cosmos and universe. Human life is enhanced by the mystery underlying the universe—what Teilhard de Chardin called the Omega Point of divine wisdom (the perfection of our consciousness) and Gerald Schroeder disclosed as wisdom inherent in the universe—transmitted to us through the noosphere. But until this wisdom resonates in our personal life experience—that is, until we experience the stirring and throbbing of the divine wisdom inherent in the universe awakening in ourselves—historical revelations will continue to remain external constructs. People worldwide will not have prepared themselves to comprehend the meaning of life fulfillment. They will not have witnessed the truth of their vital self-journey to carry out their creative vocation in the world. They will not have risen above misguided conservatism and imprudent progressivism.

In democratic societies, the participants in a genuine dialogue must engage with one another in mutual self-esteem, self-respect, and gratitude in sharing their life journey. Inspired by virtue rather than status, power, or financial gain, our consciousness must be elevated to the realm of meaning compatible with our evolving transcultural world. Spiritual awareness, which enhances our mental and emotional life, springs from the practice of the cardinal virtues. Moreover, awakening to the meaning gained from knowledge elevates our potential to stem the assault of destructive forces on planetary life-forms and strengthen our resolve to carry out our divine vocation.

This is not to be taken as a utopian dream. Freedom is our destiny. Freedom is also our burden—a source of tragedy and untold suffering. Freedom underlies the self's path to creativity and liberation. It holds the prospect of elevating consciousness to the profound mystery foreshadowing the emergence of the creative energy and spirit that gave birth to the universe. The abandonment of freedom results in a childlike neglect of the self's burden of responsibility, a neglect that blinds the self to a world fraught with suffering and injustice to which it must respond. Self-alienation is, unfortunately, a neglect of personal maturity in which the self eludes its trial of freedom—the burden of its divine, creative mission in the world.

An Era of the Spirit cannot expunge humanity's cosmological plight of freedom, which is inherent in human life and tantamount to an irreducible mystery. History teaches that the trial of freedom brings into life errors, blunders, miscalculations, and oversights that inevitably creep into the nooks and crannies of our complex personal, social, political, and economic life. Embedded in a division of labor made up of social classes, our creative vocation secured in wisdom is tasked to encounter and endure the fate of freedom. This is what it means to be human. To presume some utopian notion of perfect liberty, perfect self-adjusting markets, a perfect civil society, or a self-restorative ecology is the height of innocence and ignorance.

Humanity worldwide stands on the cusp of a possible breakthrough to a new epoch in human evolution—an Era of the Spirit capable of warding off political paralysis endemic in nation-states ruled by an unelected oligarchy.

The groundwork of an Era of the Spirit in human evolution is set in motion by discoveries that awaken humanity to the cardinal virtues and disclose the cosmic mystery discernible in human life, existentially, through the self's living experience. The four cardinal virtues—wisdom, courage, temperance, and justice—are of supreme importance in facing the global crisis in humanity. As Plato claimed, "Justice is produced in the soul, like health in the body, by establishing the elements concerned in their natural relations of control and subordination, whereas injustice is like disease and means that their natural order is inverted." Plato maintained, moreover, that virtue is "health and comeliness and well-being of the soul, as wickedness is disease, deformity, and weakness." Thus "virtue and wickedness are brought about by one's way of life, honourable or disgraceful."[356]

To repeat, a thoughtful dialogue between conservatives and progressives in our evolving transcultural world holds the promise of humanity's self-awakening to the eternal and advancement on the path of freedom that presents the self the choice of the Good (wisdom prevailing) or ill (intemperance prevailing). Humanity must embrace freedom of conscience and freedom of the spirit and renounce falsehoods, deceit, and dishonesty, which are at the core of much of human history.

In practice, capitalism in its various forms extols unlimited acquisition of wealth, presumably within a framework of competition. Based on the utility theory of value, capitalism sets free the irrational appetites from the control of reason and spiritual literacy, classifying pleasure-seeking as the prime moving force in the economic life of the self and society. In so far as the individual and the social classes function toward achieving the ends of utilitarianism—seeking to maximize pleasure—the rightful rule within the self and within society tends to be disruptive. Unmindful of spiritual literacy, the self finds itself in a state of want, subservient to the irrational appetites. Compassion and empathy for others, outside family and friendship relations, are for the most part forfeited, undermining psychological, societal, and moral well-being.

Ultimately the health of the planet's ecology and even the survival of planetary life—given the oligarchy in control of the world's nations—must be surrendered to a world community rooted in our transcultural world, united to the imperative of spiritual literacy. The Westphalian system of the world's nations grounded in their distinctive and idiosyncratic cultures will have outlived four centuries of being mired in warfare and must be transcended, thereby safeguarding the welfare of planetary life and its ecology. A universal culture rooted in our transcultural world and the imperative of spiritual literacy will hopefully thwart oligarchic consolidation of power, surmounting the global crisis in humanity of the postmodern era.

CHAPTER 11

The Global Plight of Nation States Abandoning the Cardinal Virtues and the Loss of Commonality

I

Humanity confronts a global crisis, with the world's nations finding themselves under the dominance of ruling oligarchies spawning an oppressive power structure. The nation-state system of the post-modern world is headed toward social and economic crises susceptible to appalling levels of inequity brought about by global capitalism and a market system inclined to form monopolies and massive corporations. Nations are no longer capable of shielding themselves from internal contradictions and environmental degradation (a response to climate change), the spread of infectious diseases, and contamination of the water supply. Global tensions are erupting among nations with the possibility of blundering into another world war, as escalating provocations, through a series of military stratagems among China, Russia, the United States, and other major powers, test each nation's resolve. Nations are also spiraling toward a possible ecocatastrophe: a global problem that could potentially bring about calamitous consequences, endangering life on Earth. The ill-fated presumption that humanity is free from the constraints of evolution renders humanity oblivious to the possibility of an advancement in consciousness.

Nations globally risk revolutions exacerbated by sectarian religious rivalries, terrorism, erosion of the ecosystem, and environmental deterioration to the extent that humanity may usher in its own demise. The irresponsible destruction of forests, wetlands, wildlife, and the geological and marine ecology continues to erode the planet's ecological landscape.

Mired in perpetual warfare, nations heedlessly contaminate the world's water resources, further diminishing the fertility of the soil. Deforestation is modifying the world's climate. A wanton indifference exists regarding biodiversity—the variability within and among species—in our ecosystems and the planet's life-support systems. The mass of humanity remains woefully oblivious to the state of the biosphere, atmosphere, hydrosphere, and geosphere.

American journalist Elizabeth Kolbert has studied various past extinctions on Earth and their causes. "One possibility—the possibility implied by the Hall of Biodiversity—is that we, too, will eventually be undone." This might come about, she warns, by our transforming the ecological landscape. "Having freed ourselves from the constraints of evolution, we remain dependent nevertheless on the earth's biological and geochemical systems. By disrupting these systems—cutting down tropical rainforests, altering the composition of the atmosphere, acidifying oceans—we're putting our own survival in danger." Her comprehensive study has put her at odds with scientists who have contended that "should global warming become too grave a threat, we can counteract it by geoengineering the atmosphere." Such stratagems presumably involve "scattering sulfates into the stratosphere to reflect sunlight back out to space; others involve shooting water droplets over the Pacific to brighten clouds."[357]

Kolbert warns that should humanity continue on its current course it will find itself without any evolutionary pathway to avoid the extinction of life on Earth, regardless of the hypothetical belief in the ability to geo-engineer the atmosphere. Moreover, a horrible plight confronts humanity. Nations throughout the world are awash in and saddled with the destructive power of nuclear weapons. Globally, nuclear weapon inventories are being downsized but also modernized according to the Stockholm International Peace Research Institute. According to its website, nine nations together possess approximately 15,395 nuclear weapons. Though the estimates of existing nuclear weapons are approximate, as of January 2016, the breakdown is as follows: United States possessed 7,000, Russia 7,290, France 300, China 260, India 100–200, Pakistan 110–130, Israel 80, United Kingdom 215, and North Korea 10.[358]

The survival of global capitalism itself is in jeopardy. Altered by advancing technological progress and automation, the labor force suffers mounting unemployment. Within many nations, machines and robots are estimated to replace many jobs in the coming decades. The capitalist class, as Karl Marx cautioned in the nineteenth century, "cannot exist without constantly revolutionizing the instruments of production, and thereby the relation of production, and with these the whole relations of society." This generates "uninterrupted disturbance of all social conditions, everlasting uncertainty and agitation," that distinguishes the bourgeois epoch from all earlier ones.[359] Moreover, the labor system is put in jeopardy with rapidly increasing digital technologies, which advance techniques for processing, designing, implementing, and supporting computer-based information systems, thereby reshaping the economy and bringing about a new wave of automation.

II

Nevertheless, beyond the global crisis in humanity stands a possible world-wide awakening of humanity to the twenty-first century revelations confirming energy, spirit, and freedom as the eternal foundation of the cosmos and universe. Einstein's theory of relativity (1905) and the splitting of the atom (1945) awakened humanity globally to the mystery that mass disappears when the atom is split and converts to energy. Science has played a significant part in disclosing the attributes of energy, spirit, and freedom inherent in the cosmos and universe. Einstein's discoveries gave rise to Teilhard de Chardin's *Phenomenon of Man*, the first endeavor to cobble together knowledge of a transcultural evolution regarding the advent of life on Earth. Teilhard discovered two forms of energy of mind and matter: tangential energy, which links elements with one another, and radial energy, knowable only through reflective consciousness and intuitive intelligence. With the onset of reflective consciousness in human beings, a threshold in evolution was crossed.

Seven decades after Teilhard de Chardin's work, molecular biologist Gerald Schroeder's studies confirmed Teilhard's theory of a psychic element intrinsic in matter. Through molecular biological analyses, Schroeder disclosed an aspect of mind inherent in every atom. Consistent with Teilhard's theory, Schroeder maintained that twentieth- and twenty-first-century physical sciences—beginning with Einstein's theory of relativity—replaced classical physical science. Schroeder's molecular analyses confirmed that every particle—from the atom to the human being—encompasses within it a level of wisdom.

Schroeder spelled out the profound meaning of Einstein's discoveries, awakening many of the world's citizens to knowledge of the hidden facets of the universe. Both Teilhard de Chardin and Gerald Schroeder confirmed that energy and spirit constitute the primary reality of life and being. Informed by scientific components of our transcultural world, humanity has become cognizant of the fact that we are, as Schroeder claimed, "a part of the universe that has become aware. And being part of the universe, we are able to comprehend ourselves. Our newly found self-understanding reveals that wisdom is contained within even the simplest of particles. This emergence of wisdom in the material world appears as if it is de novo only if we fail to realize that an aspect of mind is 'inherent in every atom.'"[360]

Decades after publication of Teilhard's *Phenomenon of Man*, scientists accepted the reality that the chemistry of human life, with its power of creativity and freedom, is just as extraordinary and well-tuned as the universe. Schroeder discerned that within the brain there is the consciousness of the mind, and within the human mind there is the potential consciousness of the universe. Schroeder disclosed that wisdom manifested itself from the atom, to the molecule, to the cell, and on to the cosmos. Both Teilhard de Chardin and Gerald Schroeder revealed that a creative power in the universe is eternal and infinite. Most important, they discovered that life beats the odds of chaos not by defeating entropy but by the hidden power underlying the cosmos and universe—an orderly systematic universe that embodies a creative source of energy. This signified that human beings are made of the stuff of the big bang, and as stuff of the universe, we are thinking beings who have not yet completed our evolutionary cycle. In awakening to our cosmic personality, we embrace the spirit of the earth. The human personality accordingly awakens to the faculties of love and empathy, which provide energy that inspires the affinity of being with being, developing until love encompasses all humanity and the welfare of life on earth. This constitutes humanity's evolutionary pathway necessary to avoid the extinction of planetary life.

An insightful synthesis of the major domains of knowledge constitutes the understanding of the embodiment of energy, spirit, and freedom, yet to reach the halls of higher learning. This understanding does not merely disclose new revelations of the universe; it reaffirms that factual happenings in history are immersed in and are an upshot of another world: a cosmos and universe in which the foundation of human life comprises energy, spirit, and freedom. "Whatever brought the universe into existence must of course predate the universe, which in turn means that whatever brought the universe into existence must predate time. That which predates time is not bound to time . . . it is eternal."[361]

III

Beyond the global crisis in humanity in our transcultural world, spiritual literacy confirms the possibility of humanity's awakening globally. The industrial revolution of the eighteenth century eventually required literacy for citizens in transitioning manufacturing from hand-production methods to machines, new chemical manufacturing, iron-production processes, and so forth. In our transcultural world, however, humanity's awakening to spiritual literacy posed the potential of humanity's awakening globally to the *spirit*—in its cosmic rather than its religious or mundane sense. Becoming universal, spiritual literacy enables humanity to rid itself of warfare destructive to planetary life and its ecosystems. Spiritual literacy encourages a mass awakening of humanity globally to knowledge of the metaphysical and metahistorical foundation of the cosmos and universe— energy, spirit, and freedom.

During the past fifty years, radiocarbon dating of organic remains have been cross-validated in an effort to address the question of abiogenesis—the process in which life presumably stems from nonliving matter. As discussed earlier, three scientists, Charles Thaxton, Walter Bradley, and Roger Olsen, resolved the mystery of life's origin. Their studies revealed that the time span of 3.5 to 3.8 billion years was insufficient for chemical evolution to occur on our planet. Their comprehensive study contributed a wealth of knowledge to our understanding of life's origin. Evaluating numerous studies regarding chemical evolution, they concluded that life's origin is likely an outcome of a "Special Creation by a Creator beyond the Universe." Life originating from chemical evolution as a result of random chance or accident appears more and more moot and outdated.

Unfortunately, today's war-habituated nations continue to spawn new weapon systems capable of inflicting irreparable damage on the world's resources and on human life. Wars in the twenty-first century continue to inflict the same, if not a more deadly, destructive impact on the ecosystem and on the biodiversity of life on Earth—the variability among living organisms from all sources, including terrestrial, marine, and other aquatic ecosystems and the ecological complexes of which they are a part. Beyond the global crisis, humanity's survival demands a reassessment of the nation-state system, which can no longer be regarded from a purely political and imperial perspective. Humanity must contemplate the terms of a new paradigm that fosters universal solidarity: the development of a world community enlightened by knowledge rooted in energy, spirit, and freedom—inherent in the cosmos and universe—ensuring an understanding of the global economy and the welfare of all people. Heartened by spiritual literacy—in its cosmic significance—the international, national, and local perspectives will value all human beings and strive for social justice for all. The truth is that all human beings are part of a global human family.

As early as 1932, Reinhold Niebuhr acknowledged that the future peace and justice of the nation-state system depended "upon, not one but many, social strategies, in all of which moral and coercive factors are compounded in varying degrees." Given the difficulty in avoiding both despotism and anarchy in the life of nations and the international world, Niebuhr maintained that it was "safe to hazard the prophecy that the dream of perpetual peace and brotherhood for human society is one which will never be fully realised. . . . It is like all true religious visions, possible of approximation but not of realisation in actual history."[362] Yet, Niebuhr later envisioned the possibility of a more modest goal some centuries in the future "in which there will be enough justice, and in which coercion will be sufficiently non-violent to prevent this common enterprise from issuing into complete disaster."[363] In our nuclear age, the prospect of a world catastrophe should encourage humanity to awaken to the major domains of knowledge, lighting the way forward to an Era of the Spirit and establishing a world community in which all human beings understand that they make up an offshoot of a world family.

An imperative for the survival of humanity through spiritual literacy is safeguarding a transfiguration of consciousness transculturally. Nurtured and furthered by knowledge advancing in our world, an Era of the Spirit provides humanity with a response to Niebuhr's prospect of building a world community. He saw this task as humanity's final possibility and final impossibility. "It is a necessity and possibility," he claimed, "because history is a process which extends the freedom of man to the point where universality is reached." Yet Niebuhr feared that it was "an impossibility because man is, despite his increasing freedom, a finite creature, wedded to time and place and incapable of building any structure of culture or civilization which does not have its foundations in a particular and dated locus. The world community, standing thus as the final possibility and impossibility of human life, will be in actuality the perpetual problem as well as the constant fulfillment of human hopes."[364]

In his reissue of *Children of Light and Children of Darkness* sixteen years later, Niebuhr admitted in a new foreword to not having been sufficiently prescient years earlier, given the destructive possibility of nuclear warfare that had since made its debut on the world stage. He cautiously modified his philosophical stance concerning the creation of a world community: "If we escape disaster it will only be by the slow growth of mutual trust and tissues of community over the awful chasm of the present international tension."[365] Given the terrible atrocities of wars of the past century, Niebuhr realized that continued warfare into the future would disrupt the planet's geosphere, hydrosphere, atmosphere, and biosphere. He was apprehensive of the possible harm to the ecological landscape.

Niebuhr warned that "if we should perish, the ruthlessness of the foe would be only the secondary cause of the disaster. The primary cause would be that the strength of a giant nation was directed by eyes too blind to see all the hazards of the struggle; and the blindness would be induced not by some accident of nature or history but by hatred and vainglory."[366] Indeed, another factor beyond hatred and vainglory among interdependent nation-states must be considered. Our destruction may also result, as philosopher J. Glenn Gray declared, from citizens becoming deluded by propaganda during wartime, proclaiming one's enemy to be the enemy of humanity. The enemy in wartime is thus stripped of its humanness and characterized as the embodiment of evil. In such a confused state of consciousness, citizens become grounded not in the transcendent reality of Truth, the Good, and the Eternal, but in the idolatry of their nation and culture as the bearer of ultimate reality. Presently, we bear witness to and are horrified by the violence visited on various nations and the ecological landscape by Islamist sectarian wars spreading from the Middle East to Africa.

The global crisis in humanity encourages a ray of hope, thankfully shattering the dark clouds of ignorance. New revelations shed light on the nature of the cosmos, the universe, and the eternal reality. These revelations transcend the particularity and insularity of the world's cultures and civilizations, their sectarian religious divisions, political conflicts, and penchant for warfare. Embodying the energy, spirit, and freedom embedded in the universe, they integrate Einstein's discovery of energy and spirit as the foundation of the universe; Harold Saxton Burr's experiments revealing the integral relationship of electromagnetic fields in the universe; Teilhard de Chardin's discovery of two energies of psyche and matter as the basic stuff of the universe underlying cosmogenesis and planetary evolution; Gerald Schroeder's molecular biological studies unveiling an all-encompassing wisdom that pervades the universe, including the atom; and Charles Thaxton, Walter Bradley, and Roger Olsen's assessment of the fundamental flaw in all current theories of the chemical origin of life. In addition, biomedical engineering has advanced healthcare through new diagnostics and therapies such as MRI (magnetic resonance imaging), NMRI (nuclear magnetic resonance imaging), MRT (magnetic resonance tomography), and TSM (transcranial magnetic stimulation). Thaxton and his colleagues have evaluated scientific studies and theories regarding the origin of life and have concluded that a special creation by a creator beyond the cosmos provides the most convincing explanation for the origin of life on earth. Their studies reject abiogenesis—the supposition of a spontaneous origin of living organisms evolving directly from lifeless matter.

Hopefully, our transcultural world will bring about a meaningful transfiguration of consciousness, a leap forward beyond war-habituated nations oblivious to the damage they do to life-forms and the planet's ecosystems. The sanctity of planet Earth and its relationship to the cosmos, universe, and the eternal reality confirm the divine character of human beings. Spiritual literacy enhances our capacity to educate citizens globally, thereby establishing a genuine world community, a world government, and a trans-civilizational global culture. Herein lies the prospect of rising above the enmity deep-seated in the oligarchies spawned by nation-states.

IV

Nicolas Berdyaev maintained that an Era of the Spirit will provide "a revelation of a sense of community which is not merely social but also cosmic, not only a brotherhood of man, but a brotherhood of men with all cosmic life, with the whole of creation."[367] Furthermore, Berdyaev claimed, "the coming of a new aeon presupposes a change in the human mind and the liberation of the mind from the power of 'objectness.' This change in the way people think will not come to pass in a moment. It presupposes a complex process of preparation. This is above all what is needed, a revolution in thought and a revolution in spirit, which gets rid of the desire to be alienated and ejected into the object world."[368] Berdyaev coined the term "transcendental man"—a person awakening to the eternal reality. Such a revolution in spirit requires mandatory education of children from an early age as the foremost means of bringing about a resolution to the global crisis in humanity, provided it establishes mandatory literacy in its cosmic sense.

Preparedness necessitates an extensive cadre of scholars and teachers in higher education capable of generating an evolutionary momentum beyond knowledge of the spatial-temporal reality, too often mistaken as the primary reality. Moreover, children in their elementary years of education must be exposed to the mystery of the metaphysical (the truth underlying what is perceptible to the senses) and the metahistorical (the meanings underlying historical facts), which will put an end to the notion that the empirical reality is the primary reality. Consciousness would thereby be elevated to a stage in evolutionary mindfulness in the early life of children who become open and responsive to the mystery of life and being.

Lacking wisdom and spiritual literacy, humanity's pursuit of material ends gives rise to injustice in economic, political, and social affairs. Spiritual literacy (age appropriate for children) sustains the potential to enhance wisdom in human affairs and in the communal welfare of humanity, if taken to heart and taken in a timely fashion. Moreover, knowledge of the spiritual reality poses the potential to invigorate democracy. The truth is that human beings embody the spirit of the earth, sustaining the paradoxical reconciliation of the elemental with the whole, of unity with the multitude, and the mounting power of love, empathy, and compassion until humanity acknowledges the diversity of life on Earth. Political theorist Shelden Wolin envisioned spiritually literate citizens combining "knowledge and skill with a commitment to promoting and defending democratic values, lessening the inequalities of our society, and protecting the environment."[369]

The pressing challenge is to protect our shared planetary home and to end the environmental degradation through a universal solidarity, fostered by knowledge that necessitates a return to the ancient theological virtues of faith, hope, and love and the cardinal virtues of wisdom, justice, courage, and temperance. Tragically, these virtues have been replaced by a crude utilitarianism run amok, morally and spiritually. The eventual challenge that the global crisis in humanity must face is finding a means of abolishing widespread warfare among the world's nations. This is an overwhelmingly difficult task. Self-serving oligarchies that dominate the world's nations become habituated to using the destructive power afforded them by their presumption of sovereignty, let alone in the disregard of their economic interdependence with other nations and of the appalling exploitation of the well-being of citizens.

According to Berdyaev, the "essential and fundamental problem is the problem of man—of his knowledge, his freedom, his creativeness. Man is the key to the mystery of knowledge and of existence." The human being is "the enigmatic being which, though a part of nature, cannot be explained in terms of nature and through which alone it is possible to penetrate into the heart of being." Berdyaev maintained, moreover, that the human being "is the bearer of meaning, although . . . a fallen creature in whom meaning is distorted. But fall can only be from a height, and the very fall of man is a token of his greatness."[370] Berdyaev envisioned humanity's awaking to the divine nature of the cosmos and universe—the eternal—to be of planetary significance: "In our attitude towards animals and plants and minerals, fields, forests, seas and mountains, we can break through to what lies behind this realm of bondage and necessity of strife and hostility. We can enter into communion with cosmic beauty and the spirit of community. Civilization is also chained to necessity. It belongs to the sphere of law.

It bows down before the earth in the bad sense and breaks away from the earth in the good sense."[371]

The onset of the Era of the Spirit, the era of "transcendental man," inspires the possibility of humanity's transformation: humanity's embodiment of energy, spirit, and freedom which entails the cosmic character of the eternal. This would give rise, as Niebuhr claimed, to knowledge of the resurrection of the body, expanding our understanding that time and history have meaning only in so far as they are shouldered by an eternity which transcends them. In his *Abolition of Man*, British academic, lay theologian, and lecturer C. S. Lewis warned that when absolute values are cast aside, the process "if not checked, will abolish Man." He saw this going on apace in mid-twentieth century "among Communists and Democrats no less than among Fascists. The methods may (at first) differ in brutality."[372]

This led C. S. Lewis to forewarn that traditional values are to be "debunked" and mankind to be cut out into fresh shape at will (which must, by hypothesis, be an arbitrary will) of some few lucky people in one lucky generation which has learned how to do it. The belief that we can invent "ideologies" at pleasure, and the consequent treatment of mankind as mere specimens . . . begins to affect our very language. Once we killed bad men: now we liquidate unsocial elements. Virtue has become *integration* and diligence *dynamism* . . . Most wonderful of all, the virtues of thrift and temperance, and even of ordinary intelligence, are *sales-resistance*.[373]

In her *Iliad or the Poem of Force*, the French philosopher, political activist, and Christian mystic, Simone Weil called attention to the "relations between destiny and the human soul, the extent to which each soul creates its own destiny, the question of what elements in the soul are transformed by merciless necessity as it tailors the soul to fit the requirements of shifting fate, and of what elements can on the other hand be preserved, through the exercise of virtue and through grace—this whole question is fraught with temptations to falsehood, temptations that are positively enhanced by pride, by shame, by hatred, contempt, indifference, by the will to oblivion or to ignorance."[374] Our salvation lies in the union of love and justice. "He who does not realize to what extent shifting fortune and necessity hold in subjection every human spirit, cannot regard as fellow-creatures nor love as he loves himself those whom chance separated from him by an abyss. . .

Only he who has measured the domination of force, and knows how not to respect it, is capable of love and justice."[375]

V

Neither the imperative of literacy of the cosmic spirit nor the revelation of "transcendental man" can assure humanity of a transfiguration of consciousness globally. At the heart of spiritual literacy is yet an unrevealed truth: human consciousness is so structured that it has four cognitive vistas (four directions or fields) by which the self attains knowledge of reality. Two vistas of the human mind provide direct access to knowledge of the spatial-temporal world and two vistas provide oblique, indirect knowledge.

The first vista of human consciousness is self-knowledge, which we attain from our personal experiences: what is going on in our inner world. We see ourselves as the center of the universe. About this first cognitive vista, Socrates noted: "I can't as yet 'know myself,' as the inscription at Delphi enjoins, and so long as that ignorance remains it seems to me ridiculous to inquire into extraneous matters."[376] Socrates was referring to inner knowledge and its value in conducting one's life. For without self-awareness, without consciousness becoming conscious of itself, we merely imagine ourselves as being in control of ourselves.

Russian mathematician and esotericist P. D. Ouspensky alleged that the "evolution of man will mean the development of certain inner qualities and features which usually remain undeveloped, and cannot develop by themselves."[377] He regarded human beings as self-evolving beings. Nature develops us up to a certain point and leaves us, either to develop further by our own efforts and devices or our capacity for development becomes impaired. One of the most difficult barriers in our personal development, he claimed, is lying. "A man lies so much and so constantly both to himself and to others that he ceases to notice it."[378] Ouspensky aptly suggested that one of our most creative tasks is becoming self-aware and transcending self-alienation by conquering our self-deceit.

This first cognitive vista (direct access to knowledge of our inner experiences and their meanings) is anything but a straightforward movement from psychological consciousness to self-awakening. In actuality, self-awakening prefigures an end to false consciousness attended by personal suffering. Although multifaceted interpersonal relationships cultivate social networks, they can be lacking in the personal intimacy necessary to fulfill the self's social and communal life.

The second cognitive vista concerns knowledge of the empirical world and what is going on in the world of our five senses. This is the domain of the social and physical sciences. In the second cognitive vista, the self has direct access to factual information about others and the phenomenal reality. But facts do not release to consciousness what has brought the phenomenal reality into being. The spatial-temporal reality concerns the metahistorical (consciousness awakened beyond the historical narrative of reality) and the metaphysical (consciousness elevated to the transcendent reality imperceptible to the senses). Whatever the self observes from the perspective of the world issues from the self's creative endeavors; the self's origin remains imperceptible from the perspective of the spatial-temporal reality. This is true of human creations: cities, highways, skyscrapers, bridges, houses, etc. are the embodiment of the energy, spirit, and freedom that brought them into being. But energy, spirit, and freedom do not reveal themselves to our five senses. Only through spiritual literacy in its cosmic sense are we able to grasp the embodiment of the metahistorical and metaphysical character, quality, and truth underlying the factual, historical, and spatial-temporal reality.

The third and fourth vistas of the human mind cannot be directly accessed; they relate to the inner life of other human beings. The third cognitive vista, what's going on in the inner life of another, is invisible and not directly accessible. Any information is indirect and comes by way of compassion and empathy for others. Entry into the well-protected inner life of the self of another is proffered only in so far as we are genuinely compassionate, empathic, and loving. The third vista, consequently, presupposes our initiation in the realm of spiritual literacy that strengthens our empathic sensibility.

Finally, our fourth vista: How we appear as a phenomenon to others? This vista is not directly accessible. Any information of another's inner life—their feelings, emotions, and thoughts—must come via empathy, altruism, and love for others. From the Christian point of view, this has to do with the three commandments Jesus put forth: to love the Good with our heart, mind, and spirit; to love our neighbors as ourselves; and to love our enemy and pray for those who persecute us. In sum, altruism and empathy make possible the love of others in whom self-deceit has been brought under full constraint of the spirit. We must bear in mind that knowledge is a unity. And the unity of knowledge enriched by all four vistas nurtures a life of love and empathy. Self-knowledge grounded in compassion, love, empathy, and altruism enriches our social knowledge and serves to fulfill our creative vocation as social, communal beings.

VI

Political philosopher Sheldon Wolin harbors some hopeful sentiments about reinvigorating democracy; yet, he envisions this as a rather utopian project that involves encouraging and nurturing a "counterelite of democratic public servants." He suggests that this ideal does not require neutral, above politics, technocrats, but ideally public servants of democracy who would combine "knowledge and skills with a commitment to promoting and defending democratic values, lessening the inequalities in society, and protecting the environment." He laments the fact that for "decades that ideal has been the target of corporate-inspired attacks on 'government bureaucrats' aimed at preventing a revival of effective regulation of corporate power and of social democracy." He proposed "serious changes in the quality of public discussion which, in turn, would depend upon the reclamation of public ownership of the airwaves and encouragement of non-commercial broadcasting." The contemporary version of the old struggle between "enclosure" and the "commons" (i.e., between exploitation and commonality) pretty much sums up the stakes. It is "not what new powers we can bring into the world, but what hard-won practices we can prevent from disappearing."[379]

The principal problem humanity faces in a world of sovereign nations is endless global wars. The U. S. as a superpower finds itself preparing a generation of scientists, engineers, and technical professionals for the military-industrial complex. This has permitted many communities throughout the U. S. to become addicted to military spending to satisfy the need for jobs. Many workers now depend on the production of military goods for employment. But the idea that high-tech robotic warfare will save U. S. lives will be a less expensive way to fight. Nevertheless, it may give rise to the militarization of space and a growing military dominance by the U. S. A.

A possible new epoch of the spirit would foster and fortify our creative capacity to guide, energize, and reverse the current course of human evolution. It would help nurture the inspiration of a positive outcome to our present global crisis in humanity. Catholic priest Thomas Berry made this brazen yet encouraging claim of the new epoch unfolding: "A way is opening for each person to receive the total spiritual heritage of the human community as well as the total spiritual heritage of the universe."[380] This is possible only in so far as our transcultural world embraces spiritual literacy starting early in childhood education globally.

Literacy pertaining to the cosmic spirit poses the potential of awakening future generations of children to knowledge of the eternal reality, the cosmos, and the universe in a way that arouses love, encourages unity, and embodies the utmost expression of freedom. Spiritual literacy sets us on our human journey beyond a world of diverse human families, distinct and unique to particular civilizations and cultures, under the illusion of the absolute sovereignty of the nation-state. The eternal reality having been revealed in a nuclear age of inordinate destructive power demands a human response that makes possible the establishment of a global civilization on earth. Spiritual literacy promotes—in opposition to the crippling, escalating violence based on the claim of absolute sovereignty of nations—knowledge of an Era of the Spirit in human evolution. Herein lies our conceivable resurrection that would establish a worldwide human community heartened by future generations of children schooled in spiritual literacy. So constituted, a world community and global solidarity would make possible a global human family rising above and transcending today's nations, which are engineered for endless warfare under the dominance of their reigning oligarchy—those who rule and command the power structure of the state in the name of government and its citizens.

With the advent of an Era of the Spirit, human beings will hopefully be able to press forward, restoring wisdom and truth transculturally. With planetary life at risk in the atomic age, spiritual literacy has the capacity to define afresh the meaning, cause, and significance of historical change. The modern era brought literacy to bear worldwide, expanding the industrial revolution. But literacy bound to world forces shaped by a technological civilization and an industrialization ravaging the planet ignores the limits of a historical perspective and the meaning, cause, and significance of historical change.

Shorn of spiritual literacy, humanity tends to cultivate demonic forces festering within and among the world's civilizations whose citizens are imbued with a sense that their civilization represents absolute sovereignty and autonomy in a world of interdependent and interconnected nation-states. In an Era of the Spirit, human beings awakened worldwide to spiritual literacy are bound to comprehend the significance of creating a world community; one that acknowledges the kinship of all human beings, the sanctity of all life, and the inviolability of the earth's ecosystem. An Era of the Spirit maintains the potential of awakening humanity to wisdom, truth, and freedom inherent in the cosmos and universe. Herein lies our way forward: an Era of the Spirit which transcends the global crisis in humanity and safeguards life on earth.

Advancing spiritual literacy is still a long way off. Our world is afflicted by ever-invasive systems of technology and production that cause irreparable damage to planetary resources and planetary life. Nations are seized by a world-shattering plight of internal and intercultural political and economic rivalry. Humanity remains oblivious to the fragility of the ecosystem, the biosphere, hydrosphere, and atmosphere, as our communal home becomes blighted. We continue to face the challenge of wanton warfare among the world's nations that are creating ever new, advanced means of destructive power. Our true human character—our divine personality possessing an inherent creative vocation—is ignored unfortunately in so far as the self becomes mired in mundane utilitarian ends. Citizens are inclined to take for granted that the aim of their actions should satisfy the greatest balance of pleasure over pain. Materiality reigns over spirituality. Nationally and internationally, the financial world has become so complex and infected by social injustice, greed, impiety, and inequity that the mass of citizens in democratic nations are incapable of comprehending or politically monitoring the monstrous power confronting humanity.

VII

On the occasion of the 2014 World Economic Forum in Davos, Switzerland, Oxfam International released its astonishing report on the state of the twentieth and twenty-first centuries: "the growing tide of inequality." Established internationally in 1942 by a group of independent nongovernmental organizations, Oxfam International works on the international stage to reduce poverty and injustice. Capitalism has been working for the few, with almost half of the world's wealth in the hands of just one percent of the world's population. "The wealth of the one percent richest people in the world amounts to $110 trillion. That is sixty-five times the total wealth of the bottom half of the world's population." Oxfam released these startling figures: "The bottom half of the world's population owns the same as the richest 85 people in the world. Seven out of ten people live in countries where economic inequality has increased in the last 30 years. The richest one percent increased their share of income in 24 out of 26 countries" between 1980 and 2012. "In the U. S., the wealthiest one percent captured 95 percent of post-financial crisis growth since 2009, while the bottom 90 percent became poorer." Oxfam International warns that "some economic inequality is necessary to foster growth," but "that extreme levels of wealth concentration 'threaten to exclude hundreds of millions of people from realizing the benefits of their talents and hard work.'"[381]

Previous chapters in this book sought to identify the conception of spirit beyond the realm of religion. The spirit and the eternal are disclosed in all domains of knowledge. The eternal reality ensures the advent of an Era of the Spirit beyond the Era of the Law and the Era of Redemption. An emerging globally interdependent world teaches us not to ignore fate; not to subordinate love, justice, and wisdom to power; not to abandon the unfortunate; and not to ravish and defile planetary life as we are all, despite being members of different civilizations, members of the human family sharing planetary resources. Despite the enormous and ever-burgeoning growth in human population, we must become ever mindful of wisdom and justice, not only to safeguard our own civilization but also to safeguard planetary life. A recurring theme of this book is that cultures and civilizations are the creations of human beings and thereby subject to the vicissitudes and vagaries of history.

The fate of humanity in the headwinds of freedom during the past century, since the end of the modern and the onset of the postmodern world, demands a resolution to two countervailing developments: the global crisis in humanity (the deep-seated catastrophe threatening human existence and planetary life) and the conjoining of spiritual contributions issuing from the major domains of knowledge that identify the character of the eternal. Our prospect today lies in the advent of a New Renaissance, a realization embodying knowledge that increases the clarity of thought necessary for the dawning of humanity's divine nature embedded in the eternal.

A New Renaissance, a new Era of the Spirit beyond the moral law and redemption, anticipates a transfiguration of consciousness. Such an era, Berdyaev maintained, would "recognize only the free man and the free relations which hold among free men."[382] A New Renaissance institutes an era in which humanity possesses the possibility of awakening to its divine nature transculturally. Human beings would no longer be crushed by their lower, fallen nature. The divine element in human beings, Berdyaev maintained, "is crushed not only by man's lower nature to which he falls a slave: it is crushed also by religious thought which reflects the slavery of man, by religious sanction of this slavery."[383] God is mystery, the truth underlying the world, and the freedom inherent in the world—conceptions "derived from the highest spiritual experience of man and not from experience of the world of nature and society."[384]

VIII

In answer to the need of establishing a world community in which all human beings globally become members of a world family on Earth, the extraordinary and gifted Dr. Evelin Lindner and her leadership team of physicians, scholars, and associates have begun working toward this goal. Lindner and her colleagues have the last word in this book. She and her colleagues have been journeying around the world for many years, teaching that all human beings are part of our human family. Her leadership team seeks to awaken humanity to the fundamental foundation of the cosmos and universe—the energy, spirit, and freedom that transcend the particularity of cultures and nation-states.

I was delighted to come across their work and to learn that Lindner was nominated for the Nobel Peace Prize in 2015, 2016, and 2017. Their work significantly attests to the knowledge revealed in our transcultural world and the value in spreading spiritual literacy, as discussed in this book. Linder and her colleagues are, thankfully, a global force for good in the world. Their work truly arouses our hope in the enhancement of the welfare of the human community and life globally, affirming the elevation of the dignity of all human beings regardless of civilization, culture, or religion, with comprehensive acknowledgement of humanity as a global family sharing the world's resources. Lindner's pioneering work and worldwide contributions are unique in the annals of world history. They inspire and uplift our souls, encourage us to confront and defeat the social forces mired in warfare, and awaken us to the biodiversity of all ecosystems and the world's resources.

Lindner and her colleagues have created a global movement that embraces the unique and promising challenge of transcending the global crisis in humanity afflicting our contemporary world. As a physician and psychologist, Lindner is also a transdisciplinary scholar in the social sciences and humanities. Her research focuses on human dignity and discloses the veiled truth that humiliation from a lack of honor may be one of the strongest obstacles in creating a world community. Her global movement fosters the potential of ridding humanity of the horrifying plight of perpetual warfare in a transcultural world in which nations are interdependent and interconnected. Lindner and her associates now number around 1,000 personally invited members, in addition to more than 2,000 people supporting the movement. Their website has been accessed by some 40,000 people from more than 180 countries annually. An educational initiative emerging from the network since 2011, World Dignity University sponsors students interested in a curriculum that strengthens the imperative of spiritual literacy in its cosmic sense, rising beyond nationalistic particularism, while engendering a moral universalism for future generations in a world harboring horrifying forces of destruction.

Lindner maintains that "corporations have grown to a size where they can virtually capture states, and when national interests are defended, then economic interests and security interests coincide and fuel the so-called military-industrial complex." She maintains further that "systemic pressures are such that individually, people are beholden to the status-quo of hyper-armament, wittingly or unwittingly; this includes politicians at all levels, national and international, together with multilateral organizations that were created to free the world from war." All activities which hold a promise to bring about world peace, "activities such as conflict resolution, education, poverty reduction, human rights activism, or peace work," are susceptible to being co-opted and become part of the status quo. In their World Dignity University and Human Dignity and Humiliation studies, Lindner and her associates have realized that "accepted buzzwords such as investor confidence, economic growth, or job-creation," are "sign-posts of a world that is bound up in systemic constraints that produce ecological overshoots" as "the planet's carrying capacity is increasingly being over-stretched—including a burgeoning military-industrial-media-academic complex."[385]

The approach of World Dignity University gets to the root of the problem and is consistent with the evolving transcultural world presented in this book. Lindner and her associates understand that the problem humanity faces goes deeper than the political and economic. They are aware that humanity confronts a problem that is fundamentally spiritual, in the profound sense of being a fundamental component of the universe. Their approach enhances, fosters, and broadens spiritual literacy globally, opposing the oligarchic forces within nations harmful to planetary life and the world's ecosystem that further intensify the global crisis in humanity. Global literacy lacking spiritual literacy, paradoxically, can render citizens adaptable and compliant to oligarchic forces within nations that are spreading misinformation and indoctrinating citizens susceptible to a herd mentality.

As a citizen of the world living in various countries, Dr. Lindner advises that "if we want peace, we must prepare for peace" by patiently and persistently repairing, rebuilding, and replenishing relationships. Ultimately, this will be the most practical, efficient, and sustainable path to peace in our age of interconnected nations in which enlightened people are motivated to join up and participate. The future of humanity ultimately depends on our capacity to live within our planetary boundaries in mutually dignifying relationships. Lindner proclaims that an "enduring peace requires gathering a global community of collaborators who share in this effort and maintain it over long periods of time, even in the face of adversities. The path to peace grows by cultivating mutually dignifying relationships, relationships that realize the spirit . . . 'I am because we are.'"[386]

ENDNOTES

1. Reinhold Niebuhr, *The Nature and Destiny of Man: Volume II. Human Destiny* (New York: Charles Scribner's Sons, 1964; copyright 1943), 315.

2. Ibid.

3. Ibid., 320.

4. Reinhold Niebuhr, *The Children of Light and the Children of Darkness: A Vindication of Democracy and a Critique of Its Traditional Defense* (New York: Charles Scribner's Sons, 1944, renewal copyright 1972), 159. Brackets are mine.

5. Ibid., 187.

6. See James Burnham, *The Managerial Revolution* (Bloomington, IN: Indiana University Press, 1960; copyright 1941).

7. Christopher Lasch, *The Culture of Narcissism: American Life in an Age of Diminishing Expectations* (New York: Warner Books Edition, 1980), 181–182.

8. Reinhold Niebuhr, *The Nature and Destiny of Man: Volume I. Human Nature* (New York: Charles Scribner's Sons, 1964), 258.

9. Ibid., 260.

10. Ibid., 259.

11. See Evelin Lindner, *A Dignity Economy: Creating an Economy that Serves Human Dignity and Preserves Our Environment* (Dignity Press, 2012).

12. Diana L. Eck, *Encountering God: A Spiritual Journey from Bozeman to Banaras* (Boston: Beacon Press, 1993), 129.

13. Nick Turse, *Kill Anything That Moves: The Real American War in Vietnam* (New York: Metropolitan Books, Henry Holt and Company, 2013).

14. Viktor E. Frankl, *Man's Search for Meaning: An Introduction to Logotherapy* (Boston: Beacon Press, 1992), 131.

15. Robert D. Kaplan, *The Coming Anarchy: Shattering the Dreams of the Post-Cold War* (New York: Vintage Books, 2001), 177.

16. Ibid., 179.

17. Ibid., 182–183.

18. Christian Parenti, *Tropic of Chaos: Climate Change and the New Geography of Violence* (New York, Nation Books, 2011), 7–8.

19. Ibid., 242.

20. Andrew J. Bacevich, *The Limits of Power: The End of American Exceptionalism* (New York: Henry Holt and Company, 2008), 6.

21. Ibid., 7.

22. Ibid.

23. Ibid., 182.

24. Reinhold Niebuhr, *The Irony of American History* (New York: Charles Scribner's Sons, 1952), 136.

25. Ibid., 137.

26. Andrew J. Bacevich, *Washington Rules: America's Path to Permanent War* (New York: Henry Holt and Company, 2010), 238–239.

27. Ibid., 239.

28. Ibid., 250.

29. Andrew J. Bacevich, *Breach of Trust: How Americans Failed Their Soldiers and Their Country.* (New York: Henry Holt and Company), 193.

30. Ibid., 189.

31. Ibid., 190.

32. Ibid., 191–192.

33. Cited from Eisenhower's Farewell Address, available at **https://en. wikisource.org/wiki/Eisenhower%27s_farewell_address_(reading_copy)**

34. Nick Turse, *The Complex: How the Military Invades Our Everyday Lives* (New York: Henry Holt and Company, 2008), 16–17.

35. Ibid., 30–31.

36. Ibid., 39.

37. Ibid., 255.

38. Zbigniew Brzezinski, *Strategic Vision: America and the Crisis of Global Power* (New York: Basic Books, A Member of the Perseus Books Group, 2012), 1.

39. Ibid., 192.

40. Jürgen Habermas, *The Crisis of the European Union: A Response* (Malden, MA: Polity Press, 2012), x.

41. Ibid., 69.

42. Ibid., 71ff.

43. J. Glenn Gray, *The Warriors: Reflections on Men in Battle* (New York: Harper Torchbook edition, 1967), 3–4

44. Ibid.

45. Ibid., 233.

46. Ibid., 232–233.

47. Ibid., 46.

48. Jonathan Shay, *Achilles in Vietnam: Combat Trauma and the Undoing of Character* (New York: A Touchstone Book, 1994), p. xxiii.

49. Ibid., xx.

50. See Jonathan Shay, *Odysseus in America: Combat Trauma and the Trials of Homecoming* (New York: Charles Scribner's Sons, 2002).

51. See Robert Emmet Meagher, *Killing from the Inside Out: Moral Inquiry and Just War* (Eugene, OR: Cascade Books, Wipf and Stock Publishers), 2014.

52. See David Bodanis, *E = mc2: A Biography of the World's Most Famous Equation* (New York: Berkley Books, 2000).

53. Werner Heisenberg, *Physics and Philosophy: The Revolution in Modern Science* (New York: Harper Torchbook, 1957), 197–199.

54. Gerald L. Schroeder, *The Hidden Face of God: How Science Reveals the Ultimate Truth* (New York: The Free Press, 2001), xi.

55. Teilhard de Chardin, *The Phenomenon of Man*, trans. Bernard Wall (New York: Harper Torchbook edition, 1961), 217.

56. Ibid., 216–17.

57. Ibid., 217.

58. Ibid., 219.

59. Ibid., 43.

60. Ibid., 63–64.

61. Ibid., 64–65.

62. Ibid., 51.

63. Ibid.

64. Ibid., 64.

65. Ibid., 219.

66. Ibid., 218.

67. Ibid., 220.

68. Ibid., 77. Brackets are mine.

69. Ibid., 77–78.

70. Ibid., 78.

71. Ibid., 78–79.

72. Ibid., 97, footnote.

73. Ibid., 102.

74. Ibid.

75. Ibid., 99.

76. Ibid., 99–100.

77. Ibid., 102.

78. Pierre Teilhard de Chardin, *Science and Christ* (London: William Collins & Co., 1955), 119–122.

79. Roger Penrose, *The Emperor's New Mind, Concerning Computers, Minds and The Laws of Physics*, (Oxford University Press), 21–22.

80. Teilhard de Chardin, *Phenomenon of Man*, 142.

81. Ibid., 72.

82. Ibid., 300–301.

83. Ibid., 165.

84. Ibid., 164.

85. Ibid., 165.

86. Ibid., 164.

87. Ibid., 169.

88. Ibid., 181.

89. Ibid., 173.

90. J. S. B. Haldane and J. Huxley, *Animal Biology* (Oxford: Claredon, 1927), quoted in Lee Alan Dugatkin, *The Altruism Equation: Seven Scientists Search for the Origin of Goodness* (New York: Princeton University Press, 2006), 61.

91. Ibid., 202.

92. Ibid., 271.

93. Ibid., 264.

94. Ibid., 268.

95. Ibid.

96. Ibid., 252.

97. Ibid.

98. Ibid., 260.

99. Ibid., 253.

100. Ibid., 255. The existence of pre-hominids to modern man is now dated at more than a million years.

101. Ibid., 256–57.

102. Ibid., 257.

103. Ibid., 264.

104. Ibid., 265.

105. Ibid., 171.

106. Ibid., 270–271.

107. Ibid., 272.

108. Teilhard de Chardin, *Phenomenon of Man*, 273.

109. Ibid., 274–275

110. Bodanis, *E = mc2*, 195.

111. Loren Eiseley, *Darwin's Century: Evolution and the Men Who Discovered It* (Garden City, New York: Doubleday, Anchor, 1961), 62.

112. Gerald L. Schroeder, *The Hidden Face of God: How Science Reveals the Ultimate Truth* (New York: A Touchstone Book, Simon & Schuster, 2002), xi.

113. Ibid., 179.

114. Ibid., 173.

115. Ibid., 188.

116. Ibid., 36.

117. Ibid., xi.

118. Ibid., 178.

119. Ibid., 146.

120. Ibid., xi.

121. Ibid., 59.

122. Ibid., 60.

123. Ibid., 46.

124. Ibid.

125. Gerald L. Schroeder, *Science of God: Convergence of Scientific and Biblical Wisdom* (New York: Free Press, 1997), 177. Schroeder's biblical quotations of the Old Testament are based on translations from the original Hebrew.

126. Schroeder, *The Hidden Face of God*, 45.

127. Ibid., 45.

128. Ibid.

129. Ibid., 13.

130. Ibid., 46.

131. Ibid., 181.

132. Albert Einstein, quoted in R. Jastrow, *God and the Astronomers* (New York: W. W. Norton & Company, 1987), 113.

133. Schroeder, *The Hidden Face of God*, 62–63.

134. Ibid., 63.

135. Ibid., 64–68.

136. Ibid., 78.

137. Lawrence K. Altman, "3 Win Joint Nobel Prize in Medicine," *New York Times*, Oct. 7, 2013.

138. Schroeder, The *Hidden Face of God*, 49.

139. Ibid., 178.

140. Ibid., 180. Brackets are mine.

141. Nicholas Berdyaev, *Truth and Revelation* (New York: Collier Books, 1962), 145–146. Published posthumously in 1953.

142. Reinhold Niebuhr, *Beyond Tragedy: Essays on the Christian Interpretation of History* (New York: Charles Scribner's Sons, copyright 1937, renewal 1967), 277.

143. Ibid., 284.

144. Reinhold Niebuhr, *The Nature and Destiny of Man, Vol. II* (New York: Charles Scribner's Sons, 1964), 299.

145. Ibid., 299–300.

146. C. S. Lewis, *Mere Christianity* (New York: Collier Books, 1960), 185.

147. Ibid.

148. Ibid., 186.

149. Ibid., 187.

150. C. S. Lewis, *The Abolition of Man* (New York: Collier Books, 1957), 71.

151. Harold Saxton Burr, *Blueprint for Immortality: The Electric Patterns of Life* (London: Neville Spearman, 1972), 11–12.

152. Ibid., 12–13.

153. Charles Thaxton, Walter Bradley, and Roger Olsen, *The Mystery of Life's Origin: Reassessing Current Theories* (Dallas, Texas: Lewis and Stanley, 1992), 187.

154. Ibid., 127.

155. Ibid., 189.

156. Ibid., 124.

157. Ibid.

158. Ibid., 165. Emphasis is mine.

159. Ibid., 120, footnote.

160. Teilhard de Chardin, *Phenomenon of Man*, 64.

161. Ibid., 65.

162. Thaxton et al., *Mystery of Life's Origin*, 165.

163. Ibid., 191.

164. Ibid., 191–194.

165. Ibid.

166. Ibid., 196.

167. Ibid., 211.

168. Ibid., 211–212.

169. Ibid., 182.

170. Ibid., 212.

171. Ibid., 214.

172. Ibid., 200.

173. Ibid., 201.

174. Ibid., 202.

175. Ilya Prigogine, Gregoire Nicolis, and Agnes Babloyantz, "Thermodynamics of Evolution," *Physics Today*, November 1972, 23.

176. E. F. Schumacher, *A Guide for the Perplexed* (Harper Perennial, 1977), 17.

177. Ibid., 186.

178. Ibid.

179. Ibid., 187.

180. Ibid.

181. Penrose, *Emperor's New Mind*, 557.

182. Ibid., 597–598.

183. Leo Tolstoy, *Confession*, trans. David Patterson (New York: W. W. Norton & Company, 1983), 27–28.

184. Ibid., 17–18.

185. Ibid., 29.

186. Ibid., 70.

187. Ibid.

188. Ibid., 30.

189. Søren Kierkegaard, *The Sickness unto Death: A Christian Psychological Exposition for Edification and Awakening* (New York: Doubleday Anchor Books, 1954), 157.

190. Tolstoy, *Confession*, 39.

191. Ibid.

192. Ibid., 41–42.

193. Ibid., 41.

194. Ibid., 48.

195. Ibid., 48–49.

196. Martin Buber, *Eclipse of God: Studies in the Relation between Religion and Philosophy* (New York: Harper Torchbook, 1952), 3.

197. Tolstoy, *Confession*, 52–53.

198. Ibid., 50.

199. Ibid., 51.

200. Kierkegaard, *Sickness unto Death*, 193.

201. Ibid., 195.

202. Tolstoy, *Confession*, 57–58.

203. Ibid., 68.

204. Ibid., 71.

205. Ibid., 61.

206. Kierkegaard, *Sickness unto Death*, 162.

207. Ibid.

208. Nicholas Berdyaev, *Dostoevsky* (New York: The World Publishing Company, 1957), 95.

209. Fyodor Dostoevsky, *The Brothers Karamazov*, trans. Constance Garnett (New York: Signet Classics, The New American Library of World Literature, Inc., 1963), 229–230.

210. Ibid., 231.

211. Ibid., 237.

212. Ibid., 236.

213. Ibid., 237.

214. Ibid., 239.

215. Berdyaev, *Dostoevsky*, 203.

216. Dostoevsky, *Brothers Karamazov*, 289.

217. Ibid., 288–289.

218. Ibid., 298–299.

219. Ibid., 299.

220. Ibid., 296.

221. Ibid., 297.

222. Ibid., 331.

223. Ibid., 333–334.

224. See George H. Sabine, *A History of Political Theory*, third ed. (New York: Holt, Rinehart and Winston, 1961), 674ff.

225. Friedrich Nietzsche, *The Antichrist*, trans. Anthony M. Ludovici (New York: Prometheus Books, 2000), 51, 52.

226. Gabriel Marcel, *Man against Mass Society*, trans. G. S. Fraser (Chicago: A Gateway Edition, Henry Regnery Company, 1962), 178–179.

227. Nicolas Berdyaev, *The Meaning of the Creative Act*, trans. Donald A. Lowrie (New York: Collier Books, 1962), 241.

228. Ibid., 244.

229. Frederick Nietzsche, *Thus Spoke Zarathustra*, Prologue, #5, 128, (Walter Kaufmann).

230. Berdyaev, *Creative Act*, 86.

231. See Paul Tillich, *The Protestant Era*, abridged ed., trans. James Luther Adams (Chicago: The Phoenix, 1957), 147–49.

232. Niebuhr, *Nature and Destiny of Man, Vol.* I, 121.

233. Andre Gide, *Dostoevsky* (London: Secker & Warburg, 1949), 96; quoting Nietzsche's *Twilight of the Idols*, trans. Anthon M. Ludovici, 1911, 104.

234. Nietzsche, *Antichrist*, 5.

235. Ibid., 62.

236. Dostoevsky, *Brothers Karamazov*, Translated by Constance Garnett, 295. Father Zossima: There is only one means of salvation. Make yourself responsible for all men's sins. As soon as you sincerely make yourself responsible for everything and for all men, you will see at once see that you have found Salvation.

237. Plato, *The Republic of Plato*, Cornford edition (New York: Oxford University Press, 1945), IX.

238. Ibid. Brackets are mine.

239. Simone Weil, *Oppression and Liberty* (Amherst: The University of Massachusetts Press, 1973), 62.

240. Ibid.

241. Ibid., 63.

242. Adam Smith, *Inquiry into the Nature and Causes of the Wealth of Nations*, Book V, chapter i, part 3. Some of the subsequent quotes of Smith's writing are taken from an edited version of his work.

243. Adam Smith, *The Theory of Moral Sentiments*, ed. D. D. Raphael and A. L. Macfie (Indianapolis: Liberty Classics, 1976), VI, 1, vii-xiv, pp. 214-216.

244. Adam Smith, *Wealth of Nations* (New York: The Modern Library, 1973), edited, Book I, Chapter VII, p. 56.

245. Ibid., 99.

246. Ibid., 62.

247. Smith, *Theory of Moral Sentiments*, 188. Brackets are mine.

248. Ibid., 272.

249. Ibid., 234.

250. Ibid., 166.

251. Ibid., 184, footnote 6; Smith, *Wealth of Nations*, 9.

252. Smith, *Wealth of Nations*, 55.

253. Ibid.

254. Ibid., 30. Emphasis is mine.

255. Ibid., 30–31.

256. Ibid., 47.

257. John Locke, *Two Treatises of Government* Cambridge University Press) Book II, Chapter V, para. 27.

258. Noreena Hertz, *The Silent Takeover: Global Capitalism and the Death of Democracy* (New York: The Free Press, 2001).

259. Nicholas Berdyaev, *The Meaning of History* (New York: The World Publishing Company, Meridian Books, 1962), 168.

260. Karl Marx, quoted from "Preface to a Contribution to the Karl Marx Critique of Political Economy," included in Erich Fromm, *Marx's Concept of Man* (New York: The Continuum Publishing Company, 1961), 218–219.

261. Ibid., 96.

262. Ibid., 96–97.

263. Ibid., 98.

264. Ibid., 99.

265. Ibid., 101.

266. Ibid., 106. Brackets are mine.

267. Ibid.

268. Ibid., 5.

269. Ibid., from Marx's *Third Manuscript, Private Property and Labor*, 130.

270. Ibid., 131.

271. Ibid., 131–132.

272. Ibid., 137.

273. Ibid., 206–207.

274. Ibid., 207.

275. Ibid.

276. Ibid., *First Manuscript*, 95.

277. Ibid., *Third Manuscript*, 124–125.

278. Ibid., 126.

279. Ibid., 149.

280. Ibid., 127.

281. Ibid., 140.

282. Erich Fromm, *Beyond the Chains of Illusion: My Encounter with Marx and Freud* (New York: A Touchstone Book, Simon and Schuster, 1962), 113.

283. Fromm, *Marx's Concept of Man*, Third Manuscript, 137–138.

284. Berdyaev, *Truth and Revelation*, 155–156.

285. Reinhold Niebuhr, *The Self and the Dramas of History* (New York: Charles Scribner's Sons, 1955), 229.

286. Ibid.

287. Paul Ormerod, *The Death of Economics* (Boston: Faber and Faber Limited, 1994), 206.

288. Ibid., 212.

289. Daniel R. Fusfeld, *The Age of the Economist*, Fourth Edition, 71

290. Ibid., 71.

291. Keynes, *Economic Possibilities for our Grandchildren*, 1930.)

292. Fusfeld, *Age of the Economists*, 73.

293. Daniel Fusfeld, *Functioning of a Market Economy*, 128.

294. Ibid.

295. R. H. Tawney, *The Acquisitive Society* (New York: A Harvest Book, Harcourt Brace & World, Inc., 1920; renewed by R. H. Tawney in 1948), 180–181.

296. Ibid., 12.

297. Ibid.

298. Ibid.

299. Ibid., 13.

300. Ibid., 179.

301. Ibid.

302. Ibid., 118.

303. Ibid., 183.

304. Ibid., 183–184.

305. Ibid., 184.

306. Fromm, Marx's *Third Manuscript*, 131.

307. Ibid., 132.

308. Robert Michels, *Political Parties: The Oligarchical Tendencies of Modern Democracy*, trans. from the 1911 German source by Eden Paul and Cedar Paul (New York: The Free Press, 1915).

309. Reinhold Niebuhr, *The Nature and Destiny of Man, Vol. 1*, 210–211.

310. E. F. Schumacher, *Small Is Beautiful: Economics as if People Mattered* (New York: Harper & Row Publishers, Perennial Library edition, 1989), 156. Originally published in 1973.

311. Sheldon S. Wolin, *Democracy Incorporated: Managed Democracy and the Specter of Inverted Totalitarianism* (Princeton: Princeton University Press, 2008), 44.

312. Ibid., 44–45.

313. Ibid., xii.

314. Ibid., 67, 198, 215.

315. Ibid., 241.

316. Ibid., xiii.

317. Ibid.

318. Ibid., xiv.

319. Ibid., viii.

320. Ibid., xiv.

321. Ibid., xiv–xv.

322. Ibid., xv.

323. Ibid.

324. Ibid.

325. Ibid., xvi.

326. Ibid.

327. Ibid.

328. Ibid., 64.

329. Ibid., 64–65.

330. Ibid., 65.

331. Ibid., 74.

332. Ibid.

333. Ibid., 75. Brackets are mine.

334. Ibid., 79.

335. Ibid., 80.

336. Ibid., 82.

337. Ibid., 83.

338. Ibid., 84.

339. Ibid., 85.

340. Ibid., 289.

341. Ibid.

342. Ibid. Emphasis is mine.

343. Ibid.

344. Ibid.

345. Ibid., 291.

346. Ibid., 290. Brackets are mine.

347. Ibid.

348. Ibid.

349. Ibid., 278.

350. Ibid., 284.

351. Ibid., 285.

352. Ibid., 286.

353. Ibid., 288.

354. Ibid.

355. Niebuhr, *Beyond Tragedy*, 306.

356. *The Republic of Plato*, Cornford edition, IV, 444.

357. Elizabeth Kolbert, *The Sixth Extinction: An Unnatural History* (New York: Henry Holt and Company, 2014), 267.

358. Stockholm International Peace Research Institute (SIPRI), "SIPRI Yearbook 2016." Accessed June 13, 2016

359. Marx, *Communist Manifesto*, 149–150.

360. Schroeder, *Hidden Face of God*, 178–179.

361. Ibid., 45.

362. Reinhold Niebuhr, *Moral Man and Immoral Society: A Study in Ethics and Politics* (New York: Charles Scribner's Sons, 1932), 21–22.

363. Ibid., 22.

364. Niebuhr, *Children of Light and Children of Darkness*, 189–190.

365. Ibid., x.

366. Niebuhr, *Irony of American History*, 174.

367. Berdyaev, *Truth and Revelation*, 152.

368. Ibid., 153.

369. Wolin, *Democracy Incorporated*, 291.

370. Nicholas Berdyaev, *The Destiny of Man* (New York: First Harper Torchbook edition, 1960), 11. Original copyright 1937.

371. Ibid., 150.

372. C. S. Lewis, *The Abolition of Man: How Education Develops Man's Sense of Morality* (New York: Collier Books, 1955), 84–85.

373. Ibid., 85.

374. Simone Weil, *The Iliad or the Poem of Force* (Marseilles Literary Monthly, Cahiers du Sud, Fall 1940, reprinted by Pendle Hill), 35.

375. Ibid., 34.

376. *The Collected Dialogues of Plato*, Phaedrus, ed. Edith Hamilton and Huntington Cairns (New York: Bollingen Foundation, 1963), 478.

377. P. D. Ouspensky, *The Psychology of Man's Possible Evolution* (New York, Alfred A. Knopf, 1954), Lecture 1.

378. P. D. Ouspensky, *In Search of the Miraculous* (New York: Harcourt Brace Jovanovich, Inc., 1977), 229.

379. Wolin, *Democracy Incorporated*, 291–292.

380. Thomas Berry, *The Great Work: Our Way into the Future* (New York: Bell Tower, 1999), 174.

381. Oxfam International 2014 Report, URL.

382. Berdyaev, *Truth and Revelation*, 145.

383. Ibid., 146.

384. Ibid., 114.

385. Lindner, *A Dignity Economy*.

386. Ibid.

Acknowledgments

The late Professor Joseph Smolen, University of Minnesota, contributed to the early analysis of the *Global Crisis in Humanity*.

Krista Lombardi and Victor Zuniga set up computer documents, supervised printouts, and managed computer-related aspects of the MS—*Global Crisis in Humanity*.

Mark Singer, Michigan State Professor of Communication Arts reviewed several chapters of the manuscript, providing keen and thoughtful suggestions.

David Perusek, Professor of Anthropology, Kent State University, Michigan State University Ph. D., guided and profoundly influenced the analysis of the *Global Crisis in Humanity*.

Thanks to Chris Zook for the endnotes and light editing.

The profound ideas and wisdom of my beloved Wife and Companion Margaret Petrarca Lombardi resonate throughout the Global Crisis in Humanity in our transcultural world, awakening humanity to an Era of the Spirit.

Author: Vincent L. Lombardi
Bachelor's Degree, Civil Engineering, University of Rhode Island
Master's Degree, Management Theory, University of Rhode Island
Ph. D., University of Minnesota, Psychology and Industrial Relations
Integrated Studies in the Social Sciences & Psychology, 1962 to 2007
Professor Emeritus, Michigan State University